DEATH: A HISTORY OF MAN'S OBSESSIONS AND FEARS

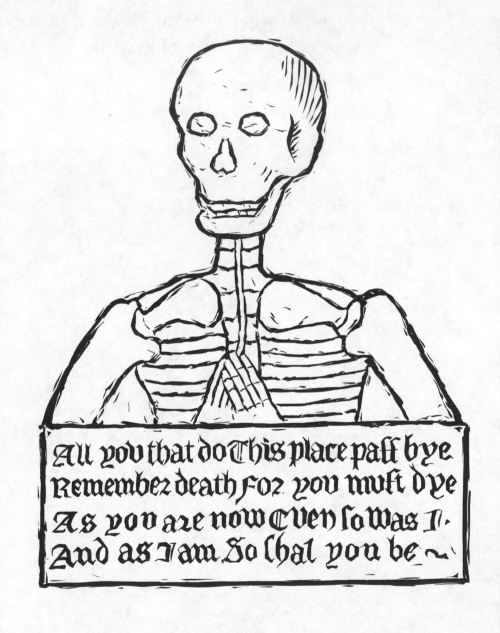

All you that do This place pass bye
Remember death for you must dye
As you are now Even so was I
And as I am So shal you be ~

Drawn by Robin Boutell from a brass plaque in Ely Cathedral

DEATH: A HISTORY OF MAN'S OBSESSIONS AND FEARS

Robert Wilkins

BARNES
&NOBLE
BOOKS
NEW YORK

Originally published as *The Bedside Book of Death*

Copyright © 1990 by Roger Wilkins
All rights reserved.

This edition published by Barnes & Noble, Inc.
by arrangement with Carol Publishing Group.

1996 Barnes & Noble Books

ISBN 0-76070-037-0

Printed and bound in the United States of America.
M 9 8 7 6 5 4 3 2 1

RRDH

CONTENTS

6

V THE FEAR OF IGNOMINIOUS DEATH

ILLUSTRATIONS

8

PICTURE CREDITS

Robin Boutell: 1,9,10,16,30,40,83. La Bibliothèque Nationale: 2. ACL, Brussels: 3,86. Mount Edgcumbe Country Park: 4. Guildhall Library,

London: 6,62. Prof. Otto Prokop, Berlin: 7. F. Schleyer, from *Methods of Forensic Science* (Interscience, 1963) Rijksmuseum Stichting, Amsterdam: 11. Dept of Medical Illustration, St Bart's Hospital, London: 12. Royal Academy of Arts, London: 13. Royal College of Surgeons, London: 14,15,18,19. Prof. M.H. Kaufman, University of Edinburgh: 17,73. Dr. Jonathan Musgrave, Bristol Medical School: 20,21. University College, London: 22. Capuchin Fathers, Rome: 23. The Wellcome Institute Library, London: 24. Dr Christopher Parish, Sidney Sussex College, Cambridge: 25. Tate Gallery, London: 26,84. Hulton Picture Library: 27,28,85. Cairo Museum Catalogue (E. Smith), 1912: 31,32,33,34. Manchester Museum, University of Manchester: 35. Museo Nacional de Antropologia y Arquelogia, Lima, Peru (Eve Cockburn and James Vreeland): 36,37,38. Museo Peruano de Ciencias de la Salud, Lima, Peru (Eve Cockburn and James Vreeland): 39. Macleay Museum, Sydney: 41,42. Silkeborg Museum, Silkeborg: 43. Forhistorisk Museum, Moesgard: 44. Revd John Paul, St James Garlickhythe, London: 45. Pitt Rivers Museum, University of Oxford: 46. Monastery of St Teresa, Florence: 47. Associated Press: 48,54,55. Congregation des Soeurs de la Charité, Nevers: 49. Deirdre O'Sullivan, University of Leicester: 50. Roberto Cuvato and the Capuchin Monastery, Palermo: 51. Arnone & C., Palermo: 52. Kina Italia, Milan: 53. Illustrated London News: 56. John Walsh, from *The Bones of St Peter* (Gollancz, 1982): 57. John Clarke, from *The Brookwood Necropolis Railway* (Oakwood Press, 1988): 63,64. Tony Hillman, Hampton, Middx.: 65. Sir Thomas Hare, Bart: 70. Muniment Room and Library, Westminster Abbey: 71,72,80 (Photo: Malcolm Crowthers). Dr A.J.N.W. Prag, The Manchester Museum and Richard Neave: 74,75. Margaret Coffin, from *Death in Early America* (Thomas Nelson, Nashville, 1976). W.Skelton: 88.

ACKNOWLEDGEMENTS

First and foremost to my wife, Anne, and my children, Katie and Gareth, for their tolerance and understanding; Margaret Coleman and Enid Forsyth at the Post graduate Library, Royal Berkshire Hospital, Reading; Julien Litten, Victoria and Albert Museum; Eve Coburn, Paleopathology Association, Detroit, Michigan, and James Vreeland, Chiclayo, Peru; Paul Woobey for many of the photographs; Robin Boutell for the line drawings; John Clarke and Tony Hillman for material concerning Brookwood Cemetery; Professor T.K. Marshall, Institute of Pathology, Belfast, whose article 'Premature Burial' spawned the idea for this book; Mr Williams and the staff at the photographic department of the Royal Berkshire Hospital, Reading; Maureen Doyle and the staff of the photographic department of St Bartholomew's Hospital, London; John Thornton, retired librarian, St Bartholomew's Hospital, London; Lady (Elizabeth) Longford; Sir Thomas Hare and Mr L. Staines, Stow Bardolph; James Curl; Ruth Richardson; Brother John Condon of Canterbury and Brother Roberto Cuvato of Ragusa; Sister Mireille Jean-Noël, Nevers; Convent of St Teresa, Florence; Miss E. Allen, Qvist Curator, Hunterian Museum, Royal College of Surgeons, London; John Evangelist Walsh; Nic Sutton; Don Brothwell; Canon F. Walters, Swithland; Pepe and Charles Rake for Spanish translations; Chris and Susan Wagstaff for Italian translations; Pam and John Dean for French translations; Dinah Eastop, Director, Textile Conservation Centre, Hampton Court Palace; Father Alexis, St Edward Brotherhood; William Schupbach and David Brady at the Wellcome Institute for the History of Medicine, London; Professor Otto Prokop, East Berlin; Michel Vovelle; Dr A. Prag, Keeper of Archaeology, Manchester Museum; Richard Neave; Dr Rosalie David and Carol Higginbottom, Manchester Museum; Father Ferber, Tuntange, Luxembourg; Enid Nixon, Muniment Room and Library, Westminster Abbey; Martin Crowthers; Deidre O'Sullivan, Department of Archaeology, Leicester University; Dr Christopher Parish, Sidney Sussex College, Cambridge; the Earl of Mount Edgcumbe and Margaret Campbell-Culver, Mount Edgcumbe Park, Cornwall; Jonathan Musgrave, Bristol Medical School; the Director, Jintan Museum, Jiangsu Province, China; Kiyohiko Sakurai, Waswedi University, Tokyo; Thérèsa Babineau, Lowie Museum of Anthropology, University of California; Professor Kaufman, Edinburgh Medical School; Mr G.M.Furlong, Archivist, University College, London; A.P. Watt and Cassell for Robert Graves's *Penthesilea* in *The Oxford Book of Death*.

To my parents, whose fears are past

APOLOGIA

In centuries before our own, life was short and early death common. A Victorian mother might have to give birth to six children in order that three might survive into adolescence. Death – intimate, cruel and obscene – plucked the young and innocent from the very midst of their families. Today we live longer and death has become remote, sanitized and mysterious. With mystery come ignorance and recoil: few adults below forty have ever seen a corpse. When death finally overtakes us, it is usually in the clinical anonymity of a hospital bed, distanced from our families and tended by strangers. Thus protected, the still-living keep their death-related anxieties to themselves.

To psychiatrists like myself, fears and phobias are the stuff of life, and anxieties concerning death are omnipresent. The only reason that we are able to lead productive lives is because most of us, for most of the time, ward off such anxieties by marshalling our defence mechanisms. Psychodynamic forces such as denial and repression push down the disturbing reality of our own mortality into the eddying nether regions of our subconscious minds. If we thought too much about death we would rush to embrace it. But our defences are never completely effective and are sometimes, albeit temporarily, breached. It is at times such as these that thoughts of death filter upwards into the conscious mind.

Death-related anxieties can be broadly divided into the spiritual and temporal. This book eschews religious considerations of after life, judgement and retribution. It deals, for the most part, with much more secular anxieties – those in which curiosity can be satisfied by direct observation rather than philosophical contemplation. Research among old people has revealed common sources of anxiety, each of which will be dealt with in a separate section of this book.

It would be a mistake to think of the fear of premature burial as one of historical interest only, since it has its origin in the uncertainty of the diagnosis of death. Many old people, given 'permission' to voice their inner anxieties, often refer, somewhat jocularly, to the hope that they will be truly dead when laid in their coffin. The precise timing of the moment of death has taken on profound medico-legal significance in matters concerned with resuscitation and organ transplantation.

Posthumous indignity is a fear that has remained widespread long after the passing of the body-snatchers. We still endow a lifeless corpse with the capacity for feeling hurt and the expectation of respect. All forms of defilement of the dead, especially the thefts or mutilation of corpses, are regarded by the majority as deeply distasteful.

Religion concerns itself with the fate of the soul and pays scant attention to the demise of the carcase. Generally speaking, thoughts about bodily disintegration become manifest only when corpses are discovered in which the normal disintegrative post-mortem processes have been arrested or attenuated. Spectacular examples include the naturally and artificially preserved mummies on display in the museums of the world. Modern interest in the preservation of bodies embraces the temporary and purely cosmetic effects of American embalming, and the cryonic movement whose members seek to freeze the newly dead in the hope of a resurrection made possible by future medical technology.

Fear of being forgotten after death is one of man's most deep-rooted anxieties. It is uncomfortable to think that we will not be alive one hundred years from now; it is even more disturbing to think that hardly anyone then alive will remember that we existed at all. It is no coincidence that presidents and prime ministers in their second terms become preoccupied with their place in history. The rest of us, who can never hope to be included in national biographies, can nevertheless have recourse to a variety of stratagems – especially ostentatious and eccentric modes of death and disposal – in order to facilitate heightened remembrance by future generations.

Although most of us have an idea of what constitutes a 'good' death, ignominious death is often capricious and quite beyond our control – a truth attested to by the large number of royals who have met with ignoble ends. So often 'ignominy' alludes to painful or lonely deaths, and it is small wonder that some pre-empt an ignominious death with a dignified suicide.

There is a widespread superstition that mere talk of death will hasten our inevitable end, while taciturnity will magically postpone our demise. Such a reluctance to contemplate forward planning has resulted in the unimaginative, look-alike funerals which we accept meekly and without complaint. The afterword is a plea for greater individuality and eccentricity to be applied to man's ultimate rite of passage.

We are all simultaneously attracted to and repulsed by death. In gathering the material for this book I have attempted to lessen my own anxiety by turning an obsession into a hobby. It has been therapeutic and, as such, needs no apologia.

I   The Fear of Premature Burial

1   BURIED ALIVE

'The unendurable oppression of the lungs – the stifling fumes of the damp earth – the clinging to the death garments – the rigid embrace of the narrow house – the blackness of the absolute Night – the silence like a sea that overwhelms – the unseen but palpable presence of the Conqueror Worm.'

Such were the terrifying images evoked by Edgar Allan Poe in 'The Premature Burial'. Poe believed that burial alive was a subject 'too entirely horrible for the purposes of legitimate fiction', and added, 'We know of nothing so agonising upon Earth – we can dream of nothing half so hideous in the realms of the nethermost Hell.' The narrator in Poe's story had more reason than most to be scared, suffering as he did from catalepsy, a neurological condition which produces intermittent episodes of profound bodily paralysis, closely mimicking death itself. Many believed, erroneously, that Poe was also prone to cataleptic attacks and that the Master of Terror himself lived his life with the ever-present dread of being placed in his family vault whilst still alive.[1]

The fear of being buried alive is one of man's oldest. More profound even than the fear of death itself. To be taken into the blackness when life is extinct is a dreadful enough prospect, but for the Grim Reaper to come calling before the appointed hour is to condemn the yet-living to a seeming eternity of suffocative horror.

Although the obsession with premature burial reached its height in nineteenth-century Europe, its history stretches back to ancient times. Pliny the Elder (AD 23–79) quotes instances of those deemed dead who had subsequently revived – if only briefly. One account told of Consul Acilius, who was solemnly placed on his funeral pyre. When the faggots were lit, his shrieks of pain alerted relatives to their terrible mistake, but before the flames could be dowsed, Acilius was dead. (Pedantically speaking, Acilius's case was one of premature disposal rather than premature burial, but the fallibility of the diagnosis of death is the common factor in both.) It is often impossible to obtain independent and corroborative evidence in the examples cited, and the truth is further obscured by Pliny's uncritical acceptance of hearsay and his reluctance to check the accuracy of his sources – a failing that became apparent as the hallmark of later writers about premature burial.[2]

An early instance of premature burial is Johannes Duns Scotus, grammarian and metaphysician, who 'died' in Cologne around 1308 and whose body was placed in a vault. Some time later, when the vault was reopened, he was found outside the coffin, having torn his hands in a futile attempt to prise open the doors of his subterranean prison. It is claimed that Thomas à Kempis (1379–1471) was denied canonization after it was pointed out that, when the coffin was opened, splinters of wood from the underside of the lid were found embedded beneath the fingernails: surely no aspiring saint, finding himself alive in his grave, would have made such frantic attempts to postpone the meeting with his Maker?

A twentieth-century example occurs in Ronald Blythe's *Akenfield*.[3] William Russ, the village gravedigger, tells how, in the 1910s, people did not hurry to bury the dead, in case they were still alive. Russ believed that 'a rare lot of folk' got buried alive, and makes particular mention of old Micah Hibble of Framlingham who was laid out for dead no fewer than three times. On the last occasion on which he drew back from the jaws of death, Hibble 'Reckoned he saw Heaven and Hell but he wouldn't say what he saw in Hell; he thought it would be too much for Framlingham.'

The anxiety concerning premature burial lies dormant in the subconscious of all of us, occasionally surfacing as a profound, but mercifully brief, paroxysm of anxiety. Nowadays it is a private terror rarely shared with others – in stark contrast to the openly expressed national hysteria of earlier centuries which reached its zenith in nineteenth-century France.[4] The renaissance of the preoccupation with premature burial can be accurately dated to 1742, the year in which Jacques Benigne Winslow, a distinguished French physician, published *The Uncertainty of the Signs of Death*.[5] The author was well qualified to write his book since he claimed to have been placed alive in his coffin *on two separate occasions*.

Winslow's thesis was simple: a body can be called a corpse only when it shows unmistakable signs of putrefaction. The practical implication of the thesis was equally straightforward: to prevent the possibility of being buried alive, it behoved relatives to keep the body above ground until the stench of decomposing flesh forced them to the conclusion that the last flicker of life had finally been extinguished.

To persuade the population of the need for such an unaesthetic practice, Winslow marshalled a large number of examples in which unseemly haste had resulted in dispatch of the dearly departed before they were truly departed. One of Winslow's more celebrated examples concerned two young Parisian lovers. The girl's father refused permission for them to marry and insisted that she wed another, much richer, man. A profound post-nuptial depression developed and the bride quickly sank into a coma so deep that she was pronounced dead. Her lover, for a reason not satisfactorily explained, suspected that she might still be alive and set about digging her out of the ground. His suspicions were well founded, and he was able to retrieve and revive her. The couple fled to England, where they lived contentedly for ten years until homesickness tempted them back to France. On a return visit to Paris the woman was unlucky enough to bump into her legal husband, who not only recognized his dead wife but immediately instituted court proceedings to have her returned to him. Although the court found in favour of the 'widower', his hopes for a resumed married life were thwarted by the lovers' fleeing to England for a second and, presumably, final time.

As is so often the case, Winslow gives too little in the way of corroborative information – names, dates, places – to allow one to come to any valid conclusions about the truth or falsehood of his accounts of premature burial.

VARIATIONS ON A THEME

Writing nearly a century later, Edgar Allan Poe cites a 'true' instance of premature burial which has an uncannily familiar ring about it:

In the year 1810, a case of living inhumation happened in France. The heroine of the story was a Mademoiselle Victorine Lafourcade, a young girl of illustrious family, of wealth, and of great personal beauty. Among her numerous suitors was Julien Bossuet, a poor *litterateur*, or journalist, of Paris. His talents and general amiability had recommended him to the heiress, by whom he seems to have been truly beloved; but her pride of birth decided her, finally, to reject him, and to wed a Monsieur Renelle, a banker and a diplomatist of some eminence. After marriage, however, this gentleman neglected and perhaps even more positively, ill-treated her. Having passed with him some wretched years, she died – at least her condition so closely resembled death as to deceive everyone who saw her. She was buried – not in a vault, but in an ordinary grave in the village of her nativity.

Filled with despair, and still inflamed by the memory of a profound attachment, the lover journeys from the capital to the remote province in which the village lies, with the romantic purpose of disinterring the corpse, and possessing himself of its luxuriant tresses. At midnight he unearths the coffin, opens it and is in the act of detaching the hair, when he is arrested by the unclosing of the beloved eyes. In fact, the lady has been buried alive. Vitality, had not altogether departed, and she was aroused by the caresses of her lover from the lethargy which had been

The Madness of Love: A Man Removing His Fiancée from the Tomb (Austria 1897)

mistaken for death. He bore her frantically to his lodgings. In time, she revived.

Her woman's heart was not adamant, and this last lesson of love sufficed to soften it. She bestowed it upon Bossuet. She returned no more to her husband, but, concealing from him her resurrection, fled with her lover to America. Twenty years afterwards, the two returned to France, in the persuasion that time had so greatly altered the lady's appearance that her friends would be unable to recognize her. They were mistaken however for at the first meeting Monsieur Renelle did actually recognize and make claim to his wife. This claim she resisted, and a judicial tribunal sustained her in her resistance, deciding that the peculiar circumstances, with the long lapse of years, had extinguished, not only equitably, but legally, the authority of the husband.[6]

Montague Summers wrote his scholarly book *The Vampire: His Kith and Kin* in 1928, close on eighty years after Poe's death.[7] In order to draw parallels between vampire legends and less supernaturally reviving corpses, Summers quotes an example of premature burial. The date was 'about 1760'; the country, France. Gabrielle de Launay, the 18-year-old daughter of the president of the civil tribunal of Toulouse, was betrothed to Captain Maurice de Serres. They were married shortly before de Serres was posted abroad. He left his bride in France at his father-in-law's insistence. Two years later news was received of de Serres' death. Subsequently, Gabrielle remarried.

In fact, he had not died and returned to Paris five years later. On passing the church of Roch, he noticed a funeral in progress and idly asked the name of the deceased. He was informed that the dead woman was Madame du Bourg, formerly Mademoiselle Gabrielle de Launay.

The rest of the story has a certain predictability about it. De Serres, in a welter of grief, bribes a sexton to exhume Gabrielle. Finding her still living, the captain then seizes the body and makes off, threading a swift course through the tombstones.

It is five years later that the inevitable meeting occurs between the revitalized corpse and her former spouse. Gabrielle fled but was seen escaping in a carriage which bore the coat of arms of the noble house of de Serres. The legal moves instigated by du Bourg to claim back his wife caused 'the profoundest sensation', Gabrielle initially claiming to be a South American orphan. The charade was finally exposed by the sudden introduction of her daughter, who positively identified her mother. The court found in favour of du Bourg but his victory was short lived, literally. Crying, 'I restore to you what you have lost,' she fell a corpse at his feet. Simultaneously de Serres committed suicide. Both deaths would appear to have been irreversible.

Readers may see many similarities between the vicissitudes of Gabrielle and de Serres and the 'true history' of Elena and Garardo by the Italian Matteo Bandello (1485–1561). Although such variations on a common theme would tend to devalue the truth of any of these accounts, it would be wrong to discount the notion of premature burial altogether. Dr Brouardel, the much-respected French professor of medical jurisprudence in Paris, was contemptuous of the vast majority of examples of supposed premature burial. In his definitive treatise on forensic medicine, *Death and Sudden Death*, published in 1902, he contended that the likelihood of a person's being buried alive was infinitely remote, provided always that a thorough examination had been carried out by a qualified doctor.[8] (Few would quarrel with Brouardel's caveat, and those who were convinced of the veracity of premature burial were quick to point out that virtually none of the victims had ever been seen, let alone been examined, by a doctor). In his book Brouardel concedes the possibility of misdiagnosis of death – and hence of premature burial, attesting to its having occurred on two occasions. Both accounts were vouched for by 'medical men'. The first concerns Mademoiselle Jonetre.

In 1867, while cholera was raging in the *département* of Morbihan, a young woman, aged twenty-four, was suddenly seized with pain in the head and various other symptoms, and her condition rapidly became serious. The people around her believed she had got cholera, and before many hours had elapsed she died. She was laid out and placed in a coffin, and sixteen hours after death her burial took place. A noise was heard inside the coffin which attracted attention. Dr Roger was summoned; he had the coffin opened and found that life remained; he had the woman removed into the church; he was unsparing in his attentions, but she died in the course of the night and was buried in earnest the following day.

This observation [says M. Tourdes, relating the facts to Brouardel] seemed to us a well-authenticated case of the burial of a living person. To make quite sure, we communicated with Dr Roger, the witness of the incident, and received from him the following reply, dated July 30, 1874: 'Yes, I was present at the exhumation of a woman buried in a state of apparent death. I am *positive* that the woman was still alive when I examined her; it is not a mere probability. Here is a *verbatim* copy of the notes taken the same evening: 'Plouigneau, Oct. 1, 1867, midnight – I exhumed at 8 pm Philomèle Jonetre, aged 24, buried at 5 pm in a grave 6 feet in depth. Several persons heard her tap distinctly against the lid of the coffin. There was no smell, no evacuation (of the bowels), but abundant evidence of respiration. Distinct rhythmical sound in the region of the heart. No *rigor mortis*. She was not dead, but like a candle the flame of which has been extinguished, though the wick continues to glow. No definite sounds of the heart; the eyelids moved in my presence. I kept her unburied until the following day.'

Tourdes continued, 'It is out of these notes that the account has been compiled; it is an authentic case of burial during life. Without doubt … the danger of being buried alive is not chimerical.'

Rather churlishly, Dr Brouardel comments: 'Without being as confident as M. Tourdes, it cannot be denied that the fact [of premature burial] is within the range of possibility.'

The other example quoted by Brouardel was a hanged criminal in Boston in 1858, diagnosed as dead by *three* doctors, who was subsequently deemed to be alive and who later died a second and irrevocable time. The account serves to demonstrate that three doctors can be as wrong as one.

Doctors Clark, Ellis and Shaw attended the hanging of a 28-year-old man at 10 a.m. The unfortunate man dropped seven or eight feet. Seven minutes afterwards the heart was heard to beat at a rate of a hundred per minute. Two minutes later it was ninety-eight, and three minutes later still it had diminished to only sixty beats per minute. In a further two minutes the heart sounds disappeared, the heart had stopped beating and the man was considered to be dead. He was taken down for burial at 10.25 am. The heart was stopped, the face was purple and the pupils of the eyes were dilated (generally considered a sign of death). At 10.40 a.m. the rope was loosened, as well as the pinions which bound the arms to the sides. At 11.30 a.m. (1½ hours after the hanging) a pulse was detected – distinctly and regularly at eighty beats per minute.

The chest was then opened! The heart was observed directly and seen to be contracting with 'force and regularity'. By midday the exposed heart was beating at forty per minute; contractions finally ceased at 3.18 p.m., five hours after the hanging. Brouardel, besides conceding his first case of death misdiagnosed by physicians, adds wryly, 'I must point out, in passing, the strange, cool manner in which these Boston physicians performed their experiments on a living man.' Indeed.

Ann Green faired better. She was hanged at Oxford in 1650. As the corpse was placed in its coffin, someone noticed that she was still breathing. Consequently '… a lusty Fellow stampt with all his Force on her Breast and Stomach, to put her out of her Pain.' Far from killing her, the blows were sufficient to revive her, and she is reputed to have lived for many more years and borne several children. A gentler method of resuscitation of a criminal was practised by Sir William Petty on a 'poor wench' hanged for a felony and destined for the anatomist's table. According to John Evelyn, the seventeenth-century diarist, Petty's successful prescription was to put the corpse 'to lie with a warm woman'.

MEDICAL ORTHODOXY

The medical profession has usually regarded claims of premature burial with deep suspicion. Most physicians, while conceding the possibility, were quick to point out its rarity. Those few doctors who believed that premature burial was a common occurrence could expect to be condemned and ridiculed by their colleagues. [One doctor held up to universal derision by his peers was Franz Hartmann, for his *Premature Burial*, published in 1895.[9] The review in the *British Medical Journal* was scathing: 'What is to be thought of the credibility of an author who gravely narrates a case of an Englishman who died of typhoid fever in 1831, who was buried four days later, and after another four days of burial in a coffin in a grave, was exhumed and found alive, and who stated that he had been conscious all the time, and that his lungs had been paralysed and used no air, and that his heart did not beat?' The reviewer had no doubt what he thought: 'A worse farrago of nonsense than that contained in this pamphlet it has seldom been our lot to come across.'[10]

Whilst the *British Medical Journal* might pour scorn on 'alarmists' who wrote about the epidemic prevalence of burial alive, the *Lancet*, an equally prestigious medical publication, regularly featured reports. Here is a chilling example from 1858: 'A case of restoration to consciousness after burial is recorded by the Austrian journals in the person of a rich manufacturer, named Oppelt, at Rudenberg. He was buried fifteen years ago, and lately, on opening the vault, the lid of the coffin was found forced open, and his skeleton was in a sitting posture in the corner of the vault.[11]

If pressed, most eighteenth-century doctors would reluctantly have conceded that cases of people buried alive might have occurred during epidemics of plague, cholera or smallpox, when, for the sake of the living, the infectious dead, or nearly-dead, had to be speedily interred. A case quoted by Tebb and Vollum in *Premature Burial and How It May Be Prevented* (1905) graphically illustrates the dangers:

> A solicitor, living in Gloucester, recently informed the editor that, when first in practice, he had as caretaker of his offices an old woman who, with her husband, had been in charge of the cholera wards, erected just outside the city, at the time of the severe epidemic of 1849, when, in Gloucester alone, there were 119 fatal cases. She told him that as soon as the patients were dead they put them in shells and screwed them down, so as to get them out of the way as quickly as possible, as the small sheds were so crowded. 'Sometimes,' she callously remarked, 'they come to afterwards, and we did hear 'em kicking in their coffins, but we never unscrewed 'em, 'cause we knew they'd got to die!' The fate of cholera victims bundled prematurely into their coffins is evoked in all its grim horror in Anton Wiertz's painting, 'L'Inhumation Précipitée.'[12]

One of the most serious problems experienced by men such as Hartmann, Tebb and Vollum was the lack of a famous case of premature burial. There may, indeed, have been many anonymous cholera victims buried alive in Gloucester, but where were the kings, statesmen or other notables who were testified as dead and who later lived again? Discounting Lazarus as a case of miraculous intervention four days post mortem, the choice for 'Premature Interment of the Famous' usually falls upon the fifth-century Emperor Zenon, who, on regaining consciousness in his tomb, is said to have eaten his shoes and the flesh of his arms and cried out for two nights, 'Have mercy on me!' It might be thought a trifle odd that some of the former emperor's subjects should hear his pleas and do nothing. Perhaps the explanation has something to do with the fact that an inebriated Zenon was *deliberately* placed in his sepulchre by his wife. Truly Zenon was buried alive, but by design not accident.

RESUSCITATED PRELATES

If not an emperor, what about a priest? Let Cardinal Archbishop Dounet, speaking in a debate in the French senate in 1866, recount an example of premature burial.

In 1826, on a close summer day, in a church which was exceedingly

L'inhumation précipitée by Anton Wiertz (1806–65). A grisly depiction of
the hazards of hasty disposal of cholera victims.

crowded, a young priest, who was in the act of preaching, was
suddenly seized with giddiness in the pulpit. The words he was
uttering became indistinct; he soon lost the power of speech, and
sank down on the floor. He was taken out of the church and carried
home. All was thought to be over. Some hours after, the funeral
bell was tolled, and the usual preparations made for the interment.
His eyesight was gone; but if he could see nothing, he could hear,
and I need not say that what reached his ears was not calculated to
reassure him. The doctor came, examined him, and pronounced
him dead. The body was measured for the coffin. Night came on
and you will easily feel how inexpressible was the anguish of the
human being in such a situation. At last, amid the voices
murmuring around him, he distinguished that of one whom he had
known from infancy. That voice produced a marvellous effect and
superhuman effort. Of what followed I need say no more than that
the seemingly dead man stood next day in the same pulpit.

Apart from the fact that hysterical paralysis would appear not to be a
solely female affliction and that Frenchmen with histrionic personality
disorders can be called to the priesthood, is this anecdote about an
obscure prelate likely to convince sceptics about the reality of premature
burial?

Perhaps we should allow the archbishop to finish: 'That young priest, gentlemen, is the same man who is speaking before you, and who, more than forty years after that event ...' The senate debate in which the archbishop was participating concerned the urgent need for legislation to forbid burial without the signature of a doctor or officer of health. Even if such a law had been on the French statute book in 1826, it would not have prevented the priest's interment since, despite Brouardel, this was a case of misdiagnosis of death *by a doctor*. [13]

The clergy are over-represented in unnerving accounts of apparent death. Abbé Prévost (1697–1763), who wrote *Manon Lescaut*, was found unconscious in the woods and was carried to the house of the village doctor, who proceeded to do a post-mortem examination. As the scalpel blade cut into the chest, the unfortunate cleric emitted a piercing shriek and promptly died. The incident was quoted in an article on premature burials in *The Popular Science Monthly* in 1880. [14] The author reports Bruchier, Prévost's biographer, as deploring this event 'as a serious loss to literature'. Many since have doubted the truth of this story. Others have argued that, even were the account to be correct, it says more about the criminal haste of the doctor than the intrinsic danger of being buried alive.

Even greater doubts have been cast on the authenticity of another autopsy on a live priest. The victim this time was Cardinal Diego de Espinosa, Bishop of Siguenza and Grand Inquisitor of Spain under Philip II. His second and final death was falsely attributed to the greatest of all anatomists, Andreas Vesalius. It was said by his enemies that Vesalius had mistakenly opened the chest of the cardinal and looked in horror and amazement at the beating heart. This account, which has been uncritically repeated, added spurious credence to to an Elizabethan's judgement that, 'Vesalius was wont to cut men up alive.'

On one occasion the 'scalpel test' had an arguably happier outcome. The case is recounted by Julia de Fontenelle in his book, *Medico-legal Researches on the Uncertainty of the Signs of Death*, published in 1834: 'A gentleman of Rouen, returning from a tour just as his wife was being borne to the tomb, ordered back the coffin, and had a surgeon to make five-and-twenty incisions on the corpse – a strange method of cherishing the remnant of existence, if he suspected any. Nevertheless, at the twenty-sixth incision, which went deeper than the rest, she mildly inquired, "What mischief are they doing me?" The woman survived to bear her husband six-and-twenty children – a pledge for every gash.'[15]

A final clerical example, also from Fontenelle. An *abbé* died, and for a reason many will understand, his friends decided to bury his cat with him, even though it was still alive. *En route* to the grave the vicar awoke and added to his agony of burial alive was the suffocation caused by his cat curled over his face: 'The *abbé* employed all his strength to drive off the incubus. The animal mewed with pain, and more regard being paid to the remonstrances of a cat than to those of an archbishop, the procession was stopped and the coffin unscrewed. Out jumped the cat, and immediately after the dead man followed, and took to his heels.'

HOW COMMON WAS PREMATURE BURIAL?

There was a young man at Nunhead
Who awoke in his coffin of lead
'It was cosy enough,'
He remarked in a huff,
'But I wasn't aware I was dead.'

Anonymous Victorian limerick

From our vantage-point in the twentieth century it is difficult to judge how realistic was the Victorians' fear of premature burial. Was the man buried at Nunhead Cemetery voicing a legitimate fear of being buried whilst merely moribund rather than definitively deceased?

The much-maligned Hartmann collected more than 700 cases of premature burial or of narrow escapes from it. Tebb and Vollum, in their book, talk of 219 narrow escapes, 149 who did not escape, ten cases of being dissected alive, three close shaves on the anatomist's table and two unfortunates who revived whilst in the process of being embalmed. And those were only the cases that were known about. What about the countless thousands whose suffering was never recorded?

When the Paris cemetery Les Innocents was moved from the centre of the city to the suburbs, the sheer number of skeletons found face down in their coffins convinced the lay public, and even some medical men, that premature burial was common. But most physicians remained sceptical: Dr David Walsh, writing in 1897, scoffed at the 'authorities' who were fond of stating that, 'One third of the human race was buried alive, and perhaps one half of those who die in their beds are not dead when they are buried.'[16]

Such seeming gullibility was easily satirized. One reviewer, pouring scorn on Fontenelle, compared cemeteries with slaughter houses and reminded his readers of the story of St Frithstane, '... who, saying one evening masses for the dead in the open air, pronounced the words *requiescat in pace*, and heard a chorus of voices from the surrounding graves respond loudly *Amen*'. Even if all of Hartmann, Tebb and Vollum's cases were validated, they would amount to fewer than a thousand – 'a rather slender counterpoise to the number of victims of passion, gluttony, drugs and physicians'.[17]

But yet the zealots persisted and asked disbelievers to provide alternative explanations for phenomena which they regarded as proof positive of burial alive.

Consider Madam Blunden, prematurely buried in the eighteenth century in the Holy Ghost Chapel, Basingstoke. As it happened, the Blunden family vault was situated beneath a boys' school. The day after the funeral the pupils heard noises. One boy ran off to tell a master but received only a thick ear for his trouble. When the noises continued unabated, the sexton was summoned and the vault was opened just in time to witness her final breath. Resuscitation was unsuccessful. In her agonies the poor lady had torn frantically at her face and had bitten the nails off her fingers.

Or the case of Virginia Macdonald, buried in a Brooklyn cemetery in the 1850s. Miss Macdonald's mother persisted so long in her belief that her daughter had been buried alive that the authorities finally granted her request that the coffin be raised and opened. 'To their horror they discovered the body lying on its side, the hands badly bitten, showing every indication of a premature burial.'

Hartmann cites a Hungarian buried in 1856, who was exhumed a few days after his interment when noises were heard emanating from his coffin. 'The fact that he had been buried alive was made evident by the condition of the body, and by the wounds which the man had inflicted by biting his shoulders and arms.'

Flesh wounds, amputated fingers and torn shrouds were ascribed to the terrors of suffocation rather than ravenous rodents.

A still higher dimension of horror is suggested by the birth of a baby to a mother incarcerated alive in a coffin. Madame Bobin sailed in the steamer La Plata from Senegal in 1901 and docked at Pauillac. She was diagnosed as suffering from yellow fever and was subsequently certified dead and then buried. A nurse had lingering doubts and shared them with the lady's father. On exhumation it was found that a baby had been born in the coffin. The father successfully sued the health officers and was awarded £8,000 damages.

A similar case was reported in The Undertakers' and Funeral Directors' Journal in 1890. Lavrinia Merli, a Mantuan peasant, died of hysterics. Two days after interment she was discovered turned over in her coffin, having given birth to a baby of seven months gestation.

The case of a soldier, Francis de Civille of Normandy, is the most remarkable of all. Born by Caesarean section to a dead mother who had been exhumed from her coffin when his father returned from a business trip, Francis became an army captain and was wounded in the siege of Rouen (almost certainly that of 1563) and buried alive in a common grave for seven hours until rescued by his servant, who had intended to dig his master a more fitting grave. Whilst he was recovering from his ordeal Charles IX's soldiers broke into the house and threw de Civille into a dung-heap, where he remained buried for three days before being rescued a second time and nursed back to health.

ALTERNATIVE EXPLANATIONS

To unbelievers, such phenomena had less macabre explanations. The different positions taken up by corpses were much more likely to be the result of externally imposed movements: bumping into walls whilst negotiating the coffin down narrow stair wells, or sudden movements produced by shying or bolting funeral horses. (Indeed, one story tells of a wife who regained consciousness as a consequence of the pall-bearers' banging her bier against the corner of a house. Some years later, when the woman was truly deceased, her husband implored the funeral director, 'Pray, gentlemen, be careful in turning corners.')

Contorted facial agonies were nothing more than the effects of rigor mortis, and coffin noise was caused by the movement of gases produced by a putrefying body. Such noxious eructations were the true explanation for a variety of manifestations taken by the simple-minded as proof of premature burial. The muffled cry for help was no more than a post-mortem belch, and a build-up of gases under pressure might cause blood to flow out of the mouth or from the nose, or a baby to be expelled from the womb. If the pressure was great enough, it could easily cause rupture of the coffin itself, giving the erroneous impression that the lid had been 'broken by its inmate in their mad endeavour to escape'. Monsieur Devergie, the physician at the Paris morgue in the last century, contended that the gas generated in corpses which had lain a long time in water was so powerful as to heave up the cadavers from their tables and hurl them to the ground.

A common tactic of disbelievers was to resort to xenophobia. Continentals, especially the French, were thought by the British to be irredeemably naïve in their acceptance of apocrypha.[18]

There were, of course, alternative explanations for the 'deaths' themselves.

DEATH'S COUNTERFEITS

Catalepsy is a mysterious condition, characterized by immobility of the muscles, which can sometimes be mistaken for death. The limbs have a 'waxy flexibility' and can be moulded into bizarre positions where they remain indefinitely. Catalepsy can occur in hysteria and hypnotism and used to be common in schizophrenia before the advent of effective drug treatment.

Didelphis virginiana has given to the English language a behaviour specifically designed to fool one's enemies by mimicking death. When attacked, the opossum will fall to the ground and roll itself up into a ball, mouth hanging open and eyes fixed in a vacant stare, pretending to be dead and hoping that its enemy will be sufficiently duped to leave it alone. When the danger has passed, the bundle of fur suddenly revives and scampers away. 'Playing possum' has saved many a soldier in the aftermath of battle when the victors roam the field doing to death anyone still showing signs of life.

'Thanatomimesis' is the name given to bodily states that may be mistaken for death. The word is derived from the Greek *thanatos* meaning death and *mimos* meaning imitation. Thanatomimesis is not the same as 'sham death' or 'playing possum' because these two descriptions imply a *deliberate* intention to deceive. What, then, are the conditions that may be misdiagnosed as death?

Faints and Trances

Fainting, or syncope, is the commonest of death's counterfeits. It is rarely prolonged and the patient recovers without serious after-effects – usually. In 1848, as King Louis Philippe of France was leaving the Tuileries to go into exile, the bodies of three National Guards lay at the gates of the garden, near the Place de la Concorde. They had probably fainted in the heat. Wishing to spare the king any fresh grief, 'some persons good-naturedly buried these bodies under a heap of sand. When they were extricated, some hours after, one of the men was still alive.'

Petrach, the fourteenth-century Italian poet and humanist, is an object lesson to those who advocate hasty burial. When he lived in Ferrara, Petrarch fell into a profound state of trance. The law at the time decreed that, for the sake of hygiene in hot climates, the dead had to be buried within four hours of death. As the funerary preparations were being made, the servants were stunned to hear the voice of their deceased master complaining about the draught. It is salutary to reflect on the loss to world literature if the poet's house had been better insulated.

Trance and coma differ in degree: it is generally accepted that in coma the sleep-like state is deeper and more likely to be irreversible than in trance. There is little doubt that in many of the examples cited as instances of premature burial people had fallen into trances or comas, similar in many respects to the mental and physical inertia produced in hibernating animals. The fate of a comatose patient may well depend on the patience and vigilance of relatives and the legal time-limits placed on the interval between death and burial.

Benjamin Disraeli, Queen Victoria's favourite prime minister, was prone to fits of giddiness in his younger days and once fell into a trance from which he did not recover for a week. Likewise the mother of General Lee, Confederate soldier in the American Civil War. Lady Burton, wife of the famous explorer, was also given to falling into trances.

But perhaps the most celebrated case was that of Marguerite Bozenval, 'The Dormouse of Menelles', who remained in a trance for twenty years. In 1883, when Marguerite was twenty-one years old, a friend told her, as a joke, that the police were coming to arrest her. She instantly became unconscious. For the next two decades she was tube-fed. On the day before her death there was an episode of violent twitching of her limbs, after which she opened her eyes and asked after her grandfather, who was long since dead. Not surprisingly, she did not recognize her mother. 'The effort to speak and rouse herself seemed more than the enfeebled frame could bear, and she ceased to breathe at nine o'clock in the morning.'[19]

Mademoiselle Bozenval illustrates the difficulty of distinguishing between bona fide trance and the self-induced variety that is sometimes seen in people diagnosed as hysterics. Much has been written, and is still being written, about hysterical paralysis. The hysterical state of unconsciousness is often preceded by an episode of strong emotion, frequently perceived by the patient as threatening and for which a trance-like state may serve as a short- or long-term solution. Marguerite, correctly, may have thought that not even the French police would put an unconscious person in gaol.

Another case with hysterical overtones was cited by MacKay and concerned a young woman on the eve of her marriage: 'The doctor was of the opinion that the girl had died from excitement – overjoy, it is said, at the prospect of being married – but the legal name for the catastrophe was disease of the heart, and with this verdict her place in society was declared vacant.'[20] The girl was duly buried but noises from within the coffin prompted the bridegroom to prise off the lid. 'The girl was found in an attitude of horror and pain impossible to describe, her eyes wide open, her teeth clenched, her hands clutching her hair.' Perhaps, just perhaps, the young lady's secret anxieties about sex had induced in her an hysterical paralysis in order to delay the ceremony. Unfortunately her solution was too permanent.

Sentient Corpses

Many people who revive from trances just in time to escape the grave give accounts of having been fully aware of what was going on around them. It would appear that physical under-activity can be accompanied by psychical over-activity. The experience of Edward Stapleton, as related in Poe's short story, *The Premature Burial*, is typical.

Stapleton, a London attorney, 'died' of typhus in 1831. When asked, his friends declined permission for a post mortem, and so the doctors, putting education above ethics, resolved to disinter Stapleton and dissect him at leisure. On the third night after the funeral, the deceased had a visit from the 'resurrectionists' (grave-robbers), who transferred the corpse to the operating-theatre of a private hospital.

At about dawn the doctors decided to proceed with the dissection. A student, however, eager to test out a theory, insisted on applying the terminals of a battery to the chest muscles of the cadaver. Someone made an incision in the pectoral muscle whilst another plunged a bare wire into the incision. With electrical contact established, the patient '... arose from the table, stepped into the middle of the floor, gazed about him uneasily for a few seconds, and then – spoke'. The words he uttered were unintelligible, but the effort required to speak at all so exhausted him that he fell heavily to the floor.

Mr Stapleton declares, '... that at no period was he altogether insensible – that, dully and confusedly, he was aware of everything which happened to him, from the moment he was pronounced dead by his physicians, to the time he fell swooning to the floor of the hospital. "I am alive," were the uncomprehended words which, upon recognising the locality of the dissecting room, he had endeavoured, in his extremity, to utter.'

One little girl quoted by Brouardel was mortified – well, almost – to hear her sister jumping up and down at the prospect of getting her necklace. Miss Eleanor Markham, writing of her experiences in *Banner of Light* in 1894, said, 'I was conscious all the time you were making preparations to bury me and the horror of my situation was altogether beyond description. I could hear everything that was going on, even a whisper outside the door, and although I exerted all my will power, and made a supreme physical effort to cry out, I was powerless.'

Dr Chew of Calcutta 'died' in 1874 soon after his favourite sister was carried off with convulsions. He had attended her funeral and was so overcome with grief that he collapsed headlong into her grave and 'fainted away'. Dr Chew relates his own demise thus:

I died, as was supposed, on 18 January, 1874, and was laid out for burial. I had been in this state for 20 hours, and in another 3 hours would have been closed up for ever, when my eldest sister, who was leaning over the head of my coffin and crying over me, declared she saw my lips move. The friends who had come to take their last look at me tried to persuade her that it was only fancy, but she persisted. Dr Donaldson was sent for to convince her that I was really dead. For some unexplained reason he had me taken out of the coffin and examined very carefully from head to foot. Noticing a peculiar, soft, fluctuating swelling at the base of my neck, he went to his brougham to get his case. He proceeded to lay open the tumour and plunged in a tracheotomy tube. A quantity of pus escaped releasing the pressure on my carotids. Restoratives were used and I was slowly nursed back to life. The tracheotomy tube was not finally removed till September, 1875.[21]

Not unnaturally, Dr Chew henceforth was overly preoccupied with the risks of premature burial. But this does not adequately explain why he found the need to open up his family vault ten years after the death of a 17-year-old relative who had died of cholera. He found the coffin lid on the floor, the skeleton half in and half out, with an 'ugly gash across the right parietal bone (skull)'. Clothes were draped over the edge of the coffin, and the bent fingers of her right hand were near her throat. Dr Chew, no doubt remembering the horror of his own close encounter with death, surmised that she had regained consciousness in the tomb, 'Fought for life, forced her coffin open, and sitting up in the pitchy darkness of the vault went mad with fright, tore her clothes off, tried to throttle herself, and banged her head against the masonry shelf until she fell forward, senseless and dead'. Either that or she was blown out of her coffin by an explosion of putrefying gases.

Fakirs, Western and Eastern

Fakirs are often credited with the power to slow down their bodily metabolism to such an extent that breathing becomes virtually imperceptible.

Colonel Townshend was a famous eighteenth-century Englishman who was able, by some mechanism under his voluntary control, to ape death itself. Dr Cheyne, in his book *The English Malady* in 1733, recounted how he and a colleague were summoned to Townshend's bedside to witness a unique experiment: he was to cause himself to die and to return to life. The colonel lay on his back. Cheyne checked the patient's pulse, Dr Baynard placed his hand over the heart, whilst Mr Skrine, an apothecary, held a mirror in front of the mouth. For more than half an hour no pulse or other life sign could be detected. The demonstration was so successful that the three attendants were convinced that Townshend had 'pushed the experiment too far'. Just as Cheyne was about to make arrangements for disposal of the body, he noticed that the pulse had returned and breathing restarted. Townshend was soon speaking of his near-death experiences. When the professionals had departed, the patient got down to more secular matters: he called for his lawyer and added a codicil to his will. Within eight hours he was dead.

Prolonged periods of suspended animation are seen today in patients suffering from electrocution, hypothermia or drug overdose, especially barbiturates.

Fakirs apart, how long might someone be reasonably expected to survive if they were inadvertently sealed in a coffin while in a state of trance? Opinions varied greatly. It was generally agreed that the available air would be no more than three to four cubic feet. Experiments had shown that dogs were able to survive in glass-topped coffins for anything up to six hours. It was reckoned that a man might last only twenty minutes – '... but is this not a century of torture?'[22]

Emma, Countess of Mount Edgcumbe, who, after burial in the family vault, regained consciousness when a sexton attempted to steal the rings off her fingers. Portrait by Sir Joshua Reynolds, since destroyed.

EMMA, COUNTESS OF MOUNT EDGCUMBE

Emma was born on 28 July 1729 and was the only child of John Gilbert, Archbishop of York, and Margaret, sister of the second Earl of Harborough. She married George, third Baron Edgcumbe (later first Earl of Mount Edgcumbe), in August 1761. Originally Mount Edgcumbe was in Devon, but a boundary-change transferred it to Cornwall in 1844.

'A most exciting and thrilling story is told regarding this lady,' began an anonymous account in a bundle of papers sent to me by Robert Mount Edgcumbe, the present earl. It continued:

The story, as related to me, was that, some years before her husband's death, she herself was stricken down by some mysterious illness which proved beyond the ken of the family doctor. And when, after a few days, she displayed such symptoms which only tended to confirm his worst suspicions and fears, the doctor had no hesitation in conveying to the Earl the sad tidings of the death of the Countess. Accordingly, all the necessary arrangements were made for her burial in the family vault at Maker Parish Church, about three-quarters of a mile away at the top of the Park. When the day of the funeral arrived the sexton came to place the body, clothed in a sheet, in the coffin.

While so doing the sexton noticed that the Countess had some very valuable rings on the fingers of the left hand, and feeling that it would be a great pity if they were allowed to remain there forever, decided to waste no time in rectifying the matter. That night, when all was dark and still, he crept down to the family vault and, opening the door, proceeded to unscrew the coffin by the light of a candle. With the lid off, he took the left hand of the corpse and attempted to pull the rings off the fingers. Encountering some difficulty he pulled more vigorously. To his amazement and horror the corpse began to sit up!

Filled with terror he let out one shriek and ran away as fast as his legs could carry him, knocking over the candle in his haste, but leaving the door of the vault ajar. The feelings of the poor Countess at finding herself in this astounding predicament must well have been beyond belief, when, awaking from her coma, she found herself in a coffin, alone in her vault, in the pitch black, and wrapped only in a sheet. The shock might well have made the bravest woman die of fright, but the Countess soon realised where she was, and guessing what had happened, slowly and painfully made her way barefooted down a little path towards the house. This path has ever since been called 'The Countess's Path'.

When she reached the house she made her way to the shuttered windows of the dining-room. Inside the family were at dinner, sadly discussing the events of the day. Suddenly a gentle tapping noise was heard. At first no-one moved, but as the tapping continued the Earl, whose nerves were very much on edge from the events of the last few days, went to the window. He slowly drew back the shutters and looked upon a white figure standing outside. Thinking he saw a ghost, he uttered a shriek, but when the figure began to speak in the tones of his wife, he summoned up his courage and opened the window. To the amazement of all, in walked the 'corpse', none the worse for the extraordinary series of adventures which had befallen her.

The Countess lived for a long time after the events recounted above, outliving her husband by some twelve years. Her portrait was painted by Sir Joshua Reynolds.

Anticipating disbelief, the author of this account testified to its accuracy by telling us that it had been told to him by William, fourth Earl of Mount Edgcumbe, when the author stayed at Mount Edgcumbe

House as a boy of fourteen. More recently the story had been confirmed by William's granddaughter, the Hon. Mrs John Parker.

It seemed to me that this celebrated case of premature burial, because it involved a member of the aristocracy, was potentially able to be authenticated. One merely had to find evidence of Emma's first demise in the Maker parish records and of her second and final departure on 26 December 1807 in 'Upper Grosvenor Street, Middlesex'. The Maker parish record of her death would fall between the date of her marriage in 1761 and the date of her husband's death in 1795.

The Maker parish records are held at the Cornwall Record Office in Truro, and the only reference is to the death of The Right Honourable *Sophia*, Countess of Mount Edgcumbe, who died on 17 August 1806 and was interred on 2 September 1806. David Thomas, who searched the records at Truro on my behalf, was sufficiently intrigued to continue delving. In Lake's *Parochial History of Cornwall,* Volume 3, in the chapter on Maker parish, was a not-unfamiliar account of a premature burial given by Polwhele (1760–1838), the Cornish historian:

> We have an astonishing instance of reviviscence in one of the Edgcumbe family, I believe the mother of Sir Richard Edgcumbe, Knight, who was created 1st Baron of Mount Edgcumbe in 1748. The family were then residing at Cutteel (Cotehele in the parish of Calstock). Lady Edgcumbe had expired. Her body was deposited in the family vault, not I suppose in less than a week after her supposed death. The interment, however, had not long taken place before the sexton, from a motive sufficiently obvious, went down into the vault, and observing a gold ring on her ladyship's finger, attempted to draw it off, but not succeeding, pressed and pinched the finger, when the body very sensibly moved in the coffin. The man ran off in terror, leaving his lantern behind him. Her ladyship arose and taking the lantern, proceeded to the mansion house. Of the authenticity of this account there can be no reasonable doubt ... as I recollect the narrative as coming from the lips of my grandmother Polwhele.

This account would suggest that it was not Emma who was buried prematurely but another Edgcumbe lady a century before. As David Thomas says: 'If this is indeed the case, then it would refer to the Lady Anne Montague, second surviving daughter of Edward, Earl of Sandwich.'

So Emma was really Anne. Unfortunately the burial register of Maker church from 1670 to 1694 does not mention Anne. Further, if Anne took the lantern and walked from Maker to Cotehele House, 'where the family were then residing', the effort would probably have killed her, since the vault and the house are some ten miles apart.

The story of Emma and Anne is told in some detail to illustrate how easily 'facts' dissolve into unsubstantiated surmise. Two ladies in two different centuries contend for the title 'Born-Again Countess' and the authority for such claims often rests on the honesty or recollections of such people as Grandmother Polwhele.

There was confusion as to the identity of 'The Lady in the Trance' as long ago as the 1870s. The then earl had this to say on the subject: 'I have never been able to get at the truth of the story, or even to the identity of the lady of whom it is told. There is an old lady living at Plymouth now who says she often heard the story from her husband's grandmother, who was housemaid at Mount Edgcumbe at the time, and opened the door for Lady Mount Edgcumbe when she walked home the night of her funeral.'[23] Considering the number of grandmothers involved, perhaps the Mount Edgcumbe saga is but an old wives' tale.

There is a none-too-flattering reference to Emma, Lady Mount Edgcumbe's age in *The Times* of January 1790. In an account of the ladies' dresses at the queen's ball, the reporter comments: 'In a dress suited to her age and person – conspicuously antique, to set modern elegance at defiance. Her Ladyship had on a coquelicot Satin, flounced all over, and marked with very broad stripes of Sable, gloomy as the view from Mount Edgcumbe to Polvrin in hazy weather.' No mention is made

Maker Church, from which the Countess made her way back to the house to be reunited with her terrified relatives, '… none the worse for the extraordinary series of adventures which had befallen her'.

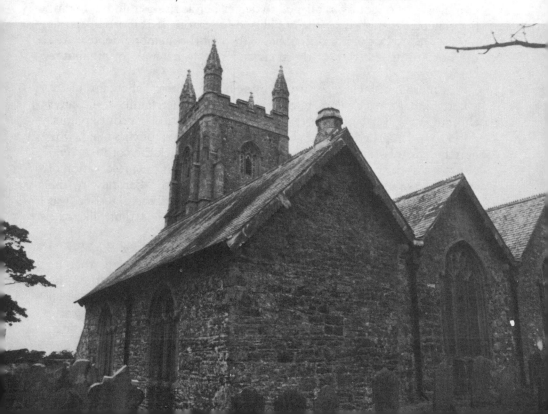

of the fact that one could be excused for looking antique if one had already been buried once.

Not only does Emma's identity become doubtful: so also does her nationality. Further reading on the subject of premature burial soon brings to light other candidates in different countries and different centuries.

The story of Frau Reichmuth Adolch antedates that of Emma and provides the template for all future variations on the theme. This lady 'died' of plague in Cologne in 1571. She revived as the gravedigger was attempting to steal her ring. In this case, the maid, a German equivalent of the Plymouth woman's husband's grandmother, opened the door to her former mistress and ran to her master to tell him the momentous news. More cynical than Lord Mount Edgcumbe, the husband exclaimed: 'It is as impossible for it to be my wife as for my horses to come out of the stable, run up into the garret and look out of the windows!' At that moment he chanced to look up to the roof and saw two stallions staring back at him. He was instantly convinced. When Frau Reichmuth was truly dead, a monument to commemorate her previous escape was erected in the Church of the Holy Apostles in Cologne.

British 'Emma clones' abound, including Lady Wyndham, the mother of the first Earl of Egremont, entombed in the family vault at St Decuman's in Somerset. Before its destruction in the blitz in the Second World War, Constance Whitney's memorial in St Giles Church, Cripplegate, London, was alleged to depict her as rising from her coffin, her slumbers disturbed by the cupidity of a sexton. It is more likely, as was attested to by the inscription beneath, that the memorial represented the hope of resurrection of the body and not an example of premature burial.

The most amusing variant is told by a French writer, Tallemant, about a certain Baroness de Panat. She was taken to her family tomb after choking on a fish bone, hotly pursued by a bunch of greedy servants. After they had prised the rings from the fingers, the baroness's maid, who bore her mistress a particular grudge, vengefully struck the corpse several blows across the neck. 'The malignity of the maid was the preservation of the mistress. Out flew the fish bone and up rose the Baroness to the complete discomfiture of the domestics. The retributive justice was complete, and the only objection to the narrative is that, like the fish-bone, it sticks in the throat.'[24]

Let us return finally to Emma. David Walsh, in *Premature Burial: Fact or Fiction'*, published in 1897, leaves the reader in no doubt that he regards all accounts of burial alive as pure fiction. He characterized the myriad 'Ring Cycle' accounts as typical of the 'From Our Foreign Correspondent' type of newspaper copy where the person, supposed and certified as dead, was committed to the grave, discovered, resuscitated

A sketch of St Giles's Church, Cripplegate, London, before it was extensively damaged in World War II, showing Constance Whitney rising up from her tomb after having been buried in a 'state of suspended animation'. This lady, like the Countess of Mount Edgcumbe, owed her recovery to the cupidity of a sexton.

and returned home to eat a hearty breakfast, all within the space of twenty-four hours.[25] He took particular exception to a letter about Emma written by Arthur Lovell of the London Association for the Prevention of Premature Burial to the editor of the Medical Press and Circular. Lovell cites as evidence for veracity the word of Sir J. Tollemache Sinclair, Bart. (formerly Member of Parliament for Caithness), who heard it from a grandson of the countess. Walsh is scathing: 'Anyone who advanced as proof of a scientific proposition, hearsay evidence of what happened three generations back would at once become a general laughing stock.'

2   THE MOMENT OF DEATH

In our graveyards with winter winds blowing
There's a great deal of to-ing and fro-ing
But can it be said
That the buried are dead
When their nails and their hair are still growing?

This anonymous twentieth-century limerick, composed to highlight
moral dilemmas in organ transplantation, neatly illustrates the notion
that we die in bits and that the hair and nails continue to grow even after
the heart has stopped beating. To certify a person as 'dead' does not
necessarily imply that all the different cells in all the organs of the body
are simultaneously dead. The practical problem is to decide the point at
which the 'process of dying' becomes irreversible, regardless of whether
the kidneys are still excreting urine or the liver still producing bile.

Fortunately when an Englishman is in doubt about anything, he can
always rely on the Bard of Avon to have had some thoughts on the
subject. In Shakespeare's *Romeo and Juliet* (Act IV, scene i) the signs of
death are listed by Friar Laurence:

...no pulse shall keep
His native progress, but surcease to beat;
No warmth; no breath, shall testify thou livest
The roses on thy lips and cheek shall fade
To paly ashes; thy eyes' windows fall,
Like Death, when he shuts up the day of Life;
Each part, deprived of supple government,
Shall stiff, and stark, and cold appear, like Death.

There is no single sign that would enable one to diagnose death; rather it
is a combination of many signs taken together.

INSENSIBILITY

A true corpse feels no pain. This fact has been used in the past to help
decide if a person is dead or not. In the nineteenth century Dr Josat
'invented' a vicious pair of forceps with sharp claws to pinch into the
nipples, on the premise that the dead would feel nothing. Another

method based on the same principle was to thrust long needles under finger and toe nails.

In earlier times attempts were often made to awaken the dead by arranging for women to gather around the body weeping, wailing and gnashing their teeth. Winslow says: 'If possible shock his Ears by hideous Shrieks and excessive Noises.' The truly dead would be oblivious to the cacophony.

Whilst on the subject of noses, consider the case of Luigi Vittori, a carabineer in the service of the pope in the 1870s, who was certified dead after an attack of asthma:

> A doctor, glancing at the body, fancied he detected signs of life. A lighted taper was applied to the nose. The body was pinched and beaten, and the taper was applied again, and so often and so obstinately that the nose was burned, and the patient, quivering in all his frame, drew short, spasmodic breaths – sure proofs, even to a non-professional witness, that the soldier was not altogether dead. In a short time the corpse was declared to be a living man. He left the hospital and resumed his duties, but his nose – a scarred and crimson beacon on his face – told till he died (which was soon afterwards) the sad story of his cure in the very jaws of the grave.[26]

Gustatory tests are rare but Winslow suggests pouring vinegar and pepper into the corpse's mouth, '… and where they cannot be had, it is customary to pour warm Urine into it, which has been observed to produce happy Effects'.

TEMPERATURE

A corpse is cold to the touch, and temperature is often used by forensic experts to estimate the interval since death took place. There are many pitfalls for the unwary, and it must be remembered that many deeply comatose patients are cold to the touch, while patients with infectious diseases such as cholera may have higher-than-normal body temperatures even though they are dead. Furthermore, a person dying at home in his own bed is likely to be kept warm by the bed clothes, whereas a hospital patient, quickly transferred to an icy mortuary, will lose body heat rapidly. The likelihood of misdiagnosis is small but not zero.

In the last century special thermometers called necrometers or thanatometers were introduced to aid in the diagnosis of death. The mercury scale was calibrated to indicate that the patient was 'alive', 'probably dead' or 'dead'. Physicians warned of the dangers of mistakes if the necrometer was used by anyone other than a qualified doctor – though one might justifiably ponder the expertise of any physician who had recourse to a thermometer which registered 'dead' before he would sign a death certificate.

With the unfortunate Luigi Vittori still fresh in the memory, it must be pointed out that hot tapers were often used on other parts of the body besides the nose. Heated flat-irons, melted sealing-wax and candle flames have all had their advocates as death tests. Unfortunately the production of a skin blister was no proof of life, since blisters could be formed by dropping sealing wax onto an *amputated* limb. A particularly dramatic test was put forward by Dr Marteno of Cordova. He would place a candle flame about half an inch from a finger or toe. If the person was truly dead, the layers of skin would separate to produce an air blister which, when it burst, would suddenly blow out the flame. Unfortunately a person does not have to be dead for this phenomenon to occur.

Brouardel favoured 'Mayor's hammer'. This entailed dipping an 'ordinary hammer' into boiling water and pressing it into the hollow of the abdomen, just below the breast bone. 'It is an excellent means of reviving a person who has fallen in a state of syncope' (faint).

RESPIRATION

The 'Mafia mirror test', so beloved of Chicago mobsters, is probably one of the most unreliable of all the tests of death. It did not work for King Lear when the body of his daughter Cordelia was brought to him (Act V, scene iii):

Lend me a looking-glass
If that her breath will mist or stain the stone
Why then, she lives.

A few lines later the regal 'feather test' proved just as inaccurate: 'This feather stirs: she lives!'

The third method of detecting respiration is the least known and the least reliable. A glass of water is filled to the brim and placed carefully on the end of the breast bone. If the water spills over the edge of the glass, the corpse yet breathes. Unfortunately posthumous hiccoughs caused by contraction of the diaphragm, or belching or breaking wind caused by expulsion of intestinal gases (Winslow's 'fermentative Motions of the Abdominal Humours') often resulted in spillage.

CIRCULATION

To most people, death is synonymous with a heart that no longer beats. But this need not be the case, since in the Reign of Terror during the

French Revolution it was not unusual for someone to have been decapitated but still have a strongly beating heart. Nevertheless cessation of the beating of the heart is generally the first sign of death checked out by a doctor. Again, mistakes are not unknown. A heart might beat so feebly as to be practically inaudible even with a stethoscope and acute hearing. Paradoxically, the longer and more intently one listens, the more difficult it is to distinguish weak beats from a miscellany of crackles and bubbles. Medical students are familiar with the fancied return of a dead man's beat – in reality what they are hearing is the sound of their own heart.

For those doctors whose hearing is less than perfect, a number of non-auditory aids have been devised to assist in ascertaining when the circulation has ceased. One, invented by Monsieur Middeldorf, consisted of a four-inch needle with a flag on the end. The needle was plunged into the heart of the patient – a still-beating heart caused the flag to oscillate.

Thankfully there were less draconian methods of testing whether the circulation had ceased. The simplest way was to open an artery and observe whether blood flowed or not – if the flow was obviously pulsatile, the heart was still beating; if there was an even, continuous flow, death was more likely.

A simpler test of circulation, propounded by Dr Magnus in 1872, is to tie a piece of string tightly around a finger. If the blood is still circulating, the end of the finger will become blue and swollen; if the finger remains white, death is more probable.

RIGOR MORTIS

When a person dies, the majority of the muscles of the body become flaccid. A dramatic depiction of this limpness is Michelangelo's *Pietá* in Florence, which shows Christ being supported with hanging head, pendulous arms and buckled legs. It is claimed that flaccidity of the jaw follows very soon after death – the lower jaw of the corpse falling open. Brouardel bemoaned the fact that this was so often overlooked by actors: 'In a performance of *Julius Caesar* at Her Majesty's Theatre a few years ago, Caesar's body, after he was stabbed and supposed to be dead, lay supine, and with the mouth closely shut. It was difficult to believe that he was not shamming.'

The relaxation of the facial muscles often produces a calm and serene countenance (Byron's 'mild, angelic air'), which is often so reassuring to the bereaved when relatives die after days of struggle and pain. Later muscular contraction '... dissipates the charm, knits the brow and draws down the mouth, pinching the features and changes a soft and soothing

The famous Wahncau case of a 45-year-old woman found dead standing upright in the corner of a timber yard. The normal muscular flaccidity which follows death has been replaced by a remarkable and instantaneous cadaveric rigidity.

expression into a look of profound suffering'.[27] It was in this state of spurious agony and terror that Sir Walter Scott had the misfortune to view the face of his dead wife.

After a variable period of time the flaccid muscles become stiff and rigid, and this gives rise to rigor mortis, in which the joints of the body become fixed. The rigidity is such that the body may be moved like a plank of wood. The fingers often become clenched at this point. The muscles around the hair roots also shorten and stiffen and result in 'goose pimples' – it is almost as if a corpse is showing sensitivity to the cold!

Rigor mortis usually starts in the neck and jaw and then spreads throughout the body, up to the face, down both arms and into the chest, abdomen and legs. When rigor mortis passes off and the muscles become soft and flaccid for the second and final time, the relaxation starts in the jaw and proceeds in the same order. The stiffness of the joints in rigor mortis can be overcome – with sufficient force an elbow joint or knee joint can be 'broken'.

There has been debate over the centuries about the time it takes for rigor mortis to develop after death – or even if rigor mortis *always* follows death. Haller, a man in whom scientific curiosity co-existed with profound grief, tested the muscles of his daughter for forty-eight hours after her death before declaring that he could not find any evidence of rigor mortis. When rigor mortis is present, it usually starts within one to six hours after death and commonly spreads to involve all the muscles of the body within a further four to ten hours. The whole process is accelerated in hot climates and when someone dies after a period of intense muscular activity, such as death in physical combat. In cold conditions, short of freezing, rigor mortis is often slow to develop – the muscles of skiers killed in the Alps may remain supple for long periods of time.

There is an important exception to the sequence of primary flaccidity – rigor mortis – secondary flaccidity, and it is a favourite of crime writers. Muscles which were *already* clenched at the point of death stay clenched and do not exhibit the initial flaccidity described above. It is for this reason that people who shoot themselves are found with their fingers tightly clutching a revolver. The same phenomenon is seen when drowning men die clutching weeds, or murder victims grasp the hair or clothing of their assailant in their clenched hands. On occasions the whole body becomes 'frozen' immediately after death, and cases are recorded of soldiers killed in action being found fixed in the act of sighting their rifles. At Balaclava a cavalry officer charged on for some time, erect in the saddle, sword drawn and levelled, despite the fact that he was quite dead – and decapitated.

There are a number of cases known of people dying whose whole body stiffens immediately without the initial period of flaccidity. There was a famous case of a woman in Germany who died standing up and whose body, instead of falling limply to the ground, remained stiff and upright.

Two other bizarre death tests depend on muscles. The first was described by Dr Collongues in 1862. He asserted that if you put the finger of a living person into your ear, two distinct noises can be heard – both sounds are described as 'rolling' and are produced by the slight movements of the finger muscles. It follows, then, that if you wish to ascertain the moment of death, you have only to stick one of the patient's fingers in your ear: when all falls silent, the patient is dead.

The second test makes use of the fact that the sphincter muscles of the anus relax after death. It is mentioned in John Snart's *Thesaurus of Horror*, published in 1817:

> The test used by the Turkish physicians seems very simple and natural, for they never think a subject dead, or even hopeless, while there is any irritability or contractile power in the *sphincter ani* muscle. The test may be easily performed by taking an ox or pig's bladder, with a tube attached to its orifice, and inflating it in the usual way, by blowing air into it from the mouth. In cold weather the bladder may be moderately heated by

immersion in hot water or by holding it in front of a fire. The tube is then inserted into the mouth of the patient, and air forced down the throat by compressing the bladder, while an assistant holds the nose and lips closed.

Death would be diagnosed by flatus passed through an anus whose sphincter muscle had lost its contractility. Snart continues, 'It is scarcely requisite to say, that the subject (for *obvious* reasons) should not be laid on a bed or other soft surface while this experiment is made. This appears so simple a test that it ought never to be omitted, even if all other trials have failed. It is within everyone's power to try it.'

So convinced was Snart of the infallibility of this test that he extracted a solemn promise from his daughter to carry it out in order to be sure he was dead: 'And upon the discharge of this paramount duty *alone* depends his future blessing and your welfare! And dreadful would it be to reflect that you had violated your father's dying injunction.'[28]

The invention of the electric coil seemed to answer the prayers of those people fearful of being misdiagnosed as dead. The solution was simple: the terminals of such a coil would be applied to the muscle of the presumed corpse; any muscular contraction would indicate that the diagnosis of death had been somewhat premature. At one time there was pressure for every parish priest to possess a Ruhmkorff's coil in order to test the muscular contractility before proceeding with the funeral ceremony. Unfortunately the test is based on a false premise: post-mortem muscle facial contortions can easily be produced in a dead person by the application of electrodes to either side of the mouth.

Ironically one of the effects of rigor mortis was actually thought by some to be a sign of continuing life rather than advanced death. It was a popular notion that discharge of semen was proof that a man still lived – in fact, the phenomenon was the result of the contraction of rigor mortis in the muscular tubules of the testicles.

PUTREFACTION

Putrefaction is the process which results in the gradual bacterial dissolution of the body into gases and liquids. It is often cited as the only truly infallible test of death.

The first sign of putrefaction is the appearance of a greenish discolouration of the skin in the lower right side of the abdomen (roughly in the region of the appendix). This is due to staining of the skin by blood seeping through the walls of vessels.

The pressure of gases produced by a decomposing body can force out stomach contents, expel a baby from the womb, tear the abdomen asunder or even burst apart the coffin. Expanding gases are also held

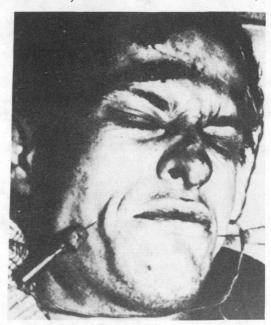

Contraction of the facial muscles following the application of an electric current forty-five minutes post-mortem shows the fallibility of this method of determining death.

responsible for the large number of Egyptian mummies found with rectal and vaginal prolapses. Brouardel says: 'When these gases are diffused abroad they create an abominable smell. To avoid this tainting of the atmosphere, I prick the bodies to let the gases escape: then I set light to them at the pricks, and long bluish flames start forth, like those of a blowpipe.' Prior to 1882, before the Paris morgue had its refrigeration apparatus, phosphorated hydrogen produced a will-o'-the-wisp phenomenon which could be seen running over and around the bodies.

The final stage of putrefaction is liquefaction of the body organs. The eyes are affected first, followed by the brain, stomach and liver. The womb liquefies last – this fact often enables pathologists to tell the sex of a body long after death and subsequent putrefaction.

The rate of putrefaction after burial depends on a number of factors, including the length of time from death to burial, the type of soil and the depth of the grave. A well-known dictum states, 'One week in air equals two weeks in water equals eight weeks buried in the ground', and this accurately reflects the ease with which microbes (and other opportunists such as flies, beetles and maggots) are able to start the process of decomposition. Some remarkably well-preserved cadavers exhumed in Transylvania prompted Dr Nathanial Shrock to investigate the subject of premature burial and to publish his results in the *Transylvania Journal of Medicine* in 1835.[29]

To retard putrefaction there was a brief vogue for india-rubber coffins in the last century. Despite the supposed impermeability of such coffins, the bodies contained within them generally succumbed to putrefaction. 'The body is destroyed in three or four years, and there is formed a liquid greasy substance, like black axle-grease, which rolls about, and when the coffin is opened gives forth an abominable stench.'[30]

So obsessed were Europeans with the misdiagnosis of death and the consequent risk of premature burial that frequent competitions were held to identify simple and reliable ways of differentiating a live body from a corpse. In 1846 Dr Bouchut won 1,500 francs merely for suggesting the stethoscope! In 1885 the French Academy of Sciences awarded a prize to Dr Maze for his protracted deliberations which finally came up with the answer: putrefaction. And in 1900 Dr Icard of Marseilles recommended injection beneath the skin of a weak solution of fluorescein: in the dead there is no effect, but if the person is alive, the whole of the skin goes yellow and the eyes green.

TWENTIETH-CENTURY UPDATE

If the concept of the 'moment of death' is such a legal fiction, when can it be said that a person is really dead, freeing his or her organs for transplantation into others?

In the years immediately following 1967, when Professor Barnard carried out the first heart-transplant operation, many people began to worry about the Montezuma Syndrome. Montezuma was an Aztec king who, besides revenging himself on Europeans by inducing severe diarrhoea, used to propitiate the sun god with human sacrifices – the still-beating hearts were scooped out of 20,000 living victims during his reign. After Barnard, the media frequently whipped up fears of modern-day Montezumas, eager for riches and fame, roaming intensive care wards on the lookout for donor hearts to implant, regardless of whether the donor was truly dead or only nearly so. Brain tracings have gone a long way to lessen the public's fears, the ghoul image giving way to a re-establishment of a surgeon's integrity. Nevertheless, since there is still no absolutely foolproof test of death, surgeons have to remain vigilant against an over-hasty diagnosis of irreversible death based on 'flat' brain tracings and have to be constantly aware of the profound, death-like but *reversible* conditions produced by hypothermia, drug overdoses (e.g., aspirin) and head injuries. There is no place or necessity for a hasty diagnosis of death. The transplant surgeon is only too aware of the maxim pertaining to organ removal: 'If in doubt, don't.'[31]

3   PRECAUTIONS TAKEN AGAINST PREMATURE BURIAL

In previous centuries the surest way to avoid being buried alive was to obtain the personal services of a doctor who could be trusted enough actually to view the corpse. Many of the instances of burial alive were the consequence of misdiagnosis by relatives or by absentee physicians who, perfectly legally, were not obliged to examine the body. A certificate of death needed only to state, 'John Smith died, as I am informed'.

The obvious answer was for your relatives to be in no doubt about the veracity of your death or, if there *was* some lingering doubt, for your relatives to be given explicit instructions how to eliminate any uncertainty.

The writers Wilkie Collins and Hans Christian Andersen always carried letters detailing the elaborate precautions they expected their relatives to observe in order to guard against their premature burial. Other people resorted to stating in their wills that no one would benefit financially until the body had been made irrevocably a corpse. The last will and testament of Francis Douce, nineteenth-century keeper of manuscripts at the British Museum and benefactor of the Bodleian Museum, left his executors in no doubts as to his wishes: 'I give to Sir Anthony Carlisle, two hundred pounds, requesting him to sever my head or to extract the heart from my body so as to prevent any possibility of return of vitality.'

Harriet Martineau, the Victorian author, was dogged all her life by ill health and deafness, which may have contributed to the precision with which she prepared for her death. 'It is my desire that my funeral shall be conducted in the plainest manner possible ... And it is my desire from an interest in the progress of scientific investigation that my skull should be given to Henry George Atkinson of Upper Gloucester Place, London, and also my brain if my death should take place within such distance of the said Henry George Atkinson's then present abode as to enable him to have it for the purposes of scientific observation.'[32] There is no more definitive method of ensuring one's death than by decapitation.

In a similar vein, another Victorian, Miss Frances Power Cobbe, had a last request designed to obviate premature burial: 'To perform on my body the operation of completely and thoroughly severing the arteries of

47

the neck and windpipe, nearly severing the head altogether, so as to make any revival in the grave absolutely impossible.' And just in case the bereaved relatives chose to ignore her instructions: 'If this operation be not performed, and its completion witnessed by one or other of my executors, and testified by the same, I pronounce all bequests in this will to be null and void.'

Others put their faith in a home-spun version of Middledorf's 'needle in the heart' technique, though it takes little imagination to predict how this particular death insurance might go fatally awry. One such case was reported in *The Undertakers' and Funeral Directors' Journal* in 1889:

Until about forty years ago a noted family of Virginia preserved a curious custom, which had been religiously observed for over a century. Over a hundred years ago a member of the family died, and, upon being exhumed, was found to have been buried alive. From that time until about 1850, every member of the family, man, woman, or child, who died, was stabbed in the heart with a knife in the hands of the head of the house. The reason for the cessation of this custom was that in 1850 or thereabouts, a beautiful young girl was supposed to be dead, the knife was plunged into her bosom, when she gave vent to a fearful scream and died. She had merely been in a trance. The incident broke her father's heart, and in a fit of remorse he killed himself not long afterwards.

For reasons that are not altogether obvious, a nineteenth-century aristocrat, Lady Burton, wife of the explorer Sir Richard, thought that it was infinitely preferable to be killed outright by an embalmer's injection, or even to come to life sliced by an anatomist's scalpel, than to recover consciousness underground. Hartmann quotes the case of a celebrated actress, Mademoiselle Rachel, who 'died' in Paris in 1858 and awoke from her trance after the process of embalming had started. Her reprieve was ephemeral, since she succumbed ten hours later as a result of the chemicals injected into her veins.

Another famous case was Hannah Beswick of Manchester. Having had a brother who narrowly escaped premature burial, she resolved that the same fate would not befall her. Consequently she bequeathed £25,000 to Dr Charles White, head of the Manchester Royal Infirmary, on the condition that he embalmed her body. Each year Dr White and two witnesses had to check that the good lady was really dead. In 1829 the mummy was given to the Manchester Museum, and tradition has it that it was placed upright in a grandfather clock in the director's office. It was insured for £10. In 1868 Miss Beswick was finally given a decent burial.

The risk of premature burial was increased in hot climates, since, for hygienic reasons, it was unwise for a body to remain above ground for too long. In the past in northern Italy the interval between death and burial was decreed to be forty-eight hours; in southern Italy this was reduced to twenty-four hours, with the greater attendant risk of burial alive.

WAITING MORTUARIES

All the experts who wrote about the risks of premature burial seemed to agree on one thing: that putrefaction was the surest sign of irreversible death. Unfortunately there were practical disadvantages in keeping the body of a loved-one unburied until such time as it began to rot. 'Waiting mortuaries' appeared to answer such aesthetic objections.

Although conceived in France, waiting mortuaries made their first appearance in Weimar, Germany, in 1791. For the twin reasons of hygiene and certification of death, such establishments received widespread approval. The ten Munich mortuaries were held up as the finest of their kind. Initially the removal of the dead to the mortuaries was optional, but following the cholera epidemic of 1869 it became obligatory. Within half an hour of a presumed death, the body was taken by a medical officer to the nearest mortuary.

The main hall at the Munich Waiting Mortuary. Corpses rested on zinc trenches filled with antiseptic and camouflaged by flowers. An intricate system of cords and pulleys attached to fingers caused bells to ring in the porter's lodge if there was any movement of the 'corpse'.

The corpse, after being washed and dressed, was placed in a sloping position on a sarcophagus under which was a zinc trench filled with antiseptic fluid. The whole was bedecked with sweet-smelling flowers, and the relatives were encouraged to take final photographs of the deceased. There were adjacent facilities for rich and poor, the only difference being the quality of the floral decoration.

The bodies remained exposed for up to seventy-two hours – less if signs of putrefaction appeared earlier. An intricate system of cords and pulleys was attached to the fingers of the corpse in such a way that the slightest movement caused bells to ring and attendants to come at the double. Staff were on duty twenty-four hours a day, made frequent inspections of the bodies and were never allowed to leave for any reason whatsoever, unless substitutes took their place. Such was the sensitivity of the system that false alarms were common, usually caused by draughts or the post-mortem movements of muscles.

It was not the theory behind the mortuaries but rather the practical financial implications that fuelled debate. Simply put, did such an expensive facility make financial sense? How many lives had been saved as a result of the use of waiting mortuaries? Opinions on this point varied from 'none' to 'one' to 'countless'. Tebb, somewhat bashfully, admits that there had been only a single unanswerable instance of recovery, and imagines the sceptic crying, 'What! Would you go to such pains and expense, when the possibility of a mistake is probably only one in 50,000 or even more?' Tebb's answer is predictable: 'Yes. Even if it were only one in fifty millions, *that one is a living human soul!*'

Brouardel was just such a sceptic. He maintained that in a hundred-year history there had been only one occasion when the bell had rung and that was when an arm fell down with the relaxation phase that followed the passing-off of rigor mortis. Tebb's single case had a comico-tragic element: 'A little child, five years old, was carried to the Leichenhauser (mortuary), and the corpse was deposited as usual. The next morning a servant from the mortuary knocked at the mother's house, carrying a large bundle in his arms. It was the resuscitated child, which she was mourning as lost. The child came to life in the mortuary by itself, and when the keeper saw it, it was playing with the white roses which had been placed on its shroud. The transports of joy that the mother experienced were so great that she fell down dead.'

COFFIN DEVICES

For those unfortunate to fall into a trance and revive in a coffin other than in Germany, all was not lost. They could always put their faith in an ingenious device invented in 1896 by Count Karnice-Karnicki,

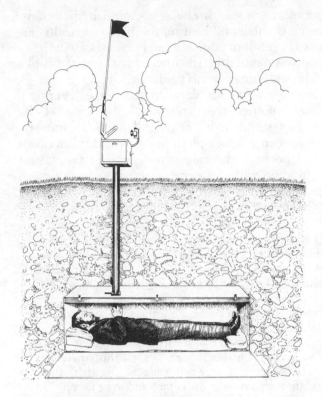

Count Karnice-Karnicki's apparatus to prevent burial alive. After a period of weeks, when it was safe to assume that death had indeed taken place, the vertical tube could be pulled from the coffin and re-used.

chamberlain to the Tsar of Russia. The count had imagined the dilemma of someone's waking up buried in a coffin, six feet underground. By what means could help be summoned? The apparatus he constructed consisted of a tube which passed vertically out of the coffin lid and ended in an airtight box above ground-level. Sitting on the chest of the corpse was a glass sphere attached to a spring which ran the length of the tube and was connected to a mechanism inside the box. The slightest movement of the chest was sufficient to move the sphere which stretched the spring which caused the lid of the box to fly open to admit air and light. The spring would also activate a flag, a light and a loud bell to attract the attention of anyone wandering through the graveyard. The tube would act to amplify the feeble cries for help.

The hire of such life insurance was deemed very reasonable, being roughly 12 shillings at the turn of the century. This would be well within the budget of all but the poorest and would give one the use of the apparatus for two to three weeks. After that length of time there was little likelihood of revival, and the tube could be pulled up and used in another coffin. The success rate of this device is not recorded, though it is not difficult to guess that most false alarms would be the result of moving muscles as rigor mortis faded, or else of abdominal eructations. How may relatives, seeing the flag and hearing the bell, frantically dug down to their loved ones as a result of post-mortem breaking of wind?

A more modest set-up was devised in 1893 by John Wilmer of Stoke Newington, London, who was buried in his garden in Church Street. A switch in his hand was wired up to an alarm in the house. Fearing a technical failure, Wilmer enjoined that 'an annual inspection of the fittings' be carried out! Not surprisingly, Edgar Allan Poe's cataleptic made much more elaborate contingency plans in case his condition was misdiagnosed as death: 'I doubted the care, the fidelity of my dearest friends. I dreaded that, in some trance of more than customary duration, they might be prevailed upon to regard me as irrecoverable.' Paranoid and fearful to the end, the story continued:

> Among other things I had the family vault so remodelled as to admit of being readily opened from within. The slightest pressure upon a long lever that extended far into the tomb would cause the iron portals to fly back. There were arrangements also for the free admission of air and light, and convenient receptacles for food and water, within reach of the coffin intended for my reception. This coffin was warmly and softly padded, and was provided with a lid, fashioned upon the principle of the vault door, with the addition of springs so contrived that the feeblest movement of the body would be sufficient to set it at liberty. Besides all this, there was suspended from the roof of the tomb, a large bell, the rope of which, it was designed, should extend through a hole in the coffin, and so be fastened to one of the hands of the corpse.

In 1896 an opportunist quack, Arthur Lovell, set up a society ostensibly to disseminate and share anxieties about being buried alive. The London Society for the Prevention of Premature Burial promised that the bodies of all members would be meticulously inspected by specially trained doctors before commitment to the sod. This might have passed as a laudable attempt to allay anxieties were it not for the fact that subscribers whose relatives failed to notify the society of their death, or those who failed to carry out Lovell's instructions to the letter, had their entire estates forfeited to the society.

II *The Fear of Posthumous Indignity*

1 DEATH AND RESURRECTION

Good friend, for Jesus' sake, forbear
To dig the dust enclosed here:
Blest be the man that spares these stones,
And curst be he that moves my bones.

The inscription on Shakespeare's tomb enshrines the inviolable right of everyone, friend and enemy alike, to be allowed to rest undefiled.[1] The fear that one's carcase may be subjected to posthumous indignity is primitive and deep-rooted.

In Britain, especially in the fifty years between 1780 and 1830, the chances of being dug up and removed from one's coffin were infinitely greater than the chances of being placed in one's coffin whilst still alive. Grave-robbing was a largely British phenomenon: long after other European countries had made sensible provision, British surgeons were *legally* unable to procure an adequate supply of dead bodies for dissection and the teaching of medical students. This potential dearth of anatomical material was readily supplied *illegally* by gangs of 'resurrectionists' or 'sack-'em-up' men, who would, for a fee, transfer a corpse from the sanctity of the grave to the indignity of the dissecting table.

The skill of a surgeon is directly related to his knowledge of anatomy. This would appear to be self-evident. When, in 1687, Louis XIV was operated upon for an anal fistula, the operation was a great success, due in no small measure to the fact that in the previous year the surgeon had practised on three lesser mortals before having the confidence to tackle the royal rump.

In the eighteenth century, bladder stones were much more common than they are today. Lithotomy, the operation to remove a stone, was attended by a fifty per cent mortality rate. William Cheselden, by dint of practice and a knowledge of anatomy, was able to pare the operating time down to a phenomenal fifty-four seconds. Reduced blood loss and less profound exhaustion resulted in greatly improved survival rates. The *Lancet* of 1828 compared Cheselden's performance to that of Bransby Cooper, a surgeon whose hallmark was incompetence and whose position was gained more by nepotism than skill. In a 'full, true and particular' account, Cooper's bungling – due in no small part to ignorance of anatomy – was accompanied by his repeated exclamations of 'Oh dear! Oh dear!' An hour-long operation was followed by twenty-nine hours of excruciating pain before the patient mercifully died.[2]

Such ineptitude could be countered only by proper training in anatomy. Unfortunately most people had such an inherent abhorrence of the idea of dissection that for centuries lower animals substituted for humans, in the misplaced hope that the anatomies of widely different species were fundamentally similar to man's. The most famous of the Greek physicians, Galen, who lived in the second century, derived his knowledge of anatomy from dissections of pigs, apes, dogs and oxen. Thus it was that for thirteen centuries the human breastbone was supposed to be segmented like that of an ape, and the liver to be divided into many lobes like that of a pig; the uterus was supposed to be in two long horns as in the dog, and the hip bones to be flared as in the ox. When, in the sixteenth century, the famous anatomist Vesalius (the same person who supposedly killed a cardinal on the dissecting-table) showed that Galen's description of the hip bone was erroneous, apologists claimed that over the centuries the human hip bone must have changed shape as a result of wearing tight trousers.

In such an atmosphere of ignorance it is small wonder that surgery made little progress. Most physicians, looking down their noses at surgeons who sullied themselves by actually examining the anatomy of a corpse, would invoke the Bible: 'He that toucheth the dead body of any man shall be unclean seven days' (Numbers XIX, 11).

In 1300 the study of anatomy was dealt a crippling blow. In that year Pope Boniface VIII issued a bull excommunicating anyone who cut up or boiled a human body. This edict was intended to discourage crusaders to the Holy Land from cutting up and boiling any of their number who died, in order that their bones could be easily packaged and sent back to Europe for a Christian burial. Unfortunately, because the bull was taken to include dissection, the scientific study of human anatomy was virtually abandoned by the medical profession, and surgery became the province of uneducated barbers, bath-house keepers, sow-gelders, executioners and vagabonds.

With the Renaissance came a renewed interest in human anatomy. The bodies used were usually those of executed criminals, and demand invariably outstripped supply. Ardour for knowledge sometimes made men contravene civilization's most powerful taboos: Rondeler, a

The Anatomy Lesson of Dr Deyman by Rembrandt (1606–69).

professor at Montpellier Medical School, dissected the body of his own dead child before a class of his students; and William Harvey, who in 1628 published his researches on the circulation of the blood, reached his conclusions 'by autopsy on the live and dead', including post-mortem dissections of his own father and sister. One would hope that Harvey's live autopsies were not performed on humans, though it is salutary to recall that the ancient anatomists of Alexandria obtained the bodies of criminals '... for dissection alive, and contemplated, even while they breathed, those parts which nature had before concealed'. In Montpellier, in the sixteenth century, the French government donated one criminal each year for live dissection.

In 1540, during in the reign of Henry VIII, an act of parliament was passed creating 'The United Company of Barbers and Surgeons'. To this company was given the exclusive right to dissect the 'bodyes of ffoure condemned persons yerely for anatomies'. Four bodies each year could never satisfy the needs of the surgeons – nor the six allowed in the reign of Charles II. The beadle of the Barbers' Company, whose duty it was to collect the bodies from the Tyburn gallows, often had to run the gauntlet of an angry mob, whipped up by the deceased's relatives, intent on preventing the corpse's being taken for dissection. In the company's accounts for 1719 the following item appears:

> Paid the Beadles expenses for going to
> Tyburn for Body for the Muscular Lecture
> when they could not get one by reason
> of a great Mobb of soldiers and others....................................... 13s 0d

Another problem, alluded to in Chapter 1, is well illustrated by the following item, recorded in 1740, concerning one William Duell, convicted rapist:

> Paid the Beadles their expenses in
> bringing body from Tyburne... £2 19s 0d
> Paid Joseph Wheeler the Company's
> Clerk his Coach hire and expenses
> in attending the Sheriffs when the
> Body came to life.. 10s 0d

Duell's sentence was commuted to transportation for life.

In 1752 Parliament passed an act whereby all those found guilty of murder were to be hanged and then handed over to the surgeons for dissection: 'In no case whatsoever the body of any murderer shall be suffered to be buried'.

John Bellingham was hanged for shooting the Prime Minister, Spencer Percival, in the House of Commons in May 1812. A detail from a contemporary drawing by an unidentified artist.

JOHN BELLINGHAM, ASSASSIN

Typical of the murderers who were publicly hanged and then dissected was John Bellingham. On an afternoon in May 1812, Bellingham walked into the lobby of the House of Commons and shot dead the prime minister, Spencer Perceval. Bellingham had previously spent two years in a Russian gaol and on his release and return to Britain had demanded retribution from the government. Although it was obvious that Bellingham was insane, in a trial described by Lord Brougham as 'the greatest disgrace to English justice' the witless assassin was condemned to be hanged and dissected.

Duly, one week later, Bellingham was hanged in front of the Debtors' Door of Newgate Prison. He uttered his last words with impressive dignity: 'I thank God for having enabled me to meet my fate with so much fortitude and resignation.' After an hour he was cut down and his body transported in a cart through Old Bailey, Newgate Street and St Martin's-le-Grand to the beadle of the Company of Surgeons in St Bartholomew's Hospital. A description of the scene has been left to us by Sir Richard Owen, himself a Bart's man:

> The college hired a house in Cock Lane, to which these bodies [Bellingham and one other] were brought from Newgate. Sir William Blizard, the President, was attired in court dress as the proper costume for the official act. They heard the shouts of the crowd and then the noise of the approaching cart. Then came the heavy steps of the executioner tramping up the stairs. He had the body of a man on his back, and entering the room, lets it fall on the table. Sir William Blizard made a small cut with a scalpel over the breast bone and bowed to the executioner. This was the formal recognition of the purpose for which the body had been delivered.[3]

Bellingham's skull was lost for over 150 years until finally located in a box in the basement of the anatomy department of St Bartholomew's Medical School. There was no problem in identification, since someone had thoughtfully written 'Bellingham' in ink across the forehead. It is eerie to compare a contemporary illustration of Bellingham, the noose around his neck, with the actual skull of this unfortunate madman.

The ignominy of dissection moved condemned men to eloquence. In 1750 William Smith, an Irish forger, was hanged at Tyburn. While in the condemned cell he composed a newspaper advertisement appealing for public subscriptions to save his body from the anatomists:

> As to my corporeal frame, it is unworthy of material notice; but for the sake of that reputable family from which I am descended, I cannot refrain from anxiety when I think how easily this poor body, in my friendless and

necessitous condition, may fall into the possession of the surgeons, and perpetuate my disgrace beyond the severity of the law ... The deprivation of life is a sufficient punishment for my crimes ... Those who compassionate my deplorable situation are desired to send their humane contributions to Mrs Browning's, next door to the Golden Acorn, in Little Wild Street.'[4]

In 1828 William Corder was tried and executed in Bury St Edmunds for the murder of Maria Martin in the Red Barn. He was subsequently dissected and anatomized. A copy of the proceedings was later bound in Corder's own skin, which was given to the town museum. His skeleton was exhibited in a glass case in the local hospital. Beneath the case was a box for visitors' contributions. By means of an ingeniously constructed spring, the arm of the skeleton pointed towards the box as soon as it was approached by a visitor. The skeleton was later given to the Royal College of Surgeons in London, where it can be seen to this day.[5]

In 1775 William Hunter, the Surgeon and brother of the more Famous John, was particularly excited by the physical development of one of the criminals brought to the Royal College of Surgeons from Tyburn. He thought the body would make ideal teaching material for students at the Royal Academy of Arts. While it was still warm and before rigor mortis had set in, Hunter posed the body in such a position as to show the muscular development to its maximum effect. He then allowed the body to stiffen, removed the skin from the corpse and made a mold. The Academy still has the cast of such a flayed criminal, 'Smugglerius'.

Of course, class distinctions extended even to murderers. Earl Ferris,

The 'Smugglerius' cast of a flayed criminal: after hanging at Tyburn the body was 'put into an attitude and ... when he became stiff, we all set to work and by the next morning we had the external muscles all well exposed'.

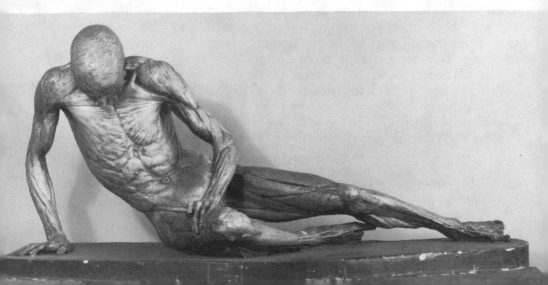

who shot his steward, was not subjected to the indignity of dissection. He was executed in May 1760 and his body taken to the Surgeon's Hall, but after a small incision had been made in the chest, purely as a formality, the corpse was returned to his relatives for 'funeral obsequies suitable to his station'.

SUPPLY, DEMAND AND MARKET FORCES

In the late eighteenth century a number of intelligent and gifted men were drawn to surgery and, as a result, the social status of surgeons slowly improved. Surgeons, jealous of their reputations and incomes, endeavoured to restrict recruitment to like-minded students. Such practices engendered profound resentment in those candidates rejected for surgical training. As a consequence, the reigns of the first two Georges (1714–60) saw the rapid growth of privately run medical schools set up to challenge the monopoly, nepotism and corruption of the established body of surgeons (who had parted company with the barbers in 1745). Since these new schools had to offer human dissection in order to attract students, the numbers of corpses available for dissection, always paltry compared to the demand, soon became woefully inadequate. Since the dead bodies needed by the private medical schools could be obtained only by illegal means, the stage was set for the flowering of private enterprise in men prepared to supply dissecting material for trainee surgeons. The reigns of George III and George IV (1760–1830) were to witness the rise of the universally loathed and reviled 'Resurrectionists'.

Although Sir Astley Cooper despised Ben Crouch, the two men were business partners. Cooper was president of the Royal College of Surgeons and had gained his baronetcy in 1829 for his 'courage' in removing a sebaceous cyst from George IV's scalp. ('Astley Cooper was also the hapless Bransby Cooper's uncle). Crouch was a drunken grave robber. Each depended on the other for his livelihood, for without Crouch, Cooper would be starved of the dissecting material he needed to keep his medical students from decamping to a rival anatomy school; and without Cooper, Crouch would have to ply an honest trade for a lot less remuneration. Cooper was the most famous surgeon of his day; Crouch was the leader of the infamous Borough Gang.

Two clues to the business that brought together such social opposites are provided by the following macabre accounts which received nationwide publicity at the time.

On a wild February day in 1809 the naked body of an old woman was washed ashore at the Bay of Nigg, near Aberdeen. The badly decomposed corpse was identified as Mrs Janet Spark, a 90-year-old widow, who might well have been regarded as the unfortunate victim of a shipwreck were it nor for the fact that this same lady had been buried in the graveyard of St Fittick's Church three days before Christmas.

In October 1826 three large casks sat on the quay at St George's Dock Passage, Liverpool, waiting to be loaded on the *Latona* for delivery to Edinburgh. The casks, labelled 'Bitter Salts', were addressed to Mr G.H. Ironson. The crew complained about the noxious smell, until finally the captain pulled out a clump of hay which had been plugging a hole in the side of one of the casks. Immediately '... the stench became almost unbearable.' Undeterred, the captain put his hand through the hole and to his horror and surprise it sank deep into putrefying human flesh. When the police opened the casks, they found the bodies of four men and seven women carefully packed in salt. The police traced the origin of the cargo to a cellar beneath a school, where they discovered a further nine men, five women, five boys and three girls. The schoolchildren had recently complained of the smell coming from the cellar but the Revd James Macgowan, headmaster and innocent dupe, had merely 'opened the windows and remarked that it was occasioned by the closeness'.

THE DIARY OF A RESURRECTIONIST

A diary which records the activities of a resurrectionist gang during a twelve-month period spanning 1811 and 1812 is now the property of the Royal College of Surgeons, London. It is probably the work of Joshua Naples, a member of Crouch's gang, and has provided a unique and invaluable insight into the clandestine activities of the body-snatchers.[6]

Five months before Bellingham was hanged and dissected, an entry in the diary testified to the fact that London anatomists had sources of bodies other than those of convicted murderers:

Sunday, 5th [of January 1812]:
At home all day. Met at 5, whole [gang] went to Newin [Newington]. Got 3 [bodies]. Jack and me took them to Wilson [James Wilson of the Great Windmill Street Anatomy School], Came home, met at 12, got 5 [adult bodies] and 2 small at Harps [Harper, probably the name of a keeper of a burial ground], afterwards went to Big Gates [probably the entrance to another London burial ground], got 3 adults, left Dan at home, trok the whole to Barthom [St Bartholomew's Hospital].

This abbreviated account of one day's work neatly encapsulates the lure of body-snatching: money, and lots of it. The deadly haul that Sunday was eleven adult corpses and two children. Each adult corpse would be worth 4 guineas, provided they had not undergone a post-mortem examination. Children's bodies were often sold by length: 6 shillings for the first foot and then 9 pence per inch. After expenses, a resurrectionist could expect to take home – or, more likely, to spend on beer – in excess of £10 per week, twenty times the average earnings of an unskilled worker.

The easiest method of obtaining dead bodies was to bribe the people who were employed to safeguard them – burial-ground keepers. These low-paid officials could be persuaded to leave gates unlocked to facilitate entry for the resurrectionists. Bribery of a keeper probably accounts for the large number of corpses obtained by the gang in February: 'Thursday 20th. Met and went to Pancress [a parish church between King's Cross and Kentish Town], got 15 large and 1 small took them to Barthol [St Bartholomew's Hospital].'

Failing such official connivance, the wives of resurrectionists would often pose as mourners, tag onto the end of a funeral party and follow the bereaved to the graveyard. The women would then make careful mental note of the precautions that the deceased's relatives had made in their futile attempt to foil the grave-robbers. The most common method was to place stones or shells in the earth covering the coffin. If any of these markers was subsequently moved, it would be evident that the resurrectionists had come visiting. This strategy had two serious flaws: firstly, any disturbance of the markers would be noticed only *after* the body had been laid out on the anatomist's table; secondly, after exhuming the body, the resurrectionists could easily replace the stones and shells in their original positions.

There were many misconceptions about the methods used by resurrectionists for lifting a corpse. Thomas Wakley, founder of the *Lancet*, gave in 1896 the following account of the *modus operandi* of the resurrectionists:

In the case of a new, or not quite new grave, the ingenuity of the Resurrectionist came into play. Several feet – fifteen or twenty – away from the head or foot of the grave, he would remove a square of turf, about eighteen or twenty inches in diameter. This he would carefully put by, and then commence to mine. Most pauper graves were of the same depth, and, if the sepulchre was that of a person of importance, the depth of the grave could be pretty well estimated by the nature of the soil thrown up. Taking a five foot grave, the coffin lid would be about four feet from the surface. A rough slanting tunnel, some five yards long, would, therefore, have to be constructed, so as to impinge exactly on the coffin head. This being at last struck (no very simple task), the coffin was lugged up by hooks to the surface, or, preferably, the end of the coffin was wrenched off with hooks while still in the shelter of the tunnel, and the scalp or feet of the corpse secured through the open end, and the body pulled out, leaving the coffin almost intact and unmoved.

The body once obtained, the narrow shaft was easily filled up and the sod of turf accurately replaced. The friends of the deceased, seeing that the earth *over* his grave was not disturbed, would flatter themselves that the body had escaped the Resurrectionist; but they seldom noticed the neatly-placed square of turf, some feet away.

Perhaps the reason that the square of turf was 'seldom noticed' was because it was very seldom there. A little thought would soon show that anyone trying to rob a grave by this method would probably be buried alive in a collapsing tunnel. To imagine that such a tunnel, eighteen inches in diameter and fifteen feet long, could accommodate a grown man, complete with grappling-tackle, and then allow him room to manoeuvre enough to prise off the end of the coffin and haul out the body! It does not take into account obstacles such as intervening

Pages from the diary of a resurrectionist (1811–12), usually ascribed to Joseph Naples, and detailing his activities as a grave robber. When the Anatomy Act was passed in 1832, Naples went 'legitimate' and joined the staff of the dissecting room of St Thomas's Hospital.

boulders, grave stones or graves; nor does it explain how to replace twenty-five cubic feet of earth in a manner that would not arouse suspicion.

The real methods used in lifting bodies were much less intricate and a lot quicker. Simplest of all was when the resurrectionist doubled as the grave-digger (or, more accurately, grave-filler), which was often the case. Working hidden from view at the bottom of the grave, he would open the coffin and bundle the body into a sack. Each time earth was thrown in to fill the grave, the sack would be raised. Ultimately the empty coffin would be buried six feet down but the sack would be left just below the surface, where it could be easily retrieved under cover of darkness.

More commonly, a resurrectionist gang, using wooden shovels to minimize noise, would dig vertically down to the head end of the coffin. They would then cover that part of the coffin with canvas sacking (again to reduce noise) and proceed to prise off enough of the coffin lid to expose only the head of the corpse. Deftly they would slip a rope noose over the head and draw the body out of the coffin and up to the surface. Francis Clerihew was a law student who would sometimes join his medical student friends to help them lift a corpse. He wrote an account of these nocturnal raids called *My First Resurrection*. As the body was being hauled to the surface, '... out flashed the moon, full on his wan, discoloured face. His dull glassy eyes were wide open, and, as I thought, leered knowingly on me; his blue lurid lips were drawn back, and showed his white teeth; his arms hung dangling to the ground, and his head rolled about on its shoulders.'[7]

An account of what it was like to be on the 'receiving end' was provided by John Macintire, buried alive in a state of trance in 1824: 'All was silent ... I heard a low sound in the earth and fancied that the worms and reptiles were coming ... The sound continued to grow louder and nearer ... Can it be possible, thought I, that my friends suspect they have buried me too soon? ... They dragged me out of the coffin by the head ... I was thrown down like a clod ... Being rudely stripped of my shroud I was placed naked on a table ... the demonstrator took his knife and pierced my bosom ... a convulsive shudder instantly followed ... my trance was at an end.'[8]

Ironically it was not a crime to steal a dead body, since, in law, a corpse did not constitute 'property'. The only items deemed property were the coffin itself and the shroud. Well aware of this legal distinction, the robbers would invariably strip the corpse and carefully place the shroud back in the coffin. The bodies – or 'things' as they are referred to in the diary – would then be transported, usually by cart, to a safe house, where they could be sorted according to age, freshness and destination. To reduce suspicion and the risk of being attacked by members of the public, the bodies were usually delivered in daylight, always assuming the robbers were not incapably drunk by dawn.

RELATIONSHIPS WITH THE ANATOMISTS

Although there was interdependence between resurrectionist and anatomist, it was usually the resurrectionist who had the whip hand. The anatomists were only too well aware that without an adequate supply of dissecting material their students would go elsewhere. Consequently, besides payment for an actual body, the resurrectionists would demand a *douceur* at the beginning of the autumn anatomy season as evidence of the anatomist's 'goodwill', and 'finishing money' at the end of the season. The anatomists were also expected to finance the resurrectionist's family if he were imprisoned, and to welcome him back with a *solatium* (financial compensation) upon his release from gaol.

Those anatomists foolish enough to argue with such overt blackmail risked the full vengeance of the resurrectionists. Joshua Brookes, (described by one of his colleagues as 'without exception the dirtiest professional I have ever met with; his filthy hands begrimed his nose with continual snuff'[9]), one of the finest anatomists of his day, once refused to pay a *douceur*. One night the resurrectionists paid him a visit. At each end of the street in which his anatomy school was located, they placed a badly decomposed body. Two young ladies out for a stroll stumbled over one of the corpses, and such was the public outcry that the police had to be called to save Brookes from the fury of the mob.

More gruesome still was the revenge of 'Old Cunny', an Irishman who used to supply bodies to the Ohio Medical College in Cincinnati. To pay back students who had played a trick on him, he dug up the body of someone who had died of smallpox and succeeded in infecting many of the students with this fatal disease.

THE WILES OF THE RESURRECTIONISTS

Competition was also fierce among the resurrectionists themselves. Alliances and rivalries would frequently change. It was not unknown for one gang to break into an anatomy school and mutilate any corpses delivered by their rivals. It was not unusual for hospitals *knowingly* to buy back the bodies of patients who had died on the wards and who had been buried in the hospital graveyard. By this means hospitals were able to preserve the fiction that paupers would receive a decent burial and not be subjected to the anatomists if they were to die. On New Year's Day 1812 Joshua Naples and his confederates dug up three adults, two in Guy's Hospital cemetery and one in St Thomas's – and then sold them back to precisely the same hospitals that had buried them.

Occasionally they would steal back bodies they themselves had delivered and proceed to resell them elsewhere. Sometimes wives of resurrectionists would call at a surgeon's premises and demand the body of their 'relative'. The received corpse would then be quickly sold a second, even third time.

Another useful role for wives was to visit local workhouses after the death of an inmate and pose as long-lost relatives. It is difficult to believe that the authorities were duped by this sham, but since it saved them the expense of a funeral, few questions were asked.

Many of the vicissitudes of plying his necessary trade are alluded to by

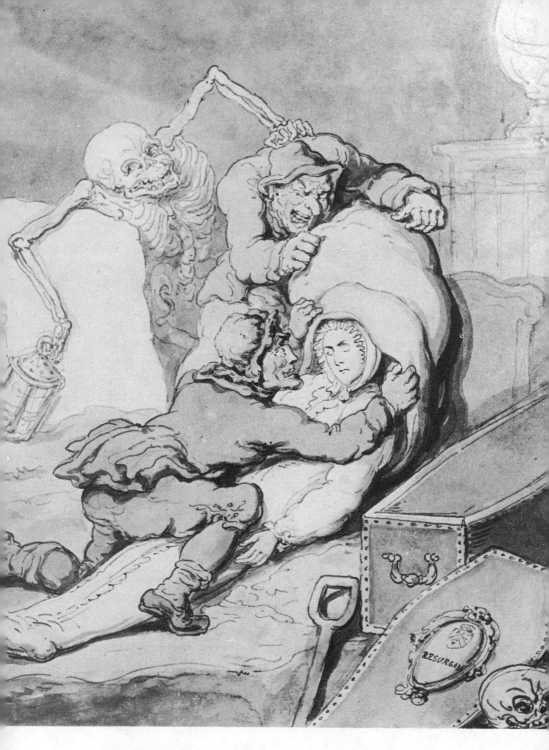

The Resurrectionists by Thomas Rowlandson (1756–1827).

Naples in his diary: 'cart broke down'; 'met the patrols'; 'moon at full, could not go'; 'Bill [Harnett] got arrested'; 'the dogs flew at us'; 'cut off extremities' (usually when a corpse had been subjected to a post mortem and only the arms and legs were intact); and 'found a watch planted' (someone guarding the grave – usually a relative who could not be bribed). Bad nights were those when they 'missed' – returned empty-handed.

On occasions the gang exhumed a corpse only to find it 'bad'. But even then all was not lost: 'Work'd two holes, one bad, drew the canines.' Anatomists were not the only professional clients of the 'sack-'em-up' men – they also had very lucrative business dealings with dentists, who would be eager customers for purchasing front teeth to make dentures for the wealthy. It is said that one resurrectionist gained entry into a family vault and managed to make off with £60 worth of teeth.

At the time of the Peninsular War, Ben Crouch and Jack Harnett (Bill Harnett's brother) went on a business trip to Spain. There they used to hover like vultures pulling the teeth from dead and moribund alike. Hubert Cole, in *Things for the Surgeon*, describes their activities: 'The battlefield quiet in the half-light, the deadly perfume of blood and gunpowder hanging over the broken remains of men and horses, and the jackal figure moving stealthily from one body to the next, pincers in hand, open haversack at his side, wrenching and twisting, then passing on, leaving each tortured face with a wider, bloodier grin than before.'[10]

Bodies were also taken for other, still more macabre uses. In an article printed in 1732, reference is made to one John Loftas who confessed to the plunder of more than fifty bodies 'not only for their coffins and burial clothes, but of their fat, where the bodies afforded any', which he retailed at a high price.[11]

BURKE AND HARE

Edinburgh, 'the Athens of the North', had a second, less flattering, sobriquet – 'Resurrectionist Capital of the World'. Such was the demand for corpses by the city's medical students that cadavers commanded high prices, and supplies were regularly transported from London and shipped from Dublin.

Orthodoxy in resurrectionism was represented by those who actually waited for the natural death of their quarry. It was inevitable that sooner or later someone would realize that *accelerating* death was much more cost-effective than waiting around for death to occur naturally.

Oft it is wondered why, on Irish ground
No poisonous reptile ever could be found

Revealed the secret stands! – of nature's work,
She saved her venom to create a Burke!
'By a Medical Officer in the Royal Navy', 1829

William Burke and William Hare, two Irish ex-patriates living in Edingburgh in the 1820s, never sullied themselves by robbing a grave. Instead, abetted by their womenfolk, they eased fifteen people, mainly prostitutes, into the world beyond (via the anatomist's table) by suffocation – or 'burking' as it came to be known.

The idea first occurred to Hare in 1827, when one of his lodgers died owing him £4. Bemoaning his ill fortune, he discussed the debt with Burke. Between them they hatched a plan to remove the man from his coffin and sell the corpse for dissection to Professor Munro. Having bundled the body into a sack, the two men asked the way to Munro's residence. A medical student directed them instead to Surgeon's Square and the house of Dr Robert Knox, who bought the corpse for £7.10s. – more than either of them could legally earn in a month! Henceforth anyone who could be inveigled back to Hare's boarding house was rendered incapably drunk and promptly suffocated with a pillow. Knox unquestioningly bought all the bodies that Burke and Hare could supply, being especially pleased with the freshness of their material compared to the rotting flesh shipped to him from Ireland.

Inevitably a number of the victims were recognized by the doctors and medical students. As Mary Paterson, a well-known prostitute, lay naked on the slab, the beauty of her body was much admired by some of her former clients. It is thought by some that Knox's assistant, William Fergusson (later president of the Royal College of Surgeons and surgeon to Queen Victoria), suggested to Burke that he cut off the woman's long golden hair in order to prevent positive identification should anyone come snooping. So proud was Knox that he postponed dissection of Paterson and had her placed in a barrel of whisky for three months. James Wilson, an 18-year-old known throughout the city as 'Daft Jamie', was instantly recognizable both facially and by his deformed and calloused feet. Fergusson promptly cut off the head and feet and quickly began the dissection.

With such medical collusion Burke and Hare had every reason to feel that their source of easy money need never be discovered. But with continued success and excess alcohol came fatal carelessness. Two of Hare's lodgers found the naked body of Madgy Docherty stuffed under a bed awaiting transportation to Knox's premises. The police were informed and the corpse was later found in the doctor's cellar.

Hare obtained immunity from prosecution by turning King's Evidence. On Christmas Day 1828 the jury found Burke guilty, and on 28 January 1829, before a delighted crowd, estimated to be between 20,000 and

Mary Paterson, an Edinburgh prostitute and victim of Burke and Hare,
whose body was sold to Dr Robert Knox, the anatomist. He so admired her
beauty that he preserved the corpse in whiskey and postponed dissection
for three months. Redrawn by Robin Boutell from a contemporary sketch.

30,000, he was hanged and his body handed to the College of Surgeons
to be publicly dissected by Professor Munro. His skeleton still hangs in
the Anatomy Museum of Edinburgh University. Pieces of Burke's skin
were tanned and sold at high prices – Charles Dickens is said to have
used one as a book-mark.

The Burke and Hare murders did much to focus attention on the
inadequate legal provision of bodies for dissection. Mob fury helped
concentrate the minds of the members of a parliamentary select
committee set up to investigate matters in 1828.

BURKING COMES TO LONDON

Although grave robbing continued after Burke's execution, the public
furore abated and the Anatomy Act of 1829, intended to provide
alternative sources of bodies for dissection, was passed in the House of
Commons but defeated in the House of Lords. Then, in 1831, public
indignation was again roused to fury by the activities of two London
burkers, Thomas Williams and his brother-in-law, John Bishop.

These men enticed a 14-year-old boy into their house in Nova Scotia
Gardens. His name was Carlo Ferrari and he made a meagre living by
exhibiting caged white mice in the London streets. Williams and Bishop
plied the youth with rum and laudanum and then rendered him
unconscious with a blow to the neck. Finally they lowered him, head
first, into a well.

Disposing of Ferrari's body proved difficult: the men tried the private anatomy schools and Guy's Hospital before arriving at King's College Hospital. The staff at King's were suspicious about the way the boy had met his death. Mr Partridge, the demonstrator of anatomy, kept the murderers waiting while he professed to get change for a £50 note. In fact, Partridge's colleagues were contacting the police. Subsequently an empty mouse cage was found back at the men's house, and at Mr Partridge's suggestion cheese was put down to tempt the incriminating white mice out from under the floorboards. A post-mortem examination showed that the boy's teeth had been removed and sold to a dentist.

Both men were hanged and dissected. Williams was sent off to St Bartholomew's, and Bishop met up for a final appointment with Mr Partridge at King's. The death of Carlo Ferrari had an immense impact on accelerating the passage of Warburton's Anatomy Act of 1832.

UPPER-CLASS RESURRECTIONISTS

In the seventeenth century medical students were expected to provide their own cadavers for dissection. In later decades, when the dangers of getting caught necessitated that such work be delegated to what Astley Cooper called 'the dregs of humanity', there were still a few surgeons who relished the challenge of procuring their own corpses.

One such was the Edinburgh anatomist and surgeon Robert Liston (1794–1847), who formed an unlikely alliance with Ben Crouch, 'the Corpse King' (on an enforced holiday from London), to lift the body of a boy who had died with hydrocephalus (water on the brain). The boy's relatives, well aware of the worth of the body to an anatomist, mounted a dusk-to-dawn vigil in the cemetery on the shores of the Firth of Forth. Many weeks after the burial two well-dressed gentlemen parked their dog-cart at the local pub, telling the landlord that they were expecting delivery of a parcel. In a little while a man dressed in scarlet livery deposited a parcel under the seat of the cart and walked away. Presently the two men reappeared and trotted off at a brisk pace. The stable boy commented that the liveryman bore a remarkable resemblance to one of the owners of the cart. At about the same time the night watch arrived at the cemetery, only to find the grave disturbed and the boy's body decapitated. Liston and Crouch had lifted the corpse in less than thirty minutes.

(To redress Liston's reputation it must be recorded that he was one of the most skilled of surgeons in those grisly pre-anaesthetic days. He once took a mere thirty-three seconds to amputate a patient's leg at the thigh – unfortunately, in so doing, he also amputated three of his assistant's fingers.)

Although the majority of the bodies dug up by London resurrectionists were delivered to the city's anatomists, there was a limited export market. Naples occasionally packed up corpses for delivery north, especially to Edinburgh.

When Laurence Sterne, author of *Tristram Shandy*, died penniless in 1768, his body was exhumed from the burial ground of St George's, Hanover Square, and turned up on an anatomist's table in Cambridge two days later. Although dying a pauper made Sterne vulnerable to falling prey to the resurrectionists (since the poor were invariably buried in shallower graves and required a lot less effort to lift), Sir Astley Cooper in his evidence to the select committee boasted that, 'There is no person, let his situation in life be what it may, whom, if I were disposed to dissect, I could not obtain.' Such arrogant self-confidence makes it improbable that Cooper was the surgeon Robert Southey had in mind in his poem 'The Surgeon's Warning':

I have made candles of dead men's fat
The sextons have been my slaves
I have bottled babes unborn, and dried
Hearts and livers from rifled graves

And my Prentices now will surely come
And carve me bone from bone
And I who have rifled the dead man's grave
Shall never have rest in my own.

METHODS OF FOILING THE RESURRECTIONISTS

The surest way to lay undisturbed in the grave was to have a large extended family who thought enough of you to mount a grave-side vigil for three or four weeks after your funeral – by which time putrefaction would have seriously dented the enthusiasm of resurrectionist and anatomist alike. In some burial grounds brick buildings were erected to keep the bodies under lock and key until they putrefied. Such a building can still be seen in the burial ground at Crail.

The putrefaction principle also lay behind the construction of the turntable storage house at Udny, just north of Aberdeen. Corpses in their coffins were loaded onto the turntable through a hole in the perimeter wall. The rotation of the table was so slow that one revolution of the carousel took two to three weeks. Consequently, by the time the body reappeared at the aperture, it was in a state of advanced decomposition and of no interest to the anatomists.

Infamy could greatly enhance the desire of surgeons to lift and dissect. Dick Turpin, the notorious highwayman, always feared ending up on an anatomist's slab. When he was hanged at York in 1739, his friends and admirers buried him deep in an unmarked grave. Despite these precautions, the resurrectionists located and stole the body. An extensive search was made, and Turpin's corpse was found in the garden of a local surgeon. This time nothing was left to chance: they packed the coffin with quicklime, a caustic substance which would rapidly dissolve flesh and mutilate the bones.

Being the relative of a surgeon or medical student could save you from dissection. The body of a child brought by Hollis, a well-known resurrectionist, to St Thomas's Hospital, was recognized by a medical student as his niece, whereupon the girl was promptly returned to her grave.

But being a relative of a resurrectionist conferred no such immunity. A Gallic trio of 'sack-'em-up' men operated out of Edinburgh: 'Merryandrew' (nineteenth-century getaway driver and in charge of the cart), 'The Spoon' (so called because of the skill with which he scooped the dead from their coffins) and 'The Mole' (who did the digging). Spoon and Mole fell out with Merryandrew over money, and when Merryandrew's sister died, they decided to take their revenge by exhuming her and selling her corpse for dissection. Just as they were hoisting the body to the surface, they were terrified by a white shrouded figure which jumped out from behind a tomb stone. As Spoon and Mole fled, Merryandrew discarded his sheet and crossed to his sister's grave. Rather than turn down the prospect of easy money, especially as a result of the endeavour of others, Merryandrew bundled his sister into a sack and made off for Surgeon's Square.

Other simple though costly expedients resorted to in order to foil the resurrectionists included deeper burial, burial in a secure vault, hire of a

Death mask of William Burke. Sentenced to hang on 28 January 1829, his body was handed over to Edinburgh University for dissection.

massive stone slab to be laid over the coffin until putrefaction set in or the construction of an iron grill, known as a mort-safe, to be placed over the grave and set in cement. Examples of mort-safes can still be seen at Greyfriars Churchyard in Edinburgh.

Sometimes bereaved relatives and friends would seek to deter resurrectionists by laying trip-wires which would fire rounds from a spring-gun. Such stratagems were usually easy to detect, and the reconnoitring wife of a resurrectionist would simply fall to the ground, weeping and wailing, and make the contraption safe by deftly cutting the wire. Occasionally things went fatally awry. When three medical students went foraging for bodies in Blackfriars Churchyard, one of them was killed when he stumbled over a trip-wire. His companions decided that they could not leave him there, so they propped him upright and tied his left ankle to one of them and his right ankle to the other. Slinging a dead arm around each neck, they staggered, as if drunk, back to their lodgings.

Bridgman's Patented Coffin

It would seem an obvious way of foiling the resurrectionists to be buried in an unopenable coffin. In 1818 Edward Lillie Bridgman invented just such a coffin that boasted no screws, hinges or movable parts, was made of wrought iron and was virtually unbreakable and impregnable. Capriciously, this boon to humanity was not welcomed, especially by the clergy, who depended upon the natural rotting of corpse and coffin to enable further burials to be made in the same place at a later date. A graveyard full of imperishable coffins would quickly become full to capacity and full for eternity. Revenue would cease and owners of burial grounds would be put out of business.

Mrs Gilbert of Holborn became a posthumous test case when the rector of St Andrew's Church refused to accept her in a Bridgman coffin. Bridgman appealed to the bishop of London, who suggested that the deceased be transferred to a more conventional coffin – a naïve suggestion since the coffin she was already in could not be opened! In June 1819, three months after her death, Mrs Gilbert's cortège arrived at the cemetery gates, which were immediately slammed shut by the sexton. In the interim the coffin was laid on top of one of the tombstones, and the undertaker told the people that the only reason the sexton was refusing permission for burial was because he feared he would be deprived of bribes from the resurrectionists. Night fell, a fight ensued and Bridgman was thrown into gaol. The long dead Mrs Gilbert spent the night perched precariously on the tombstone.

In September Bridgman finally won his fight and Mrs Gilbert went beneath the ground. Despite his victory, Bridgman's coffin never really became popular, due largely to its high cost.

Miscellaneous Deterrents

The ultimate deterrent was dreamt up by the father of a child buried in Dundee. To ward off resurrectionists, a small box packed with gunpowder was connected to the four corners of the coffin. The sexton, justifiably nervous, jumped back in great alarm after throwing in the first shovelful of earth.

The ancient Egyptians had recourse to curses as a deterrent. Threats were carved on the walls of tombs describing the consequences of any violation. The most famous of curses was Tutankhamun's. It was also the most indiscriminate. Lord Carnarvon, who financed the excavations, died in 1923, before he set eyes on the young pharaoh, while Howard Carter, the archaeologist who broke through into the funerary chamber, lived on for another sixteen years, dying in 1939 at the age of sixty-five.

One particularly vengeful mummy is thought by some to have caused the deaths of 4,190 people. It was shipped to America in 1912 in the hold of the *Titanic*.

A TALE OF TWO GIANTS

Once upon a time, in the late 1780s to the early 1800s, there were, in England, two Irish giants, Charles O'Brien (sometimes called Byrne) and Patrick Cotter (also known, confusingly, as Patrick O'Brien), both of whom claimed descent from Brian Boru, king of the Irish in the tenth century.

In those days freaks of all types could make a reasonable income by exhibiting themselves at fairs and festivals. There was, however, one great drawback – such publicity inevitably brought one to the notice of anatomists eager to probe and poke into the dark recesses of one's dead body.

Charles O'Brien was the shorter of the two men, a mere seven feet six inches. He died of alcohol-induced illness while still in his early twenties, in 1783. John Hunter, arguably the most famous of all the anatomists, had been patiently biding his time. When the news broke of O'Brien's final illness, Hunter immediately sent his man Howison to reconnoitre. O'Brien got to hear of this, and the anxiety engendered no doubt hastened his demise. Before his death the Irishman left strict instructions that his body was to be watched day and night, that he was to be sealed in a coffin of lead and then sunk far out at sea. Poor, simple

O'Brien was never a match for Hunter who had waited so long to capture this famous specimen.

Hunter may have been an exceptional anatomist and surgeon, but he was a lousy businessman. Howison took him to the public house in which a number of O'Brien's so-called minders were drowning their sorrows. Hunter offered £50, an enormous sum of money, if they would give over the corpse for dissection. He would have done better to conceal his obvious excitement. The men initially agreed but then demanded more money. Then more. And yet more. In the end Hunter had to pay £500 (some say £700) for O'Brien. Under cover of darkness the body was transferred from a hackney coach to Hunter's carriage and taken straightaway to the surgeon's house in Earl's Court. Fearing treachery, Hunter lost no time in disposing of the giant's carcase: it was cut into manageable pieces and the flesh boiled from the bone in a huge vat in the basement.

As mute testimony to the obsession of a collector and the untrustworthiness of friends, Charles O'Brien stands to this day on permanent display in Hunter's Museum, now part of the Royal College of Surgeons, London. His massive frame is in comical contrast to the minute skeleton of Miss Caroline Crachami, the twenty-two-inch dwarf who shares his glass case. [12]

Cotter died in Bristol in 1806. He was taller than O'Brien and shared with his famous predecessor the dread of dissection. (Hunter had died in 1793 but his place had been taken by other anatomists, equally fanatical.) Cotter died a richer man than O'Brien, in the bosom of friends he could trust. He left minute instructions for the disposal of his body. His corpse was to be enclosed in three coffins, an inner one of

John Hunter's copper, in the basement of his Earl's Court home, which he used to reduce the body of Charles O'Brien.

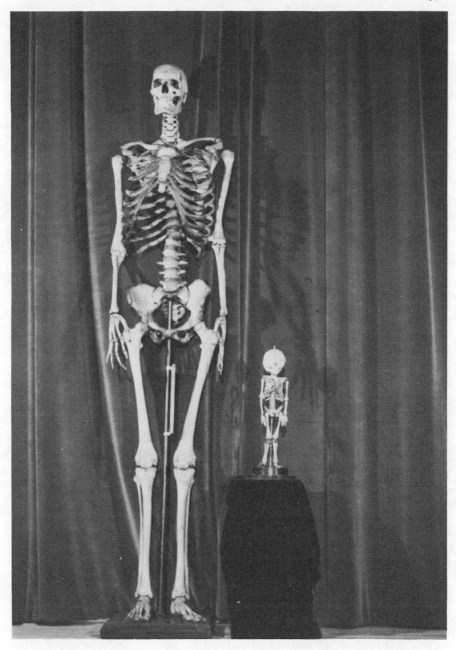

Charles O'Brien, the 'Irish Giant' (seven feet 8 inches), towers over
Caroline Crachami, the 'Sicilian Dwarf', a mere 20 inches high.

wood, an intermediate one made of lead, the whole enclosed in one of 'Mr Panting's stupendous coffins'. The outer coffin, measuring nine feet six inches long and three feet across the shoulders, was borne to the grave carried by fourteen men and lowered by pulleys into a shaft twelve feet deep, dug into the solid rock beneath the Roman Catholic chapel in Trenchard Street, Bristol. As added insurance against the resurrectionists, iron bars were embedded in the concrete above the grave.

The local anatomist, Richard Smith, went to his own grave lamenting the loss of such a prize specimen. His death-bed irritation was recounted by his pupil, George Pycoft, in 1875:

> Five and thirty years ago I was pupil to Mr Richard Smith, the senior surgeon of the Bristol Infirmary. Mr Smith was at the time the oldest hospital surgeon in England and had collected the finest provincial pathological museum in the country. Not long before he died, about the year 1843, he told me the following story. 'They tell you in London that they have got the skeleton of O'Brien in the College Museum, but they have not. They have got O'Byrne, a smaller man. Why, O'Brien was 8ft 2in; if anybody could have got out his body it would have been myself. He was buried in the porch of the Roman Catholic Church in Trenchard Street. I was determined to have him, and took a house on the other side of the street, that we might dig a tunnel under the road, and remove him quietly. But we found he was buried in a grave sunk deep in the red rock, and the stone over him secured by strong iron bars, so that we could not run a mine to him without blasting with gunpowder. So we gave the plan up.'[13]

Cotter lay undisturbed for one hundred years. In 1906 his skeleton was discovered when workmen were laying new drains. The interval between discovery and re-interment provided a golden opportunity for latter-day anatomists to examine the giant. Professor Fawcett painstakingly measured and photographed Cotter's remains. Would Cotter have minded? After what interval of time does it become acceptable to probe and poke and measure?[14]

ALTERNATIVE SUPPLIES

Before we look at the provisions of the Anatomy Act which set out to put an end to the activities of the resurrectionists, let us examine the alternative sources of supply of dead bodies for dissection prior to 1832. Besides the bodies provided by the resurrectionists, there were few other sources of supply.

The newspapers of the day were never short of suggestions. Since prostitutes spent their lives corrupting mankind, it was only right and proper that they pay for their immorality by furthering medical knowledge. Others suggested that people who committed suicide should be anatomized, and anyone who died as a result of duelling, fighting or drinking. Mr Dermott, proprietor of the Little Windmill School of Medicine, suggested that all doctors should donate their own bodies for dissection after death. Some people were willing to offer their bodies for dissection in return for 'a little bit on account' – or other people's bodies, as the following letter to Sir Astley Cooper shows:

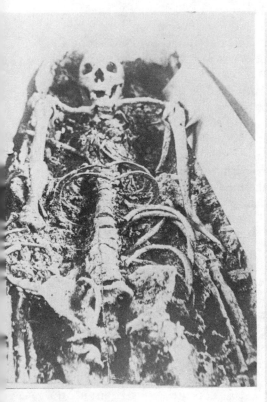

Patrick Cotter's skeleton, exhumed in 1906, 100 years after his death, lying at a depth of ten feet below the Roman Catholic Chapel, Trenchard Street, Bristol. The discovery was made during the laying of new drains.

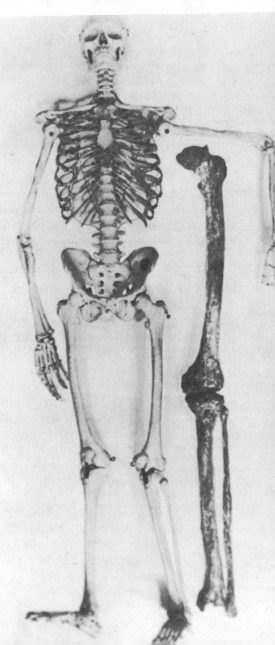

Patrick Cotter's femur compared to a teaching skeleton which measures five feet 4 inches.

Sir, – I have been informed that you are in the habit of purchasing the bodys and allowing the person a sum weekly; knowing a poor woman that is desirous of doing so, I have taken the liberty of calling to know the truth.
                    I remain, your humble servant …

No doubt suspecting a burker, the baronet replied: 'The *truth* is that you deserve to be hanged for such an unfeeling offer. A.C.' That way, Sir Astley might have got hold of a body free of charge!

Bequests were rare, though not unknown. In 1828 a mass pledge of bodies was initiated by Professor Macartney of Dublin. By 1831 more than 400 people, many of whom were said to be doctors, had signed up to donate their corpses for dissection. There is little evidence that the exercise was taken seriously – indeed, it was met with wry amusement in London medical circles.

A contributor to *The Lion* in 1829 divulged details of his will in which he left instructions for his body to be anatomized, his skin to be tanned and used to cover an armchair, his bones given to a turner to be made into knife handles, pin cases and buttons, and his flesh to be mixed in a vase with quicklime, covered with earth and planted with a rose.

Richard Carlile, who published *The Lion*, pointed out that members of the royal family were frequently embalmed and that this entailed some degree of dissection. He went on to suggest that the king might start a fashion by donating his body to the surgeons. Henry Hunt, a member of parliament who objected to Henry Warburton's ideas about the use of pauper corpses (see the Anatomy Act, p.81), was more direct. Talking about the 'rich paupers' on the Civil List he advocated that the bodies '… of all our kings be dissected, instead of expending seven or eight hundred thousand pounds of the public money for their interment'. He went on to add to his list of involuntary donors hereditary legislators and 'priests and vicars who feed themselves and not their flocks'. Colonel Sibthorp advocated that all horse-thieves should be hanged and dissected.

Others were moved to donate their bodies without thought of monetary gain. Messenger Monsey, an eccentric physician at the Chelsea Hospital, was so anxious to be dissected that in 1787 he wrote to Mr Cruikshank, an anatomist: 'Mr Foster, a Surgeon in Union Court, Broad Street, has been so good as to promise to open my Carcass and see what is the matter with my Heart, Arteries, Kidnies, &c. He has gone to Norwich and will not return before I am dead. Will you be so good as to let me send it to you?'

A Mr Boys, who died in 1835, wished to be made into 'essential salts' for the use of his female friends. In a letter to Dr Campbell, written four years before his death, he asks: 'Are you now disposed (without Burking) to accomplish my wish, when my breath or spirit shall have ceased to animate my carcase, to perform the operation of vitrifying my bones, and sublimating the rest ... And, that I may not offend the delicate olfactory nerves of my female friends with a mass of putridity, if it be possible, let me rather fill a few little bottles of essential salts therefrom, and revive their drooping spirits.'[15]

JEREMY BENTHAM AND HIS AUTO-ICON

Like the O'Briens before him, Jeremy Bentham was a giant. Though of normal physical stature, this eighteenth-century philosopher dwarfed his contemporaries in intellect and vision and is best remembered for having formulated the principles of Utilitarianism, 'the greatest good for the greatest number'. To Bentham there was no reason why Utilitarian philanthropy should not extend beyond the grave, though, as we shall see, he himself had no intention of ever being buried beneath the sod.

In 1824 Dr Thomas Southwood Smith wrote an influential article in *The Westminster Review* entitled 'Use of the Dead to the Living', in which he eloquently argued that the progress of surgery was being needlessly and dangerously impeded by the scarcity of legal sources of bodies for dissection.[16] Smith asserted that ignorant physicians and surgeons were the 'deadly enemies of the community' and highlighted the illogicality of being able to understand the workings of the human body 'without inspecting the interior of this curious and complicated machine'. Southwood Smith argued that ignorance of the course of major blood vessels had cost the life of Sir Philip Sidney, 'the light and glory of his age, cut off in the bloom of manhood'. This Elizabethan poet's 'inestimable life' would have been saved if only the medical men had known the pressure point at which to stem the haemorrhage from the severed artery.

Southwood Smith's solution in 1824 was for the bodies of paupers to be given up for dissection. By 1832 he had changed his mind and was advocating that people donate their bodies to the advancement of medicine. It was an idea that Jeremy Bentham embraced with enthusiasm. Long before, in 1769, Bentham had decided to bequeath his body for dissection, but when he read Smith's article he was determined that this surgeon was the man to carry it out. When Bentham died, in June 1832, invitations were distributed to a select number of followers and admirers:

Sir
It was the earnest desire of the late JEREMY BENTHAM that his Body should be appropriated to an illustration of the Structure and Functions of the Human Frame. In compliance with this wish, Dr Southwood Smith

will deliver a Lecture, over the Body, on the Usefulness of Knowledge of this kind to the Community. The Lecture will be delivered at the Webb-street School of Anatomy and Medicine, Webb-street, Borough, Tomorrow, at Three o'Clock; at which the honour of your presence, and that of any two friends who may wish to accompany you, is requested.
Friday, 8th June, 1832.

The dissection was a dramatic affair: a violent thunderstorm shook the building, forcing Southwood Smith, with a face 'as white as that of the dead philosopher before him', to operate between flashes of lightning.

Bentham is now supposed to have had two reasons for offering his corpse for public dissection: firstly, in order to encourage others to emulate him and to free surgeons from the need to bargain with resurrectionists; secondly, and less obviously, in order to achieve posthumous self-aggrandisement. In his will the philosopher left detailed instructions about how his skeleton was to be used after the dissection was completed. The bones were to be reassembled, joints were to be wired and the whole was to be padded out with straw and hay, seated, dressed in Bentham's clothes, with his desiccated head perched on top, replete with the glass eyes that the philosopher had carried around in his pocket for the previous twenty years.

Southwood Smith meticulously carried out these instructions: 'I endeavoured to preserve the head untouched, merely drawing away the fluids by placing it under an air pump over sulphuric acid. By this means the head was rendered as hard as the skulls of the New Zealanders; but all expression was of course gone.'[17] Obviously such an unaesthetic and shrunken head could not adorn the rest of the magnificent bulk. Consequently a wax head was modelled. The end result, Bentham's auto-icon, is still to be seen, seated grandly in a glass-fronted case, in University College, London. (The real head was initially placed in the skeleton's rib cage, but was later placed in a box. It is now kept in the university vaults.)

Bentham had some bizarre ideas about the utility of auto-icons. He saw subsequent generations doing away with burial altogether. Instead of graves and stone memorials, auto-icons, posed in their Sunday best, would adorn temples of remembrance – everyone would become a statue to be admired or reviled. He envisaged historical theatre in which the great events of history would be 'enacted' by the auto-icons of the actual characters: 'If a country gentleman have rows of trees leading to his dwelling, the auto-icons of his family might alternate with the trees; copal varnish would protect the face from the effects of rain – caouthchouc [india-rubber] the habiliments.'

For Bentham the atheist, auto-icons represented immortality of the body rather than the spirit. He was never an immodest man, as his will attested: 'If it should so happen that my personal friends and other disciples should be disposed to meet together on some day or days of the year for the purpose of commemorating the founder of the Greatest Happiness System of Morals and Legislation, my Executor will, from time to time, cause to be conveyed to the room in which they meet the said box or case, with the contents, there to be stationed in such part of the room as to the assembled company shall seem meet.' Indeed, Bentham was present at many university meetings after his death. In the minutes it would be recorded, 'Mr Bentham present but not voting.'[18]

THE ANATOMY ACT OF 1832

Henry Warburton made his first attempt to introduce an Anatomy Bill in Parliament in 1829. Essentially, Warburton's bill would have provided for the needs of the anatomists by giving them the bodies of those who were unclaimed after death. In practice this meant the pauper dead. The bill failed in the upper house because their lordships asserted that even the poorest citizen had a right to expect a decent burial. This principle of posthumous equality was enunciated in a contemporary broadsheet:

For hearts as feeling with affection pure
Dwell in the breasts of the neglected poor
As ever warm'd the sons of wealth and pride,
Who in their splendid palaces reside.

Warburton used the public hysteria surrounding the activities of Williams and Bishop to bring his second Anatomy Bill to Parliament in 1832. Although the aim of this bill was the same as the first (the dissection of unclaimed bodies), Warburton had made a number of subtle changes in order to make it appear more acceptable and to disguise the fact that, '... after death their [the poor's] bodies must be cut up and mangled for the benefit of their lords and masters.' The key clause in the first bill, 'The bodies of persons unclaimed dying in any Hospital or Workshop may be delivered for dissection', was substituted in the second bill by 'Persons having lawful custody of Bodies may permit them to undergo Anatomical Examination.' The new wording successfully obscured the reality whereby workhouse-keepers would be able to *sell* the body of any unclaimed pauper who died in their institutions. Further, it was hoped that the euphemism 'Anatomical Examination' would soothe the consciences of those who found 'dissection' too direct.

Advocates of the bill were quick to point out that there were many safeguards against abuse by the unscrupulous. Any person, rich or poor, who did not wish to be dissected had merely to express 'his Desire, either in Writing at any Time during his Life, or verbally in the Presence of Two or more Witnesses during the Illness whereof he died ...'. In

Jeremy Bentham's auto-icon sits serenely in its case at University College, London. The original head, which is shown tucked between the philosopher's feet, is now stored separately in the college vaults. The massive bulk has recently been spring-cleaned by the Textile Conservation Centre at Hampton Court.

addition, no-one would be dissected against the wishes of a surviving spouse or relative. But it was pointed out that 'none without consent' was not the same as 'all without dissent'. Warburton chose to ignore the fact that most paupers were illiterate and that workhouse-keepers might have a vested financial interest in making sure no witnesses were present. Indeed, workhouse-keepers might be tempted to supplement their income by burking their residents and legally selling the bodies.

Warburton's bill was successful. It included a clause which abolished dissection of murderers. Ruth Richardson, in *Death, Dissection and the Destitute*, neatly sums up the change in the law: 'What had for generations been a feared and hated punishment for murder became one for poverty.' She goes on to wonder whether a dying pauper would take comfort from the knowledge that he or she would be dissected on the slab *instead* of a murderer, rather than *alongside* one.

The provisions of the act were summed up by one enthusiast thus:

It has legalised human dissection in Great Britain and Ireland
    It has permitted cultured, brave and honorable members of the medical profession to escape the slimy tentacles of the resurrectionists
    It has provided the student of today with facilities for anatomical study, under such surroundings as would have brought paens from the lips of Andreas Vesalius, William Harvey and John Hunter.
    It put an end to the vocation of the 'sack-'em-up' men
    To the public – the always indifferent and stuperous public – it has given original, brilliant and life-saving surgical operations.[19]

Thus it was that the poor came to supply the needs of anatomy.

But then, as now, poverty could come swiftly to the well-to-do. In a letter to the *Lancet* of 5 June 1829, a Worcester man, who signed himself 'One of the "Unclaimed"', related how he had possessed property to the value of £20,000 but had become bankrupted by foreclosure of a mortgage. As a result of penury his wife had died of grief and his daughters of tuberculosis. He described himself as 'the poverty-striken and emaciated inmate of a workhouse, without a single relation to notice me'. He viewed the prospect of dissection with horror: 'Gracious heavens, and can this take place in England? In the abstract, dissection I should disregard, but I look with horror upon being classed with and treated like a murderer'.

The Anatomy Act of 1832 is still in force today. Happily voluntary bequests make the need for pauper corpses unnecessary.

MEMORIAL EN MASSE

Communal graves are usually associated with pauperism, pestilence or pogroms. In such burials, posthumous identity and the focus of most religious obsequies are lost.

Towers of Silence

One religious group, the Parsees, who make no provision for individuation of the dead, would argue that remembrance by the living is neither shortened nor diluted.

The Parsees are descendants of ancient Persians who fled to India to escape religious persecution. They adhere to the teachings of the prophet Zoroaster and have a unique method of disposing of their dead.

A visitor to Bombay in the 1870s asked his host about the purpose of five huge black granite towers covered with white *chunam* and disfigured by black, fungus-like incrustations. Each tower was roughly forty feet in diameter and twenty-five feet high. The oldest had stood for over 200 years. 'The parapet of each tower possesses an extraordinary coping, which instantly attracts and fascinates the gaze. It is a coping formed, not of dead stone, but of living *vultures* ... they sit there so motionless they might have been carved out of stone.' The upper surfaces of the towers were divided into seventy-two receptacles with grooved channels to convey moisture into the central drains. The receptacles were arranged in

The ossuary beneath the Capuchin Church of the Immaculate Conception in Rome. 'The ceiling of the corridor and the vaults are nicely decorated with light Baroque bonework.'

three concentric circles – the outermost for male corpses, the middle for female, and the innermost for children. The purposes of the vultures may now be divined.

'At least a hundred birds, collected round one of the towers, began to show signs of excitement, while others swooped down from neighbouring trees. The cause of this sudden abandonment of their previous apathy soon revealed itself. A funeral was seen to be approaching.' The body of a

A tableau of anatomical specimens (heart, liver, blood vessels etc.), flanked and topped by foetal skeletons, one of which is crying into a handkerchief made from placental membrane. Assembled by the Dutch anatomist Fredrik Ruysch (1638–1731). The large collection was later bought by Peter the Great.

child was taken by bearers into the tower and left uncovered in one of the receptacles. 'A dozen birds swooped down. In five minutes the satiated birds flew back and lazily settled down again on the parapet. They left nothing behind but a skeleton.' Roughly two weeks later the bearers returned and, with gloved hands and tongs, placed the bones in the central well to intermingle with the bony fragments of their ancestors.[20]

Zoroaster, who lived 6,000 years ago, taught that earth, fire and water must never be defiled by contact with putrefying flesh. Decaying bodies must be dissipated as quickly as possible, and God has provided vultures to dispose of human flesh more expeditiously by far than ants and earthworms. And the mingling of one's bones with those of others of the same faith was regarded as a symbol for communal remembrance.

Bonehouses

Although the Christian preference was for separate burial, intermingling of the bones of the dead was often the practical reality. We have already seen that shortage of land frequently necessitated the disinterment of the long dead and their replacement with the recently dead. Exhumed bones were usually collected together and placed in a charnel house, or ossuary.

On rare occasions exhumed bones were taken into the body of the church and have thus survived to the present day. Two vast bone collections which are still in existence in Britain can be seen at St Leonard's Church in Hythe, Kent, and Holy Trinity Church, Rothwell, Northamptonshire. On display in the crypt at Hythe are 8,000 thigh bones and 2,000 skulls. Experts estimate that the bones represent the remains of 4,000 people buried in, and later exhumed from, local burial grounds in the thirteenth and fourteenth centuries.

Perhaps the most awesome display of bones is to be found in the Capuchin convent in Rome. Here, and not to everyone's taste, tens of thousands of bones are arranged, rather like armorial displays in military museums, in intricate designs on the walls and ceilings. Skeletons of children hang from ceilings holding bony scales of Judgement. One may ponder on the fact that, although the individuals comprising the display are anonymous and long forgotten, the composite effect is indeed memorable.

Grimmer still, by some people's reckoning, are the works of Fredrik Ruysch (1638–1731). He used to arrange the skeletons of foetuses and children in the form of tableaux interspersed with human organs and stuffed birds. One such tableau has a foetus crying into a handkerchief made of human membrane, probably placental. Ruysch's collection was purchased by Peter the Great, Tsar of Russia.

2 DEFILEMENTS OF THE FAMOUS

Part of the price to be paid for fame in one's lifetime is sometimes to run the risk of defilement after death. Many reasons can be given for the opening of a grave or vault: to check that the alleged occupant is indeed in residence: to transfer the encumbent to a more prestigious sepulchre; to take bits for souvenirs; to raise money by ransom; or, more usually, to take revenge on an adversary. An early example of revenge-exhumation was the abuse perpetrated on King Harold Harefoot (reigned 1035–40), son of King Cnut, by his half-brother Harthacnut (reigned 1040–42). According to the chronicler William of Malmesbury, 'He [Harthacnut] ordered the body of Harold to be dug up, the head to be cut off, and thrown into the Thames, a pitiable spectacle to men! but it was dragged up again in a fisherman's net and buried in the cemetery of the Danes at London [now St Clement Danes].' Six hundred years later the need to settle old scores was again amply demonstrated by the defilement of Oliver Cromwell.

CROMWELL, THE CORPSE THEY KNOCKED ABOUT A BIT

Oliver Cromwell, Lord Protector of England, and responsible for the trial and execution of King Charles I, died of fever in 1658. He was buried in Westminster Abbey. Two years later, on the restoration of the monarchy, the followers of Charles II went looking to revenge themselves upon the regicide. Cromwell's body was disinterred from Henry VII's Chapel and was hanged at Tyburn in front of a jeering and jubilant mob. The corpse was then decapitated, and the head was spiked on the roof of Westminster Hall, where, according to tradition, it remained for twenty-five years. One stormy night, a high wind lifted the grisly relic from its spike and deposited it at the feet of a sentry, who bundled up the desiccated head and took it home.

At this point the whereabouts of the head becomes shrouded in mystery. In 1787 an actor named Russell sold it to a museum near Clare Market, which in turn sold it to Josiah Wilkinson for £230. Wilkinson would take the head, still fastened to its spike, to parties. His grandson, Horace Wilkinson of Sevenoaks, presented the head to Cromwell's old college, Sidney Sussex, in Cambridge. Questions as to the authenticity of the relic were answered by comparing the features of the head to those of the death-mask taken at the time of Cromwell's death. A distinct mark was identified on the hard, parchment-like skin over the right eyebrow, close to the bridge of the nose – the site of Cromwell's famous wart. The head has been buried at Sidney Sussex in a location known only to a small number of the college staff.[21]

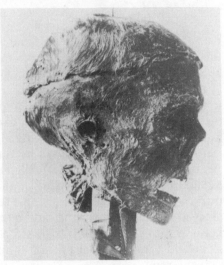

The head of Oliver Cromwell. Three years after his death, Cromwell was hanged at Tyburn and his head spiked on top of Westminster Hall, where it remained until it was blown down in a storm in 1688. It is now buried, spike and all, in a secret location in Sidney Sussex College, Cambridge.

King Charles I's Posthumous Adventures

It is one of the ironies of history that Cromwell flatly refused Charles I's wish to be laid to rest in Westminster Abbey – the very church from which Cromwell himself was so unceremoniously removed thirteen years later. Charles I was beheaded on 30 January 1648 (1649 by our modern calendar), and his body was transported to St George's Chapel, Windsor, where it was finally deposited in the vault occupied by Henry VIII and his favourite wife, Jane Seymour.

Charles II always professed to want to re-inter his father's body in the chapel of Henry VII at Westminster Abbey, 'out of whose loins King Charles was lineally extracted', but somehow he never seemed to get around to it, and by the time he gave the plan active consideration, most of the people present at the original interment at Windsor had themselves died. For this reason, and because extensive alterations had taken place in the meantime, the whereabouts of King Charles I's body had been forgotten. It was not until 1813 that the coffin was rediscovered, when a workman accidently broke into the vault during the construction of a mausoleum for mad King George III.

On 1 April 1813 the plain lead coffin inscribed 'King Charles, 1648' was opened for the Prince Regent, in a company of dignitaries which included Sir Henry Halford, physician to the king, 'who had had much to do with many crowned heads in their lifetime, and who now had the opportunity of examining the one that Cromwell caused to be removed'.[22] Inside the lead coffin was a decayed wooden one. With great care the wrappings were removed from the 'dark and discoloured' face: '...the left eye, in the first moment of exposure, was open and full, though it vanished almost immediately: and the pointed beard ... was perfect. The face bore a strong resemblance to that of Charles the First as preserved on coins and medals, and in the pictures of Vandyke.' Not surprisingly, the head could be easily removed from the trunk, and was quite wet. The hair was found to be cut short at the back, either to help the axeman's aim or else as a consequence of mementoes having been taken by friends. The fourth cervical (neck) vertebra was sliced clean through. No examination was made of the rest of the body, and the head was replaced and the coffin soldered.

Henry Halford has been accused of having palmed the king's cervical vertebra and having it mounted in a case of lignum vitae lined with gold, to show his dinner guests. The bone was finally returned by one of Halford's heirs and placed back on the king's coffin in 1881 by order of the Prince of Wales (later King Edward VII). Halford was not the only one who carried off a memento of his visit: it is claimed that a workman crossed to Henry VIII's coffin and removed a finger bone which he subsequently had fashioned into a knife handle.

John Milton (1608–74), author of *Paradise Lost*, was a supporter of Cromwell. After the restoration of Charles II, Milton lived quietly in the country and was buried in St Giles without Cripplegate in London. Nineteen years later his grave was opened and desecrated:

A journeyman named Holmes produced a mallet and chisel, and forcing open the coffin so that the corpse (which was clothed in a shroud, and looked as if it had only just been buried) might be seen. Mr Fountain, one of the overseers, then endeavoured to pull out the teeth but, being unsuccessful, a bystander took up a stone and loosened them with a blow. There were only five in the upper jaw, but they were quite white and good. They, together with some of the lower ones, Mr Fountain and two others divided between them. A rib bone was also taken and the hair from the head, which was long and smooth, was torn out by the handful. After this the caretaker, Elizabeth Grant, took the coffin under her care, charging sixpence to anyone who wished to view it. Later she reduced her fee to threepence and finally to twopence.[23]

DEFILEMENT BY EXHUMATION: VERSES BURIED AND RETRIEVED

Dante Gabriel Rossetti (1828–82) is principally remembered as one of

Ophelia by John Everett Millais (1829–96). The model was Elizabeth Siddal, later to be exhumed from her grave at Highgate in order to retrieve poems which her husband, Dante Gabriel Rossetti, had buried next to her cheek. For added realism Millais had Siddal lie for hours in a bath of water.

the founder members of the pre-Raphaelite Brotherhood, which advocated a return to pre-Renaissance ideas about art. But Rossetti was also a poet of great distinction. This macabre tale concerns the retrieval of some of his long-buried verses.

In 1860 Rossetti married Elizabeth Siddal, the beautiful model of many of his paintings. Two years later Elizabeth, suffering from tuberculosis, took her own life with an overdose of laudanum. Rossetti was overcome with grief. As she lay in her open coffin, in a gesture of eternal love he placed, between her cheek and her famous golden-red hair, a book of manuscript poems which he had written for her. Elizabeth was then buried at Highgate Cemetery.

Alas, his need for secular fame as a poet began to cast doubts on the propriety of such a romantic, but futile, gesture. Rossetti wanted the poems back but agonzied for seven years on how the retrieval might be brought about. Finally, in October 1869, with permission from the Home Secretary, a gang of neo-resurrectionists began digging in the Rossetti plot. The poet himself stayed at home, consumed with guilt, 'in a state of agitation and torturing suspense'. By the light of lanterns the coffin was opened and the poems reclaimed for the benefit of the living. After disinfecting and drying, they were taken to their author. They were published as *Poems* in 1870.

When he enquired, the poet was told that Elizabeth's pale beauty remained unimpaired by seven years underground. One is tempted to observe that his informers were unlikely to report otherwise, in order not to upset the artist's sensibilities.

GRAVE-ROBBERY, ANCIENT AND MODERN

It might be thought that the best method of ensuring that a corpse is safe from the attention of thieves is to enclose it deep within a vast edifice of stone with all routes of entry securely blocked. Such was the theory behind the construction of the pyramids. Unfortunately for the pharaohs, the reality was very different, since such a gigantic temptation always proved irresistible to plunderers, who would invariably find a way of stealing its funerary treasures. It is for this reason that all the pyramids are now empty. It is also the reason that ostentatious burial went out of fashion in ancient Egypt and was replaced by unadorned shafts burrowed in secret locations in the Valley of the Kings. Of course, the vast amount of treasure that was needed to ensure the pharaoh's status in the Other World remained a powerful lure, and discoveries of undisturbed tombs, such as that of Tutankhamun, are exceptional.

In 1875 an Egyptian peasant out searching for his lost goat came across a deep shaft. It was the entrance to a tomb in which had been buried generations of pharaohs and which for thousands of years had escaped the attentions of robbers. By the light of a candle he could make out the mummified remains of many of the most mighty rulers of the ancient world: Amenophis I, Thutmose II, Thutmose III, Seti I, Rameses II – forty in all. For six years the Abed el-Rasul brothers and their extended family systematically rifled the treasures of the tomb. Given time, they would undoubtedly have turned their attention to the mummies themselves.

For many centuries rich Europeans regarded mummy wrappings as a cure for all ills, a veritable panacea. Before long, entrepreneurs argued that, if the wrappings were so powerful medicinally, how much more potent must be the actual body! Thus was born a thriving trade in pulverized mummies. Some famous Renaissance physicians, notably Ambroise Pare, railed against the practice of desecrating the dead that they might serve as 'food and drink for the living'. Pare maintained that a mummy *caused* rather than *eased* stomach pains and was more likely to worsen bleeding than staunch it. But still the demand for mummies continued to outstrip supply, and the limited source soon became seriously depleted. It was then that criminal resourcefulness came into its own: fresh corpses were stolen from modern Egyptian cemeteries, eviscerated, soaked in a blackish material called asphaltum and finally left in the sun to dry. After a few weeks the bodies were ready for powdering in flourishing mummy factories. This cannibalism ceased only when the Egyptian government taxed the factories out of existence.

The export of *whole* mummies from Egypt to the museums of Europe and North America continued long after the trade in powdered mummies had ceased. Some were later subjected to the minutest scientific examination, including dissection thousands of years post mortem. Margaret Murray in Manchester was a pioneer in the field.

MODERN THEFTS OF BODIES

Examples of thefts of famous bodies for ransom or barter include an elaborate plot, hatched in 1876, to steal the corpse of Abraham Lincoln and exchange it for the freedom of a gaoled counterfeiter. The gang were discovered and the plan was foiled when they had lifted the wooden coffin half out of the sarcophagus. As body-snatching *per se* was not a crime, each was gaoled for a year for violation of a tomb. Twenty-five years later, to discourage a copy-cat crime, Lincoln's coffin was embedded six feet deep in steel and concrete.

Bungling is the hallmark of the majority of instances of thefts of bodies for ransom. In December 1881 a gang of neo-resurrectionists broke into the vault of Dunecht House, Aberdeenshire, and stole the body of Alexander William Lindsay, twenty-fifth Earl of Crawford and Balcarres, who had died a year before in Florence and whose embalmed body had been shipped back to Scotland. An anonymous letter was received by the family: 'Sir, The remains of the late Earl of Crawford are not beneath the chapel at Dunecht as you believe, but were recovered hence last Spring, and the smell of decaying flowers ascending from the vault since that time will, on investigation, be found to proceed from another cause than flowers. Signed Nabob.'

The letter did not have the effect intended, since it was regarded as a tasteless hoax and ignored. Two months elapsed before the exasperated grave-robbers were forced to dispense with subtleties: they returned to the vault, tore down the iron railings which had enclosed the entrance and propped up the granite slab leading to the crypt. The police were called and Inspector Cran descended into the vault. An empty coffin stood in the middle of the floor, its inner lead shell peeled back like an opened can. The smell referred to in the letter was the stench of the impregnated sawdust in which the body had been packed.

Charlie Chaplin's empty
grave at the cemetery of
Corsier-sur-Vevey, overlooking Lake Geneva. Chaplin
died, aged eighty-eight, on
Christmas Day 1977. The
coffin was stolen in March
1978.

Charlie Chaplin's coffin,
recovered 2½ months later in
a maize field ten miles away,
before being reinterred in a
cemented vault back at
Corsier-sur-Vevey.

Another letter soon followed, demanding £6,000 for the safe return of the corpse. What happened next often bordered on farce. The police called in the services of a bloodhound called 'Morgan' – which preferred to chase rabbits. In July 1882 the earl's body was eventually found wrapped in blankets and buried in a shallow grave less than 500 yards from the house, and shortly afterwards, following a tip-off, the police arrested Charles Soutar, a mole- and rat-catcher. The earl was then deposited with his ancestors in a more secure vault in Wigan. Part of his inscription reads:

> He shall give his angels charge over thee
> He that keepeth thee will not slumber.

Body-snatching is not unknown in our own times. In March 1978 the coffin containing the body of Sir Charles 'Charlie' Chaplin was stolen from the cemetery at Corsier-sur-Vevey, overlooking Lake Geneva in Switzerland. Charlie Chaplin had died the previous Christmas Day, aged eighty-eight and had been buried in the village where he had spent the last twenty-five years of his life, following allegations of political and moral offences in Hollywood. The theft followed two attempts to steal the remains of other celebrities: the ashes of the opera singer Maria Callas disappeared from a Paris cemetery on the day on which Charlie Chaplin was buried, and in August 1977 four men had attempted to steal the body of Elvis Presley from its marble mausoleum.

It was accepted that the theft of Chaplin's body had no political motive. Other explanations included exhumation so that he could be reburied in Westminster Abbey, in Britain, the country of his birth; so that he could be reburied in a Jewish cemetery; theft by an insane fan; or else ransom, pure and simple. Chaplin's widow, Oona, daughter of the playwright Eugene O'Neil, refused to pay a ransom and was reported as saying, 'My husband lives on in my heart and mind, and it really doesn't matter where his remains are.'

Chaplin's coffin was finally found eleven weeks later, in a shallow grave in a cornfield about ten miles from his former resting-place. Two men, a Pole and a Bulgarian, were charged with having demanded a ransom of £400,000 and with having disturbed the peace of the dead. The Pole, reckoned to be the 'brains' of the operation, was gaoled for four years; the Bulgarian, regarded as the 'muscle man with a limited sense of responsibility and a background of family problems', was given a suspended sentence. Charlie Chaplin was reinterred in a concrete vault.

SAINTLY BITS AND PIECES

The more pious a man's life, the more likely he was to have his anatomical parts stolen and venerated after death. Saintly bits and pieces are enshired in gold and silver throughout the churches of Christendom. In addition to the intrinsic religious significance of such holy relics, they invariably brought great prestige to the church or city that owned them. Cologne benefited financially from the pilgrims who journeyed to see the shrine of the Three Wise Men or Magi.

Pedants would even attempt a hierarchy: heads, arms and legs were the most venerated bits, fingers and teeth the least. Very important relics were divided up and widely distributed. John the Baptist's face ended up in Amiens, the top of his head in Rhodes, the back of his head in Nemours; his brains went to Nogent-le-Retrou, his jaw to Besançon and a bit of ear to Saint-Flour-en-Auvergne.

Relics were traded in the political arena much as gifts are exchanged in contemporary state visits. A patriarch of Jerusalem gave Queen Radegund of France a finger which once belonged to St Mamme, and the monks of Mount Sinai presented one of St Catherine's ribs to Henry II of Brunswick and a finger to Rouen Cathedral. On the death of St Hugh of Lincoln, the corpse was decapitated in order that the value of the relics could be instantly increased. During his life, whilst on a pilgrimage to Normandy to venerate the alleged remains of St Mary Magdalen, Hugh had bitten off two pieces of bone from the saint's arm to take back to England as souvenirs.

During the Reformation Henry VIII was responsible for a precipitous reduction in the number of relics. On his orders the bones of Thomas à Becket were plundered from his shrine at Canterbury and burned – though his skull is reputed to have been preserved and to lie now under the corona at the east end of the cathedral. (It is a mischievous apocrypha to suggest that Henry intended to put the skeleton of Becket on trial for treason more than 400 years after the martyr's death.)

In 1542 Henry's henchmen meted out the same treatment to St Cuthbert, lying peacefully in Durham Cathedral. They broke into the shrine and found Cuthbert's body uncorrupted. Because of the remarkable preservation, the superstitious king ordered that the saint be reinterred beneath a plain marble slab. Some authorities maintained that Cuthbert's body was removed by monks and buried in a secret location. To check out this rumour, Cuthbert was dug up again in 1827 – this time by the cathedral authorities. By that time the body had become corrupted and Cuthbert was a skeleton swathed in fabric. The saint's identity was no longer in doubt when his gold cross with a garnet at its centre was discovered in the coffin. Incredibly, in 1899 he was exhumed yet again, before finally being placed back under his marble slab inscribed 'Cuthbertus'.

The bones of many less saintly notables still sometimes come to light. In 1896, a box of bones was found on a shelf in the Louvre Library. The bones, allegedly collected after the rifling of the royal tombs of the cathedral of St Denis in 1793, included a scapula of Hugues Capet, a femur of Charles V, a tibia of Charles VI, a vertebra of Charles VII, a rib of Philip the Fair and one of Louis XII, and the lower jaw of Catherine de Médicis.

Galileo's fifth lumbar vertebra (a bone in the spine) was stolen in 1757 and now rests in the Gabinetto Fiscio in Padua; the astonomer's withered finger was placed in a glass vase in the Museo di Storia Naturale in Florence.

The English king Edward the Martyr was murdered in 979, stabbed by his stepmother. The bones were moved from Wareham to Shafesbury Abbey, Dorset. They disappeared when Henry VIII sacked the monasteries but reappeared in 1931 when a gardener unearthed a casket while digging in the abbey ruins. When the owner of the land died in the 1950s, her two sons disagreed on the most appropriate disposal of the bones: one wished to reinter them in the abbey grounds; the other wanted them to be given to the St Edward Brotherhood, who had promised to enshrine them at Brookwood Cemetery, Woking. Until recently the royal bones were deposited in a cutlery box in a vault in the Midland Bank, Woking, but today Edward's remains lie secure at Brookwood.

NAPOLEON'S PRIVATE BIT

It was not only holy men who ran the risk of exhumation and of having bits of their anatomy removed after death. When Napoleon died, his chaplain, Père Vignali, helped himself to a number of anatomical relics, including a 'mummified tendon'. This specimen, whose diminutive and shrivelled appearance gave a new meaning to 'Not tonight, Josephine', had had many owners over the years before being auctioned at Christie's in London in 1969. It failed to reach its reserve price.

DISTURBING THE DEAD IN SEARCH OF A KING

That antique pile behold,
Where royal heads receive the sacred gold:
It gives them crowns, and does their ashes keep,
There made like gods, like mortals there they sleep;
Making the circle of their reign complete,
These suns of empire, where they rise they set.

Thus Edmund Waller (1606–87) described Westminster Abbey's dual function – to crown and bury English monarchs. Francis Beaumont, the Elizabethan dramatist, had also alluded to the abbey's pre-eminence as a royal cemetery:

Gruesome proof that defilement of the dead did not cease with the passing of the resurrectionists. Modern-day vandals have broken into this coffin and peeled away the leaden inner shell to expose the skeleton inside.

Think how many royal bones
Sleep within these heaps of stones: ...
Here's an acre, sown, indeed,
With the richest royallest seed.

The area around Westminster also had a third function: it served as a royal residence. This was in stark contrast to Saint-Denis, the burial place of the French kings – not only did French monarchs never live at Saint-Denis, they rarely ever visited the place during their lifetime. Louis XIV chose to live at Versailles in part because from Saint-Germain he would still catch sight of the towers of the hated abbey in which he would finally be laid to rest.

James I, the first Scottish king of England too, died in March 1625 and was buried in Henry VII's Chapel at the eastern end of Westminster Abbey. Unfortunately no one knew precisely whereabouts in the chapel the king lay, since the abbey records were contradictory. The mystery was not solved until 1869, when Dean Stanley finally tracked down James's final resting-place. The story of the search weighs in the balance scholastic curiosity and the disruption of the peace of the royal dead.[24]

Since one of the earliest records, written only fifty-six years after his burial, sited James's grave 'in a vault on the north side of the tomb of King Henry VII', this seemed the most logical place to start the search. Duly the marble pavement was carefully lifted, and a spacious vault with four coffins was discovered immediately. To Stanley's surprise and disappointment, the occupants proved to be the second duke and duchess of Argyll and their two daughters.

Next Stanley decided to strike out to the south-west of Henry VII's tomb, where he soon received another surprise. He found a single coffin of lead 'rudely shaped to the human form', to which was attached a silver plate giving the name and title of Elizabeth Claypole, the favourite daughter of Oliver Cromwell. The isolated position of this vault probably explains why Elizabeth was not disinterred with her father and the other members of the Cromwell family on the restoration of the Stuart monarchy.

North-west of Henry VII is the Sheffield Chapel, containing the remains of the first duke of Buckingham of the third creation (1648–1721). On lifting the pavement, a vault was discovered which conformed precisely in dimensions to the one in which an abbey record, dated 1723, places the bodies of James VI/I and his queen, Anne of Denmark. In the centre of a large vault was the lead coffin bearing the inscription 'Regina Anna'. The six-foot seven-inch coffin, corroborating accounts of Anne's remarkable height, was badly corroded and had collapsed inwards over the queen's face and body.

Anne of Denmark had been found but there was no trace of her husband, despite accounts that the two had been buried together. In the west wall of the vault two leg bones and a piece of skull were found, and it occurred to some that they might be all that was left of the first Stuart King of England, defiled at the hands of Parliamentarian soldiers who had once occupied the abbey. The search for James henceforth took on a new urgency. An eastern wall closed off another vault with an impure atmosphere containing several coffins belonging to members of the Buckingham family.

If James had not been interred with his wife, perhaps he lay with his mother. Consequently attention now turned to the vault of Mary, Queen of Scots, situated in the south aisle of the chapel. It was here that the remains of this unfortunate queen had been brought from Peterborough Cathedral by her son. A flight of stone steps was soon uncovered, leading to a large vault beneath Mary's tomb. 'A startling, it may almost be said an awful, scene presented itself. A vast pile of leaden coffins rose from the floor; some of full stature, the large number varying in form from that of a full-grown child to the merest infant, confusedly heaped upon the others, whilst several urns of various shapes were tossed about in irregular positions throughout the vault.'

The first coffin to be identified was James VI/I's elder son, Henry Frederick, Prince of Wales. A soldered case contained his heart, below which was discerned the Prince of Wales's feathers. Through the collapsed lead casing could be seen the still lifelike appearance of this Stuart prince, in whom so much hope had once been invested.

Arabella Stuart lay on top of the corpse of Mary, Queen of Scots. Also lain to rest were the bodies of Mary, Princess of Orange, Prince Rupert and Anne Hyde, James VII/II's first wife. Then there were the multitude of smaller coffins, representing 'the numerous progeny of that unhappy family … infant after infant fading away which might else have preserved the race'. First there were the ten children of James VII/II, including one whose existence was unknown hitherto – 'James Darnley, natural son'. Then the eighteen children of Queen Anne, only one of whom, William, Duke of Gloucester, lived into childhood. The most notable absentee was James VI/I.

The search then diverted to the north aisle and the tomb of Elizabeth I and Mary I. In contrast to the Stuart vault, the Tudor vault contained only the two coffins, Elizabeth lying on top of Mary. There were no signs of disorder or decay. Elizabeth's coffin, made of elm and oak, was decorated with the Tudor rose, the initials 'ER' and the date 1603.

With the two aisles fully explored, only the central floor of the chapel remained to be investigated. A shallow vault in front of Henry VII's tomb contained the body of Edward VI, the son of Henry VIII, who died in 1553 at the age of sixteen. Identification was aided, if such was needed, by the fact that no hair was attached to the skull, coinciding with the description of Edward's fatal illness: 'Eruptions came out of his skin, and his hair fell off.'

In the south-east of the chapel, opposite the vault which contained James's queen, excavations revealed not a vault but an earthen grave containing a leaden coffin in an advanced state of decay. There was evidence that the body had been embalmed. The skeleton was of a man, roughly six feet tall, with good teeth. There was no identity plate. Could this, at last, be the body of James VI/I? It was thought most unlikely on two counts. Firstly, the abbey records clearly refer to the building of a vault to receive James's body, there being no reference to an earthen burial. Secondly, and more conclusively, James was of short stature. It was probable that the skeleton was Charles Worsley, Parliamentarian general and, with Elizabeth Claypole, the only Cromwellian to remain buried in the abbey after the Restoration.

At this stage it would appear that every conceivable space in Henry VII's Chapel had been explored, save only the tomb of Henry himself. There was a great reluctance to accept the idea that the first Stuart king would have elected to be buried away from his queen and in the vault of the founder of the Tudor dynasty. Nevertheless, before James could be said definitely not to lie within the chapel (unless represented by the bones in the wall of Anne of Denmark's vault), it was imperative to investigate Henry's tomb. The vault was approached from the west, and before too long an entrance was discovered under a firestone arch.

'It was with a feeling of breathless anxiety amounting to solemn awe, which caused the humblest of the workmen employed to whisper with bated breath, as the small opening at the apex of the arch admitted the first glimpse into the mysterious secret which had hitherto eluded this long research. Deep within the arched vault were dimly seen three coffins, lying side by side – two of them dark and grey with age, the third somewhat brighter and newer ...'

The copper plate soldered onto the coffin on the northern side was inscribed:

Depositum
Augustissimi
Principis Jacobi Primi, Magnae Britanniae
Franciae et Hiberniae Regis

The long quest for James, 'King of Great Britain, France and Scotland' was finally over. The other two coffins were indisputably those of Henry VII and his wife, Elizabeth of York, the latter wedged uncomfortably between the two kings.

It is a curious historical coincidence that James VI/I's son, Charles I, came to share the same vault at Windsor as Henry VII's son, Henry VIII, and his wife Jane Seymour.

The coffin of King James VI/I was finally located in 1869, lying between King Henry VII and Elizabeth of York. Redrawn by Robin Boutell from an original by George Scharf in Arthur Stanley's *Historical Memorials of Westminster Abbey*: John Murray, 1869.

3 NECROPHILIA AND VAMPIRISM

NECROPHILIA

Penthesileia, dead of profuse wounds,
Was despoiled of her arms by Prince Achilles,
Who, for love of that fierce white naked corpse,
Necrophily on her committed
In public view.

Graves, Penthesileia

Necrophilia, the most reviled of all perversions, is taken to mean pleasure derived from sexual intercourse with a corpse, and represents posthumous indignity in its grossest form.

Necrophilia, especially the incestuous variety, was a favourite theme in the writings of the Marquis de Sade. Henri Blot indulged his necrophiliac perversions on a number of disinterred corpses, including an 18-year-old ballet dancer whom he dug up at Saint-Ouen in 1886. When he was finally brought to trial, he offered a bizarre defence: '*Chacun à son gout, le mien est pour les corps*' – 'Everyone to his own taste. Mine is for bodies.'

It has been suggested that within the ranks of undertakers and embalmers necrophiliacs are over-represented and that the problem was recognized in ancient times. Herodotus, describing Egyptian embalming techniques, commented that, 'Wives of prominent men and women of great beauty are not delivered at once to the embalmers, but only after they have been dead three or four days. This is done in order to prevent embalmers from having carnal relations with these corpses.'

In the strictest meaning of the word, necrophilia was never considered a variety of sadism, since sadism infers inflicting pain – which is impossible on an insensible corpse. Yet emotions were sometimes strongly felt towards the dead victim: a gravedigger's assistant defended himself against a charge of necrophilia by saying that, since he could find no live woman to yield to his desires, he saw no harm in giving affection to dead women – indeed, they never repulsed his tender advances. Monks keeping vigil over the dead, and soldiers at the front sharing cramped quarters with dead comrades, were also thought to pose an increased risk of necrophilia, because of long-suppressed sexual drives.

Ariès, in his *The Hour of Our Death*, retells a story first attributed to the surgeon Antoine Louis in 1740. A monk was asked to keep vigil over the recently dead body of a beautiful young girl. Indeed, so lovely was she that the monk quite forgot his vows of chastity. 'The monk made love to the corpse.' Only she was not a corpse. The dead girl revived after the monk's departure and gave birth to a baby nine months later.[25]

Doctors were thought not to be immune – many attribute sexual motives to Robert Knox in his behaviour towards the naked body of Mary Paterson, referred to on p. 67. A contemporary cartoon showed the 'Day of Resurrection' in a London anatomy school and featured a woman demanding the return of her virginity, lost since her arrival.

VAMPIRISM

Vampirism, as most of us understand the notion, is the return from the grave of the 'living dead' to feed off the blood of those still living. Bram Stoker's 'Count Dracula' is the archetypal vampire, replete with needle-sharp incisors to feast on the jugulars of sleeping virgins. But 'necrophilia' and 'vampirism' are terms which often overlap and are used to describe the activities of the *living* who become sexually aroused by corpses – including the sucking of blood from the dead. There are many well-documented cases of necrophiliacs who have indulged in 'vampirism'. In 1827 a 29-year-old man violated and mutilated the body of a 12-year-old girl and drank her blood. Fritz Haarman, 'the Hanover Vampire' was executed in 1925 after having killed twenty-four adolescent men and indulged in vampiristic and necrophiliac activities.

In the early part of the eighteenth century it was not unusual in Eastern Europe to dig up the bodies of the dead to check if they had become vampires. The spur for such activities was often the death of a suicide, murder victim or drowning victim whose burial had been followed by a spate of unexplained deaths. If, on exhumation, the body was identified as that of a vampire, staking through the heart was reckoned to rid the community of his unwanted attentions.

In 1725 Peter Plogojowitz died in Kisilova, in Serbia. Within a week nine others went to their graves, each claiming on their death-beds to have been visited by Plogojowitz. Hysteria soon resulted in a clamour to open his coffin. This accomplished, the tell-tale signs of a vampire were not hard to find: the hair, beard and nails had continued to grow since burial; the skin had peeled away and a fresh layer had grown to replace it; his erection testified to his post-mortem sexual desires; the body showed no signs of decomposition; and, as final proof to persuade the sceptics, there was fresh blood trickling from the corner of the mouth, sucked from his victims in his nocturnal feasting. Plogojowitz was staked through the heart and burned, and his ashes were scattered.

A second exhumation is cited by Paul Barber in his *Vampires, Burial and*

Death. It concerns a shoemaker in Breslau who cut his throat in 1591. For a while his widow persuaded everyone that he had died naturally of a stroke, but rumour remained rife and concerned numerous sightings of the ghost of the shoemaker, who was prone to come into people's beds, lie beside them and squeeze so hard as to leave finger-marks on their necks. On 18 April 1592, eight months after his death, the shoemaker-cum-vampire was dug up. The body was found bloated and foul-smelling but supple and undecayed; a second skin had grown; the throat wound gaped red; and a mysterious mole had appeared on his big toe. The corpse was later decapitated and dismembered, had the heart cut out from the back and was finally cremated.[26]

Many of the so-called signs of a vampire will be recognized as natural post-mortem phenomena: growth of hair and nails; the peeling off of the upper layer of skin to expose a 'new' skin underneath, whose red colour was taken as proof of ingestion of blood from living victims. The pressure of gases formed as a consequence of putrefaction can adequately explain a variety of vampire signs – the erection, the oozing of blood from the mouth, the bloated, well-fed appearance of some of the corpses. The groan of the vampire as he was staked through the heart was due to the forcible expulsion of gas from the chest cavity out through the mouth.

'SIR ASTLEY HAS MY HEART'

Thomas Hood (1799–1845) wrote a comic poem, 'Mary's ghost: a pathetic ballad' in which he described the disposal of various bits of a lady's anatomy after she had been delivered into the hands of the anatomists. Her ghost complains to her lover:

> The arm that used to take your arm
> Is took to Dr Vyse
> And both my legs are gone to walk
> The Hospital at Guy's.
>
> I vowed that you should have my hand,
> But fate gives us denial;
> You'll find it there at Dr Bell's
> In spirits and a phial.
>
> I can't tell you where my head is gone
> But Doctor Carpue can;
> As for my trunk, it's all packed up
> To go by Pickford's van.
>
> The cock it crows – I must be gone!
> My William, we must part
> But I'll be yours in death, altho'
> Sir Astley has my heart.

III *The Fear of Bodily Disintegration*

1 MUMMIFICATION IN EGYPT

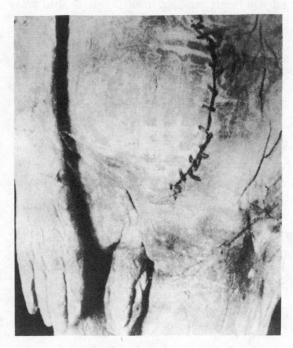

The stitched incision in the left side of the abdomen through which the internal organs, except the heart, were extracted during mummification.

Many people who can face the prospect of death with equanimity baulk at the thought of the slow disintegration of the body in its grave. Numerous civilizations have attempted to arrest or delay this process.

In ancient Egypt it was necessary for the body to be preserved since it was believed that the soul of the dead would return to re-occupy its former carcase. It was imperative, therefore, that the soul should be able to recognize its own body, since only by this means could the deceased hope for life in the next world. Consequently the Egyptians' fear of bodily disintegration was rooted in religion.

The art of mummification in Egypt evolved over a prolonged time scale. Before 1500 BC mummification was crude and experimental; it became elaborated and refined in the period from the Eighteenth to the Twenty-first Dynasty (roughly 1500 to 1000 BC), after which it went into

104

slow decline. Much of what we know today about the embalming methods used by the Egyptians was recorded in the fifth century BC by the Greek historian Herodotus.

The first step in the mummification process was the removal of the brain.[1] Herodotus tells us how this was done: 'They [the embalmers] drew out the brain through the nostrils with an iron hook, taking part of it out this way, and the rest by pouring in drugs.' Archaeological examination of a mummy's skull usually reveals a hole in the delicate bones which form the base of the nose, through which the brain substance was scooped out. It is believed the hook, after breaking through into the cranial cavity, was moved in numerous lacerating sweeps in order to liquefy the brain and facilitate its flow down the nostrils in a face-down position. Sometimes the operation was bungled, resulting in gross mutilation of the nose – such a lack of expertise accounts for the noseless face of Tausert, priestess of Amun in the Twenty-second Dynasty. Another method of removal of the brain was to decapitate the body and spoon out the tissue through the natural hole in the base of the skull through which the spinal cord exits.

The brain was never preserved, even in its liquid state, since the Egyptians considered it an unimportant organ – the heart, not the brain, was considered the seat of the soul.

The eyes, the other organs prone to rapid putrefaction, were also removed at this initial stage. Interestingly, on some occasions the eyes were left *in situ*, having shrunk to the back of the socket. Sometimes it has been possible for scientists to rehydrate the eyeball, allowing it to re-expand to its former size, presenting a greyish cornea between half-open lids.

REMOVING THE INTERNAL ORGANS

There were two types of Egyptian embalmers: *parischistes* and *taricheutes* – cutters and salters. Using a sharpened Ethiopian flint, the *parischistes* would cut into the left side of the abdomen, either a vertical cut from the ribs down to the pelvis or a transverse cut just above and parallel to the groin. Although the incision was rarely more than six inches long, the hole made into the abdominal cavity was sufficient for the embalmer to insert his hand and draw out the viscera: intestines, stomach, liver and spleen. The kidneys, lying, as they do, flat against the back wall of the abdomen, were generally left undisturbed, as was the bladder.

To reach the inside of the chest the embalmer would cut through the diaphragm that divides the chest from the abdomen. By this route and by plunging his arm up to the armpit, the embalmer was able to reach the back of the throat. He would then cut the trachea (windpipe) and oesophagus (gullet) and extract the lungs through the abdominal incision. The heart was always left in place, since it was regarded as the seat of all emotions and the core of a person's character, and therefore vital for eternal life.

Next the chest and abdominal cavities were cleansed with water and palm wine. The excised organs were preserved separately by being treated with molten resin, wrapped in linen and placed in canopic jars, each topped with a representation of the head of one of the four sons of Horus, guardians of the entrails. The jars were sealed and kept for burial with the body – sometimes inside the body itself.

The female reproductive organs – uterus, tubes and ovaries – were always removed. A linen tampon was placed inside the vagina, and the external genitalia were covered in a resinous paste. A man's penis and testicles were almost always left in place, except in the cases of Seti I and Rameses II, when they were removed and preserved inside a statuette of the god Osiris.

DEHYDRATION OF THE BODY

The Egyptians would have known about the drying-out of bodies when

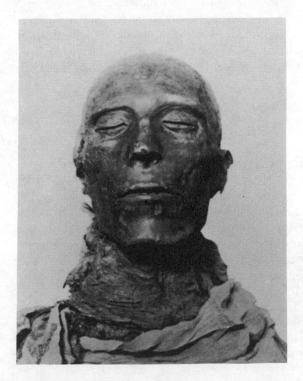

The mummy of Seti I (1312–1298 BC). When the mummy was found and unwrapped by Maspero in 1886, it was 'completely intact and admirably preserved', with a face which retained 'an awe-inspiring expression of greatness and serenity'. His genitals had been cut off and mummified separately.

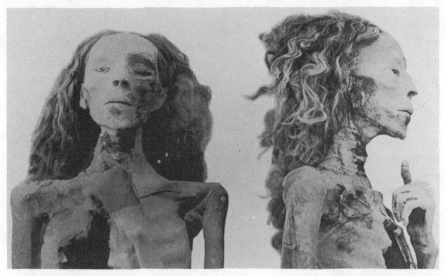

The mummy of Hatchepsut (1520–1484 BC), female pharoah. 'This extraordinary woman dressed as a man and insisted that her portraits depict her with a beard.'

buried in shallow graves beneath the hot desert sun. But such a natural dehydration process would have been impractical because of the length of time necessary for mummification. Consequently the embalmers had recourse to a chemical method of dehydration, using natron, a mixture of sodium carbonate (washing soda) and sodium bicarbonate, found in deposits along the shores of lakes between Cairo and Alexandria.

There has been a lot of controversy and much heated debate among Egyptologists as to exactly how the natron was used as a dehydrating agent – as a solid substance or in liquid form.[2] Some experts thought that the bodies were weighted down in huge vats of liquid natron. As the natron began to work, bits of flesh would separate from the body and float to the surface. Vigilance would have been needed to ensure that bits and pieces from different bodies were not mixed up – lack of proper surveillance was given as the explanation for the finding of some mummies with missing legs and others with three arms. The question was finally settled by Lucas, who compared the preservation of pigeons when immersed in a solution of natron or buried in dry natron. The pigeon treated in natron solution was quickly reduced to an offensive-smelling carcase from which all flesh had been dissolved. The bird packed in dry natron was recognizable, dry and well preserved, although a little shrunken. It seems certain now that the Egyptians packed the body, inside and out, with dry natron which they left for forty days. After that time the dehydrated corpse was then washed and dried with towels.

STUFFING AND BANDAGING

The embalmers usually began by pouring hot resin into the hole through which they had drawn out the brain. Then the body cavities were stuffed with lichens, sawdust or bundles of cloth impregnated with resin. Sometimes onions were put in the abdomen. For greater realism, painted onions were placed in the eye sockets – as in those of Rameses IV.

What emerged from the dehydration process was a dry, hardened and stiff corpse which had to be made supple before bandaging. The softening of the skin was achieved by massaging the body with sweet-smelling oils and grease. The constituents of the ointment included cedar oil, oil of turpentine, cummin oil, incense and minerals.

Resin was then poured into the cavities and left to solidify around the stuffing. The abdominal incision was rarely stitched. Usually the two edges of the cut were brought together and hot wax poured over to make a seal. Next the mouth and nose were filled with cloth, and the body was painted red for men and saffron yellow for women. Later refinements, in the Twenty-first Dynasty, included methods of making the corpse less emaciated by packing mud, sand and sawdust between the cheeks and gums, and between the muscles and skin of the neck, thighs, buttocks and limbs.

There were a number of ways of arranging the arms of a mummy: often they were crossed upon the chest, hands touching the shoulders; at other times the arms were laid out straight, the hands touching the thighs in women and covering the genitals in men.

The bandaging of a mummy was a complex and time-consuming procedure which could take anything up to two weeks to complete. The bandages were made of linen impregnated with resin. It is clear that the wrapping of a mummy was carried out in stages – two mice which had burrowed into the bandages were trapped when fresh layers were added, their skeletons being discovered during unwrapping 3,000 years later. Some high-ranking mummies had ornate gold funerary masks placed over the head and shoulders, while other, lesser worthies had to make do with a cardboard covering called a 'cartonnage'. In later times portraits painted on wood covered the face.

SOCIAL STANDING AND MUMMIFICATION

The mummification process as described above was lengthy and costly and restricted to the rich. The less affluent dead risked their chances of eternal life in the afterworld by having to submit to 'bargain basement' procedures. The method of preservation of the working classes was 'evisceration *per ano*' which consisted simply of injecting large amounts

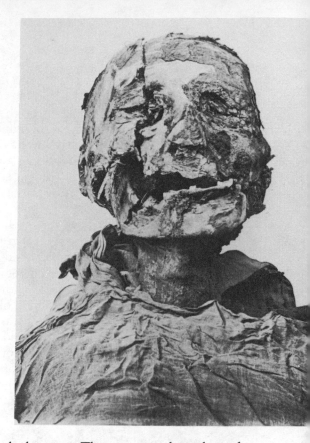

The best efforts of the embalmers ruined by tomb robbers: mummy of Ramasses VI, the face scarred with a knife.

of cedar oil into the bowel through the anus. The anus was then plugged and the body laid in natron for a number of days. After this time the liquefied contents of the abdomen – intestines, stomach, liver and spleen – were allowed to pour out of the anus. The corpse was then bandaged and buried.

A third method, reserved for the poorest classes, consisted merely of a purge and natron treatment.

An intriguing sidelight of embalming practices was provided by the discovery of the mummy of Princess Makare. She was a priestess and a virgin – so how did such a celibate come to have the mummy of a baby occupying her coffin? Had she succumbed to earthly temptation, become pregnant and been condemned to death with her child? The mystery was finally resolved in 1968, when an X-ray of the baby showed it to be a baboon: Makare had been buried with her pet to keep her company in the afterlife.

Embalming of animals was very common in ancient Egypt, and countless thousands of mummified animals were buried in huge necropolises: animals such as bulls, rams, cats, dogs, ibises, crocodiles (worshipped in the town of Crocodilopolis) and many other species. In 1859 a cat graveyard was discovered, and 300,000 mummified felines were disinterred and shipped to Britain for use as fertilizer.

SUCCESSES AND FAILURES

The expertise with which some of the pharaohs were embalmed has resulted in their preservation for thousands of years. Rameses II (1298–35 BC) died in his ninety-sixth year, having reigned for sixty-five years, married 200 women and sired ninety-six sons and sixty daughters. Today, at Cairo Museum, he can be seen in such a good state of preservation that it is even possible to identify the blackheads on his face. Hatchepsut (1520–84 BC) retains her royal dignity more than three millennia after her death. She can be seen with her left hand folded over her breast as if holding a sceptre, and her long brown hair falling about her shoulders. (This extraordinary woman proclaimed herself pharaoh and insisted on dressing as a man and having herself depicted in portraits with a beard.)

The embalming of Sequenenre (at the end of the seventeenth Dynasty) was much less successful, probably because he died a violent death. Whether he died in battle or was assassinated is uncertain. What is obvious for all to see are the wounds which brought about his end. Sequenenre's brain was not removed prior to embalming, and his body had already begun to decompose. Even today people comment on the revolting smell given off by his mummy. The head shows multiple fractures of the forehead, eye socket and cheekbone, probably caused by

Margaret Murray and her colleagues unwrapping one of Manchester Museum's mummies in 1906.

an axe. A javelin penetrated below the left ear and embedded itself in the top of his spine.

The mummy of Henattaui fared just as badly. Poor technique resulted in excessive mud being injected under the skin. Instead of its producing a more life-like appearance, her skin split and separated from her face, producing a grotesque effect. Rameses VI is equally grotesque, but his appearance is the result of knife cuts wielded by grave-robbers. Amenophis also suffered from the attentions of robbers, who pulled off his right hand and both feet. A fascinating sidelight on the examination of Amenophis in 1974 was the faint scent still given off from a 3,000-year-old spray of delphiniums.

2 MUMMIES OF THE WORLD

Talk of mummies usually conjures up images of Egyptian pharaohs, particularly the magnificently ornate mummy of Tutankhamun discovered by Howard Carter in the Valley of the Kings. But centuries-old corpses, preserved by natural or artificial means, can be seen in countries as culturally diverse and as geographically separated as Peru and Australia, Japan, America and Italy.[3]

PERUVIAN MUMMIES

Preservation of corpses can occur by natural and artificial means and has produced the wonderfully intact Peruvian mummies on display in our own time. The desert climate of coastal Peru, with its negligible rainfall, and the rarefied atmosphere and intense cold of the Peruvian Andes are both ideal for the retardation of decomposition and the production of natural mummies. Artificial preservation processes – evisceration, smoke-curing and embalming – were also used prior to the Spanish conquest of the Incas in 1532.

It is estimated that in Egypt more than half a billion (500 million) corpses were mummified, since people of all social classes wished to ensure life in the other world. In contrast, mummification in Peru was much more the prerogative of the rich, especially the Inca kings. Unfortunately no Peruvian equivalent of Tutankhamun exists: although the royal mummies were known to have been put on display in Lima in 1560, their whereabouts thereafter are shrouded in mystery. In Egypt, mummification was usually performed for religious reasons, whereas in Peru ancestor-worship was thought to be the major incentive to preserving the corpses of chiefs and royalty – those in possession of the mummies of powerful ancestors became powerful themselves.

The earliest Peruvian mummies date back to 4000 BC: two adults and two children were found as natural mummies in a cave 12,000 feet above sea-level. The adults were wrapped in cloaks and trussed up in a typical flexed position, knees drawn up against the chest. In Quiani, on the coast, artificial mummification dating back 3,000 years has been discovered, with mummies showing brain removal, evisceration, limbs reinforced by sticks, and painted faces with wigs fastened over the heads.

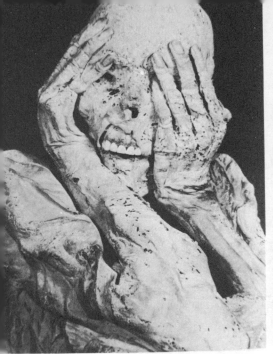

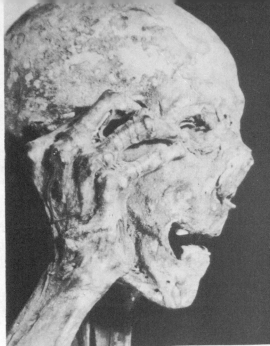

Peruvian mummy I: An adult male with extensive insect damage and remains of cord bindings between fingers.

Peruvian mummy II: An elderly male with cotton fibre in the eye sockets and remains of string laced between fingers.

Peruvian mummy III. An adult male with tattooing on wrists and cords used to bind corpse in flexed position.

Peruvian mummy IV: Mummified trophy head showing perforation in forehead and cactus spine pinned through lips.

114

Perhaps the most characteristic method by which Peruvians preserved their dead was by tightly flexing the body, hands opened flat over the face and secured with cord, covering with a shroud or poncho, and placing the cadaver, in a seated position, inside a coiled basket. Whether the bodies were artificially treated or not before being bundled has remained a contentious issue: some experts declare that evisceration and smoking preceded bundling; others believe that natural desiccation, together with the use of cotton wrapping to absorb the decomposition fluids, was the only process utilized. Sometimes the bundle was topped with a false head and painted mask. X-rays of such bundles have shown skeletons with bracelets and other jewellery, sitting squat and snug on top of the radio-opaque mass of decomposition fluids.

Recently such a bundle (*fardo*) was opened before an audience by Dr Jimenez-Borja. The bundle appeared so auspicious, weighing 300 pounds and needing four men to move it, that there was a great deal of optimism that an important archaelogical find was about to be revealed – the

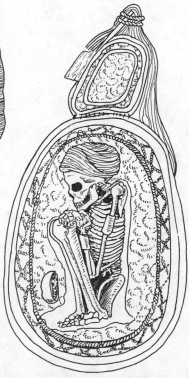

A Peruvian *fardo* with false head. The cross-sectional view shows the mummy in its typical flexed position. Redrawn by Robin Boutell from Simone and Roger Waisbard's *Masks, Mummies and Magicians* (Oliver & Boyd, 1965).

mummified body of a pre-Incan princess perhaps. In reality the bundle contained cloth, linen, sand, branches of guamo trees, cotton balls, a tunic, pots of maize and parrot feathers – but no mummy. What was revealed finally has defied explanation: in the last pile of feathers was the tiny mummified left foot of an adolescent girl, almost certainly severed while she still lived. Did it represent an accident, a punishment or a symbolic sacrifice? Some have suggested that the body may have been eaten by pumas or swallowed by a water snake and that the foot was all that remained. With a macabre humour, she has been dubbed 'Cinderella of Sugar Loaf Mountain'.

The most elaborate post-mortem preservation rituals were reserved for those at the top of the social ladder: the Inca kings. Flexed, trussed and wrapped in cotton, the royal body waited forty days before being placed in its sepulchre. The deceased's every need was catered for – bags of old clothes, jewels, food, drink, wives and concubines were placed in the vault. Special custodians were appointed to wait upon the dead king in perpetuity, their duties including feeding him, washing his clothes, whisking away flies and lifting the bundle when they deemed that the king wished to urinate. On state occasions the royal mummies were dusted down and taken out of their sepulchres to be borne on stretchers and exhibited to the people. No mummy of an Inca king survived the Spanish conquest but descriptions of their preservation allude to embalming with balsam or bitumen.

AUSTRALASIA

Mummification of the dead in Australia and south-east Asia relied mainly on augmented natural processes and was not intended to preserve the corpse indefinitely. Mummification was generally part of a mourning ritual and was not a preparation for an afterlife. Consequently very few Australasian mummies exist for study. Probably the most famous is the mummy found by Sir William Macleay in 1875 on Darnley Island in the Torres Strait, between Australia and New Guinea, and displayed in the University of Sydney.

The Macleay mummy is an adult male suspended on a ladder-like wooden frame by cords passing under the armpits. Natural sagging in the vertical position has brought the shoulders level with the ears. The body was thickly coated with red ochre. Shells were placed in the eye sockets, on each of which was painted a black spot to represent the pupil. The nostrils were plugged with coral. The brain had been removed through an incision at the nape of the neck, and the intestines had been removed through an incision in the left flank. The genitals were complete but there was no discernible pubic hair.

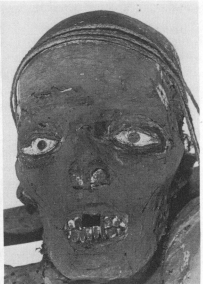

Detail of the head of the
Torres Strait Mummy with
artificial eyes of shell and
nostrils plugged with coral.
The missing teeth were found
by X-rays to be in the throat
and chest.

The Torres Strait Mummy
found on Darnley Island in
1875 by the Australian zoolo-
gist, Sir William Macleay.
The body had been dried,
lashed to a wooden frame and
then painted with a thick
layer of red ochre.

Holes had been made in the knee and elbow joints and between the
fingers in order to allow drainage of putrefying fluids: expulsion of these
fluids was facilitated by stroking and kneading the limbs. The fingernails

and toenails were absent; so was the skin off each palm and sole – these items, together with the tongue, would have been presented to the surviving spouse.

After many months of drying out in the heat of the sun, the mummy would have been decorated and the frame tied to the central post of the dead man's house. In time, the bodies usually fell to pieces, only the head being retained by the relatives. On some of the Melanesian islands the skull would have been given to the nearest relation for use as a drinking-cup.

The body of a Torres Strait infant, aged roughly thirty months, is in the collection of the Royal College of Surgeons in London. It is tied to a rectangular wooden frame and, in most respects, was prepared by the same methods used in adult specimens. There is one intriguing mystery: the abdominal incision, through which the viscera were removed, is only 47 mm long – much too small an aperture for an *adult* hand to enter. Could it be that, in the same way in which men were employed to embalm men, and women to embalm women, children were employed to embalm infants?

MUMMY MISCELLANY

American mummies have usually been desiccated by natural processes. The bodies are most often flexed, wrapped in fur and stored in caves. The majority have been found in Arizona, Colorado and Texas. But perhaps the best-known American mummy was discovered in 1875 by two men in Kentucky. Known as 'Little Alice', she was found lying on a ledge in Salts Cave. In 1958 she was examined at the University of Kentucky and promptly rechristened 'Little Al' on the discovery of external genitalia. The mummy is of a boy about ten years old, probably a Woodland Indian, deposited in the cave roughly 2,000 years ago.[4]

In Japan nineteen mummies are known, fifteen of whom were priests who voluntarily sought self-mummification for religious reasons. The four secular mummies are the grandfather, father, son and grandson of the Fujiwara family who lived in the twelfth century in north-east Japan. The priests achieved 'self-mummification' by starving themselves to death and then being interred in an underground stone chamber for three years, after which time they were exhumed, dried, displayed and venerated whilst patiently awaiting Maitreya-bodhisattva, who would appear on Earth 5,670 million years after the Buddha's attainment of Nirvana. One priest, Tetsumonkai Shonin, is reputed to have extracted his left eyeball and cut off his penis and scrotum before starving himself to death.

Only a small number of Chinese mummies have been discovered – one female mummy, in a remarkable state of preservation, has such suppleness of her limbs that the arms can be flexed with ease.

THE BOG PEOPLE

The most perfect examples of bodily preservation must surely be the 'Bog People' of northern Europe. These people, most dying around the time of Christ, have been remarkably preserved in the unique chemical conditions found in peat bogs.[5]

The most famous of the Bog People were uncovered in Denmark in the years following the Second World War: three in Borremose, Tollund Man and Grauballe Man. So well preserved is Tollund Man that his facial expression makes him appear merely asleep. His serenity belies the fact that a rope is tied tightly around his neck and was obviously the cause of his death. He was found naked apart from a cap, lying on his side, his knees flexed upon his abdomen. Grauballe Man had also met with a violent end: his throat was cut so deeply that the laceration had severed the gullet. Most experts believe that the bog bodies represent human sacrifices to the fertility goddess Ertha.

The most poignant sacrifice was uncovered in Schleswig in 1952, when workmen noticed a foot and a hand rolling off a peat conveyor belt. It proved to be the upper part of the body of a girl of about fourteen. She had lain naked with a bandage over her eyes and a collar around her neck. Experts believe that she had been led blindfold to her death and drowned, weighted down in water by a large stone placed over her.

A British bogman was discovered by workmen in a peat deposit in Cheshire in 1984. Lindow Man, or 'Pete Marsh' as he was irreverently christened by the British press, was dated (using radio-carbon techniques) to about 300 BC. As investigations by experts continued, it became clear that the unfortunate man had been simultaneously hit on the head and garrotted, probably as part of a ritualized killing.

A year earlier, in 1983, the skull of a woman had been dug up in the same vicinity. The find comprised an incomplete skull with some hair and the left eyeball intact. Living near Lindow Moss at the time was Peter Reyn-Bardt, whose wife had disappeared more then twenty years before. When the local police told Reyn-Bardt of the discovery of a skull, he promptly confessed to his wife's murder and was duly tried and convicted. The hapless husband would have been well advised to remain silent, since Lindow Woman was subsequently dated at Oxford University to 210 AD, give or take eighty years.

THE LATER HISTORY OF EMBALMING AND PRESERVING BODIES

From its heyday in ancient Egypt until its renaissance in modern America, the art of embalming went into a decline – though it was never totally abandoned. In ancient Babylon, embalming was accomplished by immersion in honey, and it is said that the body of Alexander the Great was treated in this fashion. The tale is told of twelfth-century visitors to

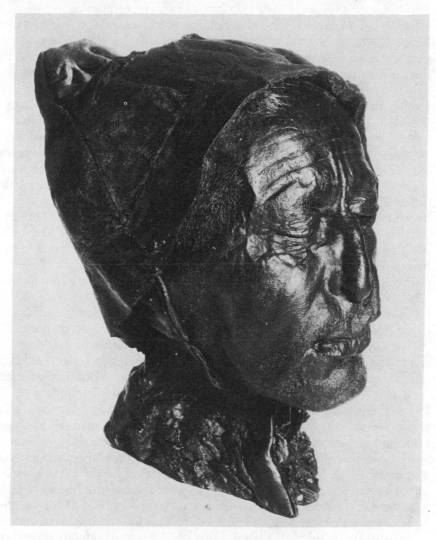

The perfectly preserved head of Tollund Man, found in 1950, wearing a calfskin cap and with a rope, made from two braided thongs, pulled tightly around his neck.

Giza who happened across a sealed jar containing honey, which they proceeded to dip into and enjoy. But their appetites precipitously diminished when one of them scooped out a handful of hair. On emptying the jar they were horrified to find the corpse of a small child, fully clothed, bejewelled and in a remarkable state of preservation.

The ninth-century Emperor Charlemagne was embalmed, as were many members of English royalty, including Canute and Henry I. Henry died in Lyons-la-Forêt, near Rouen, in 1135. His entrails, brain and eyes were buried in France, and the body was embalmed for shipment to Reading Abbey. Such was the advanced state of decomposition of the king's corpse that the surgeon assigned to do the embalming died of infection, 'the last of many whom Henry destroyed'. The body was sewn in a bull's hide and carried to Caen. Despite the coldness of winter, the corpse deteriorated further, prompting one mourner to observe. 'Note the vileness of human flesh. It gives cause for humility.' In contrast, when Edward I died in 1307, the body was so expertly embalmed that when his tomb was opened 500 years later, the king was found in an excellent state of preservation. Catherine de Valois, widow of King Henry V, was embalmed in 1437. When her grandson, King Henry VII, pulled down the chapel in which she was buried, he kept the preserved body above ground in an open coffin. And so she remained for 200 years. In 1669 the diarist Samuel Pepys saw, '... by perticular favour, the body of Queen Katherine of Valois, and had her upper part of her body in my hands. And I did kiss her mouth ...'

Preservation in pickling solutions was occasionally resorted to: during alterations to Danbury church in 1779 the village doctor came across the grave of Sir Gerard de Braybroke who died in 1422. The elm coffin and inner lead shell were opened to reveal a tolerably preserved corpse lying in an aromatic fluid which the doctor proclaimed, after tasting, resembled Spanish olives in mushroom ketchup. Nelson, after his death at the Battle of Trafalgar in 1805, was delivered back to Britain immersed in a barrel of brandy. Some years earlier Suzanne Curchod, wife of Jacques Necker, minister to Louis XVI, left instructions that her body was to be preserved in a huge tank of alcohol within a mausoleum to be built on their estate on the shore of Lake Geneva. Her daughter wrote, 'Perhaps you do not know that my mother gave orders so singular and extraordinary ... [that] she believed the features of her face would be so perfectly preserved that my poor father would spend the rest of his life looking at her.' When the mausoleum was opened in 1804 to receive the body of her daughter, Necker and his wife were found 'in a black marble basin, still half filled with alcohol'. Necker's face was perfectly preserved but his wife's head had fallen off.

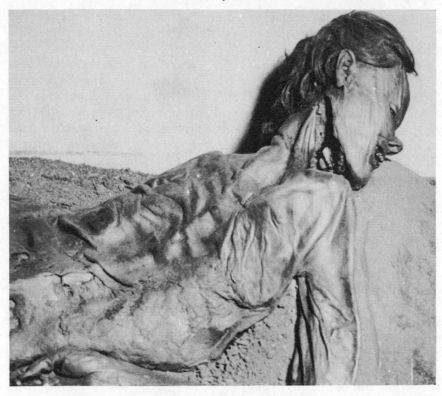

Grauballe Man, found in 1952, his cut throat leaving us in no doubt as to
the cause of death, some 1,500 years ago.

EMBALMING AND ENGLISH ECCENTRICITY

It will probably never be known with certainty just how Hannah Beswick
came to end up as a mummy, but a mummy she indeed became, and it
was more than a hundred years after her death before she was finally laid
underground.

Miss Beswick was born in 1688 into a rich Manchester family. For
many years before her death in 1758 she was a patient of Charles White,
a distinguished local surgeon with an interest in anatomy. The reason
given for her embalming was her terror of being buried alive, though
many have pondered the relative agonies of suffocation in a coffin and
under layers of resinous bandages. No request for embalming appeared in
Miss Beswick's will, and many contemporaries were unjustly suspicious of
White's motives, inferring that he had embalmed the spinster for
monetary gain – it was rumoured that she had instructed him to arrange
her funeral, any change out of £400 to be kept by the surgeon. White's

enemies suggested that he had embalmed the body in order to pocket all of the money. In fact, he received only £100 as his fee for medical and executor services.

For whatever reason, Hannah Beswick *was* embalmed, and White kept the mummy in his possession until his own death in 1813. Thomas de Quincey in his *Autobiography* recounts that as a child in Manchester he was taken to see Charles White's museum of anatomical specimens and that the mummy had been 'Placed in a common English clockcase, having the usual glass face; but a veil of white velvet obscured from all profane eyes the silent features behind'. After White died, his anatomical collection, including Hannah Beswick, was given to the Manchester Natural History Museum. When the museum closed its doors in 1868, Hannah Beswick was finally buried 'without stone or tablet to indicate the spot'.

It is not known whether Mrs van Butchell was eccentric or not, but her husband most decidedly was unhinged. Martin van Butchell was a dentist and truss-maker who had once been a pupil of John Hunter, the brilliant surgeon who melted down O'Brien, the luckless 'Irish Giant'. In 1775 van Butchell's first wife died when she was only thirty-six years old. It is unclear why she was embalmed – some say that the widower loved her too much and was loath to bury her. Others invoked a clause in the marriage settlement to the effect that Martin van Butchell could dispose of some property in any way he saw fit, '*always provided his wife remained above ground*'. The first explanation would seem to be more credible according to the sentiments of the lady's epitaph:

Epitaph on Mrs Vanbutchel
whose remains, preserved by a curious and newly invented method
embalment, are the object of her fond husband's daily attention.

Here, unintombed, Vanbutchel's comfort lies,
To feed a husband's grief, or charm his eyes;
Taintless and pure her body still remains,
And all its former elegance retains.
Long had disease been preying on her charms,
Till slow she shrunk in Death's expecting arms;
When Hunter's skill in spite of Nature's laws,
Her beauties rescued from Curruptions jaws;
Bade the pale roses of her cheeks revive
And her shrunk features seem again to live:
– Hunter who first conceived the happy thought,
And here at length to full perfection brought.
O! lucky Husband! Blest of Heav'n
To thee the privilege is given,
A much loved wife at home to keep,
Caress, touch, talk to, even sleep
Close by her side, when e'er you will

As quiet as if living still:
And, strange to tell, that fairer she,
And sweeter than alive should be;
Firm, plump and juicy as before
And full as tractable, or more –
Thrice happy mortal! Envied lot;
What a rare treasure thou hast got!
Who to a woman canst lay claim
Whose temper's every day the same!

The Hunter referred to in these sexist, McGonagall lines is not John but his elder brother William, who had invented a method of embalming in order to preserve his surgical specimens. The process consisted of three stages: first, the injection of turpentine and vermilion 'to fill the arteries and veins'; second, the removal of the organs in the chest and abdomen and the emptying of the bladder and rectum; third, the injection of turpentine and vermilion, again into the blood vessels and organs. The viscera were then replaced in the body, and the cavities packed with a mixture of camphor, nitre and resin. After sewing, washing and drying, the body was rubbed with fragrant oils and placed in a box half filled with plaster of Paris to absorb excess moisture. Hunter recommended that the process should not be hurried and that it should not cost less than 100 guineas.

From a document written by van Butchell it would appear that he entered into the embalming personally and with gusto:

14th January 1775. At half past two this morning my Wife died ... At half past two this afternoon Mr Cruikshanks injected at the crural arteries 5 pints of Oil of Turpentine mixed with Venice Turpentine and Vermilion.
15th. Dr Hunter and Mr Cruikshanks began to open and embalm the body of my Wife. Her diseases were a large Empyema ... with Pleuropneumony.
17th. I opened the abdomen to put in the remainder of Powders.
18th. Dr Hunter and Mr Cruikshanks came and put my wife into a Box on and in 130 pounds of Paris plaister at 18 pence a bag. I put between the thighs three Arquebusade bottles, one full of Camphorated Spirits very rich of the Gum; one containing 8 oz of Oil of Rosemary; and in the other 2 oz Oil of lavender.
11th February. I unluted the glasses to clean the face and legs with Spirits of Wine and Oil of Lavender.

A great deal of interest and curiosity was generated by the embalming, and a stream of visitors presented themselves at van Butchell's house in order to view his late spouse. So great was the demand that he had to publish a notice in the St James's Chronicle on 21 October 1775: 'Vanbutchell (not willing to be unpleasantly circumstanced, and wishing to convince some good Minds they have been misinformed) acquaints the Curious, no Stranger can see his embalmed Wife, unless (by a Friend personally) introduced to himself, any Day, between Nine and One, *Sundays* excepted.'

The first Mrs van Butchell shared her home with her husband's second wife.

On the death of Martin van Butchell in 1814, his son offered the embalmed body to the Royal College of Surgeons. The generous gift was accepted. In 1857 a visitor to the college commented thus on a certain exhibit: 'No doubt extraordinary pains were taken to preserve both form and feature; and yet, what a wretched mockery of a once lovely woman it now appears, with its shrunken and rotten-looking bust, its hideous, mahogany-coloured face, and its *remarkably fine set of teeth*. Between the feet are the remains of a green parrot – whether immolated or not at the death of its mistress is uncertain – but as it still retains its plumage, it is a far less repulsive object than the larger biped.'[6]

Fortunately or unfortunately, the body is no longer on show – it was finally cremated in 1941, when a German bomb landed on the college during the Second World War.

John Sheldon gained his diploma in surgery in 1775 and joined the staff of Lock Hospital. Miss Johnson, one of his patients, was a beautiful woman of twenty-four who was dying of tuberculosis. She asked Sheldon to embalm her when she died. One can only speculate on his motives but Sheldon, after embalming the dead woman, took the body to his home and placed it in his bedroom, laid out on a bed under glass. A visitor from France was asked to admire the fine brown hair and to feel the flexibility of the arms and the elasticity of the bosom. Sheldon had used spirits of wine and had tanned the skin with finely powdered alum. Much camphor was used, as Sheldon's widow was to attest to when she offered the body to the College of Surgeons: 'I recollect putting a little favourite Bird in the room in which the case stood that contained the Body; in the morn that Bird was found dead, which Mr Sheldon attributed to the smell of camphor.'

Alas, Miss Johnson fared no better than Mrs van Butchell. In 1899 a writer in *The British Medical Journal* commented that Sheldon's mummy no longer had '… any semblance of life but was shrunken and hard as a board, the skin of the arms, neck and chest quite white but the face, where apparently the colour injected had remained, a dull red, all the more ghastly for its colour, and the long brown hair is beautiful no more.'[7] So much for Sheldon's optimism that the bosom would retain its elasticity for centuries!

JIMMY GARLICK

Jimmy Garlick is one of the rare examples of natural mummification that can be seen in Britain. In 1839, during excavation work being carried out

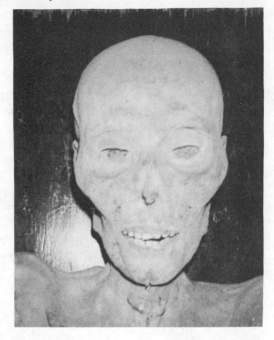

The body of a young man who lived 300 years ago, discovered in 1839 near the altar at St James Garlickhythe, London, and affectionately known as 'Jimmy Garlick'. At present he resides, snug and warm, in the boiler room of the church, but plans are in hand to move him to a more dignified resting-place.

in St James Garlickhythe in the City of London, the calcified body of a young man was found buried near the altar. Nothing is known about him except that he is at least 300 years old. He is known affectionately as 'Jimmy Garlick' and presently stands in an upright box in the snug warmth of the boiler-room in the basement of the church. He shows no signs of having been embalmed. Plans are far advanced to provide a permanent place in the body of the church to exhibit this unusual relic.

WITH HEART AND HEAD

The ancient Egyptians regarded the heart as the most important organ of the body and took special care to leave it embalmed within the chest cavity. The advent of Christianity saw the decline of embalming, since resurrection of the body in no way depended on its state of preservation. Dead Christians were to be committed to the ground, happy in the knowledge that their chances of eternal life would depend only on the quality of their earthly existence and not upon the quality of their corpse.

Tampering with the dead was officially frowned upon, and in 1299 Pope Boniface VIII was moved to issue a vigorous edict prohibiting any dismemberment of the dead on pain of excommunication. Despite such papal threats, the practice of Christian heart burial, begun in the twelfth century, continued with increasing momentum in succeeding centuries.[8]

Much of the interest in affording the heart special treatment after death came about because of the wish of many medieval crusaders to have their heart buried in the Holy Land. Despite Boniface's edict, papal dispensations were sometimes granted to facilitate the burial of the hearts of the pious and famous in Jerusalem.

Two stories are told about the fate of the heart of Robert the Bruce, King of Scotland, who died of leprosy in 1329. The king's wish was recorded in a translation of Froissart's Chronicles: 'I will that as soone as I am trepassed out of this worlde that ye take my harte owte of my body, and embawme it, and take of my treasoure as ye shall thynke sufficient for that enterprise ... and present my harte to the holy Sepulchre where as our Lorde laye, seying my body can nat come there.' Other sources claim that Bruce merely wanted his heart to be taken to Palestine to be blessed and then brought back to be buried at Melrose.

In one account, James Douglas, to whom the organ was entrusted, carried it to Jerusalem and buried it in a gold box before the altar of the Church of the Holy Sepulchre. An alternative, and more authentic version tells of how, passing through Spain en route to the Holy Land and with the silver casket containing the heart hung around his neck, Douglas did battle with a troop of Moors. Surrounded by the enemy, he flung the casket, saying, 'Pass first in fight as thou wert wont to do. Douglas will follow or die!'

Douglas died, his body falling on the casket. The heart was recovered and sent home and was subsequently buried at Melrose.

More recently, in 1900, another illustrious Scot, John, Marquis of Bute, had his body buried in Scotland, but his heart, in its golden casket, came to rest on the Mount of Olives.

There were other, more pragmatic, reasons why the Catholic Church finally came to condone the practice of separating the heart from the rest of the corpse. Firstly, there was the economical use of space within a church – such was the demand of clergy and laity alike to be buried inside a church, rather than in the graveyard outside, that an expedient compromise was to bury the corpse without and an urned heart within the church precincts. Antiquaries have long commented on the large number of urns found under the floorboards of old churches and cathedrals containing the shrivelled-up remnants of hearts.

The Catholic Church also came to accept the separation of the heart from the body in order to satisfy the demand for holy relics, since, as we have seen, saintly hearts could be bartered and traded in the political arena. But the practice of separate heart burial found greatest favour with European royalty and the aristocracy. Jeanne, Queen of Navarre, kept the heart of her husband King Philip, who died in 1343, until her own death, when on her orders it was enshrined in the same urn as her own and placed at the Jacobins' church in Paris.

English royalty embraced heart burial with gusto. Richard the Lionheart directed that his body be placed with his father Henry II at Fontevrault Abbey, but that his heart be presented to the citizens of Rouen as a sign of his gratitude – the leaden box containing the heart was rediscovered in Rouen Cathedral as recently as 1838, 'withered to the semblance of a faded leaf'. A less romantic version of the story has the Cœur de Lion's heart buried in a church in Barking.

Even more ignominious is the fate of the hearts of the two Tudor queens: they were deposited in the same vault in Westminster Abbey, where they remained undisturbed until 1670. In that year, when the vault was opened for the funeral of the duke of Albermarle, a boy named William Taswell opened up two urns, one labelled Queen Mary (Tudor), the other Queen Elizabeth. The urchin dipped his hand into each and took out a red, glutinous substance 'somewhat resembling mortar'.

But perhaps the greatest posthumous indignity befell James II and VII who died in exile in Paris. His heart, encased in lead and enclosed in a casket of silver-gilt, was deposited at the Chapel of the Visitation at Chaillot and later removed to the Chapel of the English Benedictines in Paris; his other viscera were divided between Saint-Germain-en-Laye and the English College at Saint-Omer; his brain, in a bronze-gilt urn, was given to the Scots College in Paris. The body was deposited with the English Benedictines in the forlorn hope that sometime in the future James would be permitted to rest with his peers in Westminster Abbey. When seen in 1793, the corpse was found to be swaddled like a mummy in bandages smelling strongly of vinegar and camphor. All hopes of Westminster Abbey were dashed when James's coffin was broken up by the revolutionaries for the sake of its lead. The interment of the relics that remained took place at Saint-Germain in 1824.

Occasionally people other than the aristocracy would have their hearts disposed of separately. David Livingstone's heart was buried in his beloved Africa. Shelley's heart refused to burn and is preserved at Boscombe Manor House in Hampshire. A story, probably apocryphal, recounts that a cat stole and ate Thomas Hardy's heart as it was being prepared for burial in 1928; the more accepted version has Hardy's heart buried in the churchyard of St Michael's in Stinsford, Dorset. Almost 200 years earlier, when a duke of Orléans was being embalmed, a great dane pounced on his dead master's heart and had eaten 'a good quarter' before it could be retrieved.

When John Hunter died in 1793, he requested that his body be buried but that his heart be preserved in his famous museum. His wish was ignored (perhaps deservedly when one recalls how Hunter had ignored the wishes of Charles O'Brien). He was buried in the crypt of St Martin-in-the-Fields where his coffin was 'lost' for over sixty years. In 1859, when the vaults were to be cleared, Frank Buckland went searching for, and eventually identified, Hunter's coffin among the hundreds that lay sequestered there. Hunter was subsequently reinterred in the place in which James II would have dearly wished to have been buried – Westminster Abbey.

A unique heart memorial was contrived for Johannes Wepfer. When this great anatomist died, his friends decided to honour the man, who was the first to describe the link between damage to the cerebral blood vessels and strokes, by bringing out a posthumous edition of his works in 1727. The book began with an illustrated account of the author's autopsy, and in a drawing captioned *Memoria Wepferiana*, the cause of Wepfer's death is plain to see, since the dissected heart and blood vessels show gross hardening of the arteries.

HEAD-SHRINKING

Just as Jeanne of Navarre stored her husband's heart until her own death, Sir Walter Raleigh's widow held on to the head of the Elizabethan hero. After his execution, Sir Walter's embalmed head was carried around in a leather bag until his wife's own death. Such practices, unusual in England, were more reminiscent of the head-hunters of South America, who would collect the heads of relatives or vanquished enemies for ritual and religious purposes.

There have been many misconceptions about how Amazonian tribes were able to shrink the bones of the skull and jaw in order to produce a shrunken head. In reality, only the skin and soft tissues were reduced in size, the bones being discarded at an early stage. The first step was to remove the head from the body. The incision was made through the neck as close as possible to the chest. The bones of the spine were then cut through with a sharp blade. A short length of wood was pushed through the victim's mouth, exiting at the cut end of the gullet. In such a way the head could be hung from the waist while the victorious natives made off to shrink the heads at leisure.

A long incision was made at the back of the neck and extended up to the crown of the head. The scalp was then peeled away from the skull beneath. Separation of the skin from the bone was relatively easy when working on the back of the head but became increasingly more intricate when separating the face from the deeper structure. The skull and the lower jaw were detached and discarded. The eyelids were sewn together, and slivers of palm wood held the mouth closed. Water was then boiled in an earthenware pot in which were placed the scalp and face. After two hours the specimen was taken out of the water, and the two halves of the scalp were sewn together to produce a 'bag' open at the neck. Into this pouch were placed large, hot stones, whose effect was to shrink the skin

A shrunken head.

tissues. As shrinkage occurred, smaller stones were successively used. Hot sand was poured in, to produce a final reduction to about the size of a large orange. To maintain the proportions of the facial structures to the head, the eyelashes and eyebrows were plucked to the correct lengths. Next the head was smoked overnight by suspension above a fire. In this way the skin became dark and leathery, and the features of the face, especially the nose and the mouth, were manipulated to make it resemble its original state. Finally the face was painted and ornamented.

In the late 1800s many European museums vied with each other to obtain shrunken heads for their collections. Consequently a brisk trade in 'counterfeit' heads grew up, with practices reminiscent of the British resurrectionists: the bodies of paupers were either stolen or exhumed by the Indians, who would then decapitate them and shrink the heads – for roughly $25 each.

3 THE INCORRUPTIBLES

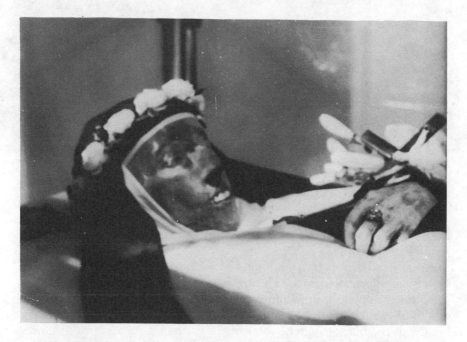

St Teresa Margaret of the Sacred Heart (1747–70). Exhumed in 1783, the body was found to be 'perfectly incorrupt'. In 1805 it was declared to be 'surprisingly elastic and pliable'.

Most experts categorize mummies in two groups: those that have been naturally desiccated, by burial in hot desert sand for instance, and those that have been artificially produced, by processes akin to embalming. But some cite a third group, consisting mainly of saints, whose bodies have resisted decay by virtue of their sanctity. These are 'the Incorruptibles'.[9]

To the devout there are many examples of holy corpses that have defied the natural disintegrative processes. Besides the absence of decay, these relics often have a number of other things in common. Unlike natural and artificially produced mummies, whose hard and dry corpses invariably show signs of rigidity and shrinkage, Incorruptibles retain their suppleness and flexibility despite the passage of centuries. They are often described as 'sleeping' rather than dead. Naturally sceptics disagree about the need to invoke miraculous intervention to explain what they would regard as bodies accidentally preserved by dint of unusual circumstances.

The remains of St Francis Xavier (1506–52) being borne in procession to
the Basilica of Bom Jesus, Goa, India, on their final exhibition in 1975.
Many bits of the saint's anatomy had been taken away as holy relics.

Let us take as an example St Teresa Margaret of the Sacred Heart, born
Anna Maria Redi (1747–70).

Anna was born in Italy and entered a Carmelite convent in Florence
in her middle adolescence. During her lifetime she was credited with
performing numerous miraculous cures. She herself died of a gangrenous
condition which caused her eighteen months of excruciating pain. On
her death the black gangrene soon began to change into a faint rose hue,
'... which gave her a more angelic beauty than when she was alive'. Two
days later her hands and feet 'changed to the glow of living fresh' and she
seemed to be 'quietly sleeping'. Two days later still her face was even
more beautiful, her lips were fresh and naturally red, limbs pliable, and
the whole body was enveloped in 'a most delightful odour'. In short, St
Teresa had become an Incorruptible.

Fifteen days post mortem she was examined by an archbishop,
numerous minor clerics and three physicians. All was unchanged, there
were no signs of putrefaction, and the sweet fragrance persisted. Thirteen
years after burial, when the body was exhumed in order to move the saint
to a drier location, it was found to be perfectly incorrupt. In 1805 she was
again disturbed and was described thus: '... Healthy flesh colour;
somewhat dry but, nevertheless, surprisingly elastic and pliable ... the
colour of the hair on the head livid and fresh ... eyebrows golden-blonde
... [and a previous wound in the right foot] healed and of good colour'.
Teresa was canonized in 1934, and her body, now dark and dry 'but still
perfectly incorrupt', can be seen in the chapel of the monastery of Santa
Teresa dei Bruni in Florence.

To Catholics, St Teresa is an example of miraculous incorruption. Others have mooted alternative explanations. The most secular reason for the rosiness and fragrance of the corpse was a clandestine attempt at post-mortem cosmetics in order to make the deceased look more attractive and to try to dissipate the colour and offensive odour of gangrene. Indeed, covert embalming is the most common explanation put forward for the incorrupt appearance of saints, especially in the case of one of the most famous of all the Incorruptibles, St Francis Xavier (1506–52).

Francis Xavier died in China, but ten weeks after his burial he was exhumed and shipped to Malacca. Five months later he was dug up for a second time and taken to the basilica of the Bom Jesus, in Goa, where he remains to this day. His body was deemed incorrupt and, to scotch talk of secret embalming, Dr Cosmas Sairauia in 1556 declared on oath that no artificial preservatives had been used. At that time the doctor noted, but did not comment upon, an incision which had been made in Xavier's chest. In 1614 the body was described as 'beautiful and whole', the right eye open and fresh, while the legs and fingers were fresh but dry. In the same year the saint's right forearm was removed to join St Ignatius Loyola as a holy relic in Rome.

When the rest of the body was examined by priests 142 years after death, the saint was described as having black, lively eyes, bright reddish lips, vermilion-tinted cheeks, a moist, flexible tongue and a beautifully proportioned chin, and the body had all the appearance of being a living man'. (A number of the saint's toes were missing, one having been bitten off by Donna Isabel de Carom in 1544). Bits of Xavier have been distributed throughout the world: besides the right forearm in Rome, the rest of the right arm went to Japan, a toe went to Spain, the left hand to Cochin, a shoulder blade to Malacca. What remains, dry and shrunken, stayed in Goa. The body was last exhibited in 1974, when a priest commented that it looked 'as though the saint was only sleeping'.

Believers dismiss all talk of clandestine embalming and cite Dr Sairauia's examination of the body. What is usually omitted is that the examination took place by candle-light and that the body was not stripped. Ambrose de Ribera, representing the Inquisition, noted a wound in the abdomen which had been missed by the doctor. This abdominal incision may have been made by embalmers; others contend it was made in order to remove the internal organs to satisfy the insatiable demand for relics. [10]

The central tenet of advocates of miraculous intervention is the belief that the saints have remained incorrupt for centuries in conditions which would have rapidly reduced any other body to a putrefied mass. Since moisture is a major catalyst of putrefaction, how is it that Charbel Makhlouf remained incorrupt despite floating for four months in mud at

134

the bottom of a flooded grave? Or St Josaphat, incorrupt after a week in a river? Or, most remarkably, St Andrew Bobola: flayed alive, hands hacked from his body, tongue torn from his head, splinters driven under his fingernails, exhumed after forty years in a grave so damp that his vestments were rotted, yet described as a soft, flexible body showing no evidence of decay. Whilst eschewing accusations of false witness, sceptics wonder out loud why, after being 'incorrupt' for centuries, most present-day examples of incorruption are hard, brittle, blackened bodies who would be deemed dead and not sleeping. A specimen which does appear to be better preserved, St Catherine Labouré (1806–76), lying in the chapel of Our Lady of the Sun in Paris, is known to have been injected with a solution of formaldehyde, glycerine and carbolic acid at the time of her exhumation in 1933 'to ensure preservation'.

AN UNHOLY INCORRUPTIBLE

In 1981 a remarkably well-preserved body was found at St Bees Priory in Cumbria. Although buried close to the monks' cemetery, this, the only preserved body among a host of skeletons, was the corpse not of a holy man but of a medieval knight. The nobleman had been wrapped in shrouds over which a wax-and-honey mixture had been poured. The body was then enveloped in a sheet of lead and packed with clay inside a

The well-preserved body of St Bernadette Soubirous (1844–79), who saw her first vision of the Virgin Mary at Lourdes in 1858. She was exhumed in 1909 and again in 1919 before being placed in a coffin of gold and glass in Nevers.

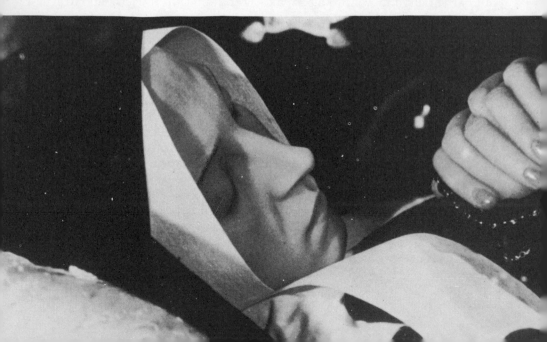

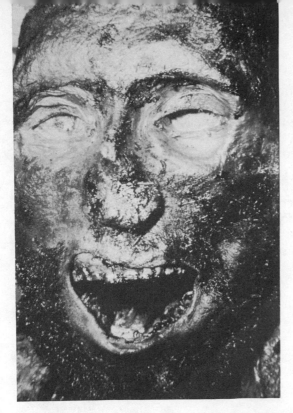

The head of a medieval nobleman found at St Bees Priory, Cumbria, in 1981. Preservation had been enhanced by rapid embalming of the corpse, which had then been wrapped in lead and packed in clay. The body was later reburied.

wooden coffin. Inside this micro-environment the normal disintegrative processes had been arrested. When the body was unwrapped, the knight was exposed for the first time in seven centuries, naked except for two pieces of string, one around his neck, the other around his penis. The pink hue of the skin quickly faded but the eyes were well preserved and the heart and intestines intact. The liver, when cut, appeared bright pink initially, and the vessels in other organs appeared to contain 'fresh' blood. Experts believe that such an unusual body was produced by a combination of rapid embalming and a unique combination of environmental conditions.

THE CAPUCHIN CATACOMBS AT PALERMO

This truly remarkable burial-place dates back to 1599. Initially it was intended as the last resting-place of the Capuchin monks of Palermo, but over the centuries the inordinate demand of others to be buried there led to its division into sections: for monks, men, women, children, professors and priests. At the present time there are over 8,000 bodies in varying degrees of preservation.

Although a small number of the bodies were preserved by being dipped in solutions of arsenic or lime, the vast majority have been mummified by simple desiccation. The corpses were first laid on grills made of terra-cotta tubes in a hermetically sealed cell. After six months the bodies were removed and placed in a bath of aromatic herbs and vinegar before finally being exposed to the Mediterranean sun. The bodies were then dressed and placed in niches. These long-dead Sicilians are arranged along the walls of the catacombs, some horizontally, others vertically, some as if only sleeping, many appearing to be grinning grotesquely – the very stuff of nightmares.

One of the most remarkable of all the bodies on show in the Capuchin church is that of a child, probably one of the best examples of embalming to be seen anywhere in the world. Two-year-old Rosalia Lombardo died in 1920 and was embalmed by a local physician, Dr Solafia. Ironically, he himself died shortly after the embalming and took the details of his technique with him to the grave.

The central corridor of the Capuchin Monastery in Palermo, Sicily.

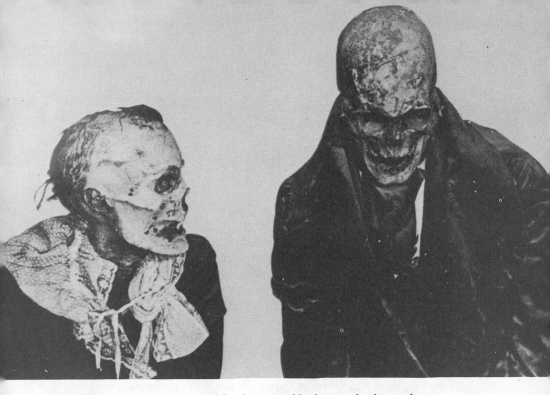

A husband and wife: two of the desiccated bodies on display at the
Capuchin Monastery in Palermo, Sicily.

The body of Rosalia
Lombardo on view at the
Capuchin Monastery in
Palermo, Sicily. The child
died in December 1920, aged
two years, and the body was
preserved by injections given
immediately after death by
Dr Salafia.

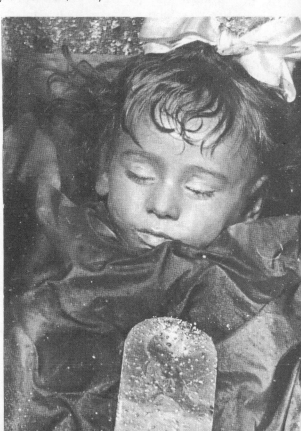

4 TWENTIETH-CENTURY EMBALMING

Embalming, an art long dead in Europe, has had a twentieth-century renaissance in North America. Embalming in the United States has become an integral and essential part of the highly profitable business centred on the disposal of the dead. But embalming American-style bears very little resemblance in either its purpose or practice to the methods of bodily preservation used by the ancient Egyptians. In the Egyptian religion it was essential to maintain the body's physical integrity in order that the *ka* (soul) should be able to recognize and reoccupy its former carcase and thus ensure eternal life. In modern America bodies are embalmed for purely cosmetic reasons, and its effects last little longer than the length of time it takes to put the corpse underground.

Dr Jesse Carr, head of pathology at the San Francisco General Hospital, was quoted by Jessica Mitford in *The American Way of Death*, her book about American funeral practices, as saying, 'An exhumed embalmed body is a repugnant, moldy, foul-looking object. The body itself may be intact, as far as contours and so on, but the silk lining of the casket is all stained with body fluids, the wood is rotting, and the body is covered with mold.'[11] Burial in a sealed metal coffin makes matters worse, not better, since anaerobic bacteria, those that thrive in airless conditions, reduce a body to a putrefied mass even more quickly. In contemporary America, according to Carr, the *ka* would have a hopeless task!

What, then, are these modern embalming methods which compare so unfavourably with those used thousands of years ago?

Modern American embalming can be said to have started with Dr Thomas Holmes (1817–1900). During the Civil War, Holmes was asked by President Lincoln to devise a method of preserving the bodies of Union soldiers long enough for their transportation from the southern battlefields to their homes in the north. Holmes's method was crude and temporary: he would inject into an artery a solution of bichloride of mercury. Although it is not recorded, it is to be hoped that his technique had improved by the time he was called upon to give his services to the president himself.

After the Civil War there was little call for embalming, due to a combination of the poisonous effects that mercury solutions had upon the embalmers, and their ineffectiveness in producing an aesthetically pleasing preserved corpse. Arsenical solutions replaced mercurial ones, but the results were often just as unsatisfactory. Both arsenic and mercury, as well as lead, zinc and other metals, were subsequently banned as preservative substances for medico-legal reasons – they constituted a poisoner's charter, whereby the evidence of murder could be masked by the embalmer's chemicals.

Other embalming techniques were equally as primitive. 'Cavity embalming' consisted merely of injecting large amounts of preservative solutions into the chest and abdominal cavities through a wide-bore needle called a 'trocar'. Such injections were often combined with moistening the face with a preservative mixture of aluminium sulphate and mercury bichloride. 'Cranial injection', as its name implies, consisted of inserting a trocar into the skull through either the base of the neck or the corner of the eye or up through the nostril. Embalming only really rose out of the doldrums with the discovery of the preservative properties of formaldehyde.

Blum discovered the hardening action of formaldehyde in 1893. This substance, injected into the blood vessels of a corpse, has the dual effect of disinfecting and preserving. Much used to be made of the disinfecting properties of formaldehyde, but with greater candour it is now conceded

Princess Grace of Monaco, formerly the film actress Grace Kelly, lies in state in the Palatine Chapel. Her famed beauty is preserved despite the serious injuries she sustained in the fatal car crash.

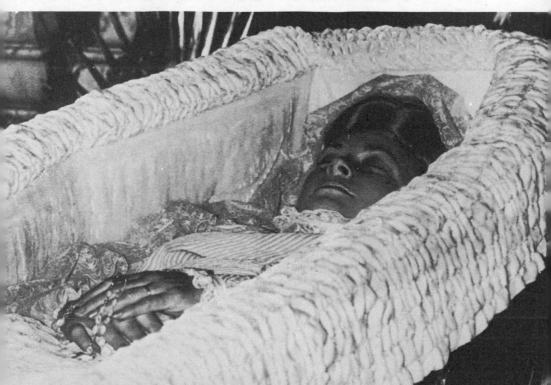

by most American undertakers that the sole function of embalming is to produce a short-term, superficial but aesthetically pleasing preservative effect for the benefit of grieving relatives. The embalmer's job is to enhance the 'memory picture', a psychologically dubious concept supposedly comprising the bereaved's last glimpse of the deceased. In a defensive style, one of the standard embalming textbooks says, 'It is our purpose to serve the living ... not to create museum specimens for the amazement of those who may populate the earth many centuries in the future. Few intelligent people fear or object to the eventual return of the body to the dust from which it originated. What they do fear and abhor is the thought of the putrefactive or rotting process ... Embalming eliminates the putrefaction or rotting and permits the body to return to its component elements through the gradual, clean process of oxidation and dissolution.'[12] Perhaps this is not the place to enquire too deeply into the differences between putrefaction and 'clean' dissolution.

The theory and practice of arterial embalming have changed little from the time of William Hunter – only the particular chemicals differ. In the living, the heart pumps blood into the arteries, which feed into a vast system of smaller blood vessels called capillaries, from which the blood drains into veins and is directed back to the heart for the cycle to start over again. At any one time the majority of the capillaries are empty, and this potential space allows embalmers to inject large quantities of solution into the vascular system without noticeable distention of the corpse. In practice, embalming essentially consists of the draining from the body of blood and its replacement by formaldehyde pumped in under pressure – the formaldehyde in the arteries pushes blood ahead of itself which is then drained from the body through a vein. Favoured arterial injection sites include the carotid artery in the neck, the brachial artery in the arm, the femoral artery in the groin and the aorta. Drainage veins include the jugular in the neck, the brachial and femoral veins and the inferior vena cava – the large abdominal vein tracking back to the heart. The sooner embalming begins, the better; in this way the blood remains fluid and can be easily drained from a vein. In Britain, where there is likely to be considerable delay between death and embalming, the blood has often clotted, and it then becomes necessary to withdraw blood via a large trocar inserted into the heart itself.

In the capillaries the preservative solution reacts with the protein within the body cells to produce an insoluble substance. The effects of formaldehyde depend on its concentration: too strong a solution fixes the tissues too rapidly, coagulates the blood and causes obstruction in the blood vessels; too weak a solution often has insufficient preservative action. Strong formaldehyde solutions also cause shrinkage by dehydration, and over-hardening, and produce a brown discolouration.

The dehydration is counteracted by adding glycerine to the formaldehyde solution, and borax is used to keep the blood fluid and to help break up blood clots. Dyes such as saffranine, methyl red and eosin yellow are mixed in the embalming fluids to create the illusion of the 'soft, warm glow of life'.

STEP-BY-STEP EMBALMING

In general, the sooner embalming is started, the fewer the difficulties, especially those problems brought about by coagulation of the blood. Nevertheless, cleanliness and good hygiene are paramount considerations at all times: consequently the embalming process begins with a thorough washing of the dead body with soap and water.

Next the embalmer chooses the vein he will use to drain the blood from the body, and the artery through which preservative will be injected into the body. Sometimes *two* drainage veins are used – the femoral (in the groin) below the heart, and the axillary (in the armpit) above the heart. Massaging in the direction of the heart helps to break up small clots that may have formed in the blood vessels. By clearing such obstructions the injection of fluid can be facilitated. If the axillary artery in the armpit is used, two or three pints of preservative are injected in the direction of the hand. Fluid will begin to fill the arm, and the veins on the back of the hand will become prominent as the fluid circulates towards the heart and eventual drainage out of the body. When the fluid is directed towards the head, the cheeks become fuller and firmer, and the eyeballs and surrounding skin become harder.

When between four and six pints of fluid have been injected, it is time to start draining from a vein. It is axiomatic that inadequate drainage will result in poor preservation and premature decomposition.

Initially the fluid that is drained is thick blood, but as the embalming fluid circulates in the body, the blood draining out becomes thinner and thinner. If drainage from a vein proves difficult, it may become necessary to drain directly from the heart by using a wide-bore trocar. Circulation of the embalming fluid is facilitated by devices such as hand-held vibrators and roller massagers, or even by manual shaking or rocking of the table. Over-enthusiastic massage is to be discouraged, since the skin of a corpse is extremely vulnerable to trauma. In extreme cases, when drainage is meagre, outflow can sometimes be enhanced by delivering a heavy blow with a closed fist onto the breast bone in order to loosen blood clots. Less draconian methods of encouraging drainage include the simple expedient of raising the deceased's feet off the table by ten to fifteen inches.

The embalming procedure just described will generally ensure that the vessels of the torso, limbs, head and neck are drained of blood and replaced by preservative fluid which will harden the tissues and delay decomposition. But what of organs such as the intestines which harbour countless millions of bacteria and which are not reached by the embalming fluid? 'Cavity embalming' has been introduced to prevent such organs causing rapid decomposition and putrefaction.

The principle of cavity embalming is simple: a trocar is plunged into the abdomen just above the navel and is thrust in all directions in order to pierce the stomach, intestines, rectum, bladder and liver (which is usually engorged with blood), sucking out bits of tissue, blood clots, food, faeces, intestinal gases and urine. The instrument is then pushed through the diaphragm and into the chest, and the lacerating and sucking continue. (The process is akin to sucking out a blocked drain.) When suction through the trocar is complete, concentrated preserving fluids are introduced into the abdomen and chest in order to reduce the likelihood of decomposition.

Special attention is paid to the face, since this is the part of the body left uncovered. At death the lower jaw falls downwards and backwards, and the mouth hangs open. The embalmer closes the mouth by an intricate process of internal stitching. A needle is passed from the inner surface of the lower lip, up in front of the gums, through into one nostril, across to the other nostril and back again into the mouth behind the upper lip. The thread is drawn tight, pulling the lower jaw upwards and forwards. Another method is to take the needle from behind the lower lip, down below the bone of the lower jaw, up through the floor of the mouth, out between the teeth and into the nose. Dentures are replaced before the knot is finally tied. If there are no dentures, cotton wool is placed between and in front of the gums in order to give a more natural appearance.

A great deal of an embalmer's expertise is in producing a natural and pleasing contour to the mouth. Most embalmers aim for a slight separation of the lips after a pumice has been used to polish any exposed teeth. 'A colourless nail polish may be applied [to the teeth] with pleasing effect.' Alternative procedures (done only with the family's permission) include loosening protruding teeth with forceps and realigning, and removal of protruding teeth and their replacement with a cardboard strip.

The appearance of the eyes is important: they must be neither bulging nor sunken. Contact with concentrated preserving fluids tends to produce dehydration, wrinkling and hardening of the eyelids. Sunken eyes can be corrected by slipping a thin piece of cotton or tissue paper under the lids; those that are grossly sunken can be corrected by an injection of cream directly into the eyeball. Eyelids can be helped to remain closed by coating the margins with vaseline or eye cement.

Modern embalmers do not aim to preserve a corpse for longer than a week or so. Nevertheless, there are a small number of outstanding examples of exceptionally well-preserved bodies – Lenin and Eva Peron are two cases in point.

The embalmers of ancient Egypt were often treated in a very ambivalent way, being venerated and despised. They were essential to preserve a body for use in the afterlife, yet because of abhorrence of the idea of mutilating the dead, the 'cutters' were ritually stoned after they had made the first incisions. Today embalmers are neither venerated nor despised, though social commentators openly question the precepts upon which these expensive practices are based.

PRESERVATION BY FREEZING

The fact that bodies can be preserved almost indefinitely by low temperatures was poignantly demonstrated in 1954 with the discovery of 'the Inca Prince' on Mount Cerro El Plomo in Chile. The body of a 10-year-old child was found by a shepherd near Santiago at an altitude of 14,000. He had died 500 years before, probably after having become lost, and had squatted in the cave to keep warm. The state of preservation was remarkably good. He was dressed in a tunic, wore embroidered leather slippers, carried a doll carved from shell and had a coloured bag containing his nail parings, cut hair and milk teeth. Since there were no obvious signs of violence, it seems unlikely that this child was murdered, although it is known that, as part of Inca religious ceremonies, youths were often taken up into the Andes, made intoxicated with alcoholic corn beer or narcotic coca leaf and sacrificed by strangulation.

CRYONICS

The reports of my death are greatly exaggerated.

Mark Twain (1835–1910)

The 'science' of cryonics depends upon two basic premises: that the human body can be preserved indefinitely if stored at very low temperatures, and that, given enough time, medical science will find a cure for the disease that killed you, reverse its pathological effect (death) and bring you back to life.

At the time of writing it is estimated that between eleven and fifteen corpses have been frozen and are patiently awaiting future thawing – though not all of them can be accurately described as 'corpses', since some, the people who opted for neurosuspension alone, at a saving of rougly $60,000, are stored as disembodied heads.

Cryobiologists, those scientists who study the preservation of organs and tissues at low temperatures, accuse cryonicists of being charlatans who have found a lucrative income by merchandizing a totally unrealistic method of achieving immortality. 'They're freezing meat not living cells,' as Dr David Pegg, a cryobiologist at Cambridge University, so succinctly puts it.

Essentially, the biologists maintain that the freezing process itself produces such profound and irreversible damage to the cells of the body that resuscitation and restoration to normal function will never be possible. The riposte from the cryonicists is that nothing will be impossible to the technologies of the future, not even the repair of the very cellular damage caused by today's imperfect freezing methods. The maxim of cryonics is that it is better to have even a small prospect of immortality – however enormous the statistical odds might be *against* cure and resuscitation – than the absolute certainty of total bodily destruction which is brought about by burial or cremation, religious afterlife notwithstanding.[13]

THE FREEZING PROCESS

The persuasiveness of the cryonicists' arguments owes much to the subtle interweaving of fear of death and hope for immortality, all couched in scientific jargon. Unfortunately much of the published scientific material is quoted out of context and consequently often has little or no relevance to the issues being debated. Death is divided by cryonicists into three stages:

1.   the cessation of respiration and circulation of the blood – i.e., the failure of the lungs and heart. In this stage resuscitation is possible given the close proximity of medical expertise and equipment;
2.   that at which resuscitation is no longer possible with *today's* technology, but in which not all the cells of the body are dead;
3.   that at which all the individual cells are irreversibly dead.

Stage two is sometimes called 'suspended death' or 'cryonic suspension' and is the time during which the 'body can be thought of as dead, but not very dead'. It is in this second stage that cryonicists believe the death process may be ultimately reversed by the scientists of the future.

The first cryonic suspension took place in 1966. A woman was frozen but was later thawed and buried when the relatives had second thoughts. The distinction of being the first freezee must therefore go to James Bedford, a 73-year-old psychology teacher who was frozen in 1967 by the

Cryonic Society of California, an organization run by Robert Nelson, a television repair man. Three years later a newspaper reporter discovered the abandoned and decaying bodies of eight of Nelson's clients. Nelson was sued and ordered to pay $900,000 to the families of the deceased. Bedford, however, was not one of the eight, having been previously transferred to the care of another cryonic organization. Financial problems bedevil cryonic organizations, and a number of them have had to return bodies to the relatives when funds to pay for the liquid nitrogen have run out.

The wish to be frozen after death is a highly personal decision, with both legal and financial implications to the freezee, and is not a procedure that can be instigated at your death-bed by yourself or your relatives. Freezing must be planned years before, preferably when you are young and healthy, in order to make adequate financial provision. Even with such fiscal forethought, it would appear that the chances of successful freezing are inordinately affected by the location in which you die. If you are a client of Alcor Life Extension Foundation, the optimal place to have your heart attack is within the greater Los Angeles area (always assuming that living in LA would not accelerate hardening of otherwise healthy arteries), since that is the base of Alcor's Emergency Response System (ERS), a complex network of trained technicians on twenty-four-hour alert. 'Less sophisticated' networks are located in northern California, Indiana, Florida and Britain.

Paid-up members wear a metal tag at all times in order that brief instructions can be gleaned by passers-by about emergency stabilization. This advice would then be supplemented by telephoning the freezer centre, which would dispatch the Los Angeles Rescue and Transport System (LARATS) to the scene, its fully equipped ambulance carrying a state-of-the-art Mobile Advanced Life Support System (MALSS), including heart-lung machine, pumps, oxygenator, heat-exchanger and independent power-supply. 'For members living within the LARATS region, rapid response in the event of an emergency is often just a phone call away.' And for the rest of us? With enough prior warning, technicians will be sent to 'stand by at the patient's bedside'.

When death is diagnosed, the corpse is promptly connected up to a Heart-Lungs Resuscitator (HLR) to maintain circulation and respiration. Drugs such as anticoagulants are adminstered, and external cooling begins by packing in water ice. The femoral vessels in the groin are used to facilitate further cooling. Outside the LARATS area the body is taken to the local mortuary, and the blood is replaced by Tissue Preservation Solution (TPS), packed in ice and airlifted, with minimum delay, to California.

Besides preservation of the tissues, there is the need to protect the tissues from injury brought about by the freezing process itself. Such

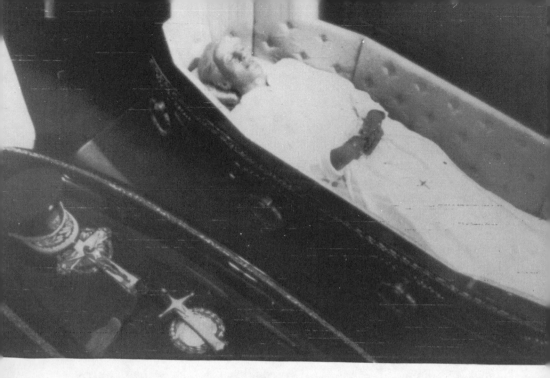

Juan and Eva Peron, reunited in death, lie side by side in the Presidential Chapel in Olivos, 10 December 1974. Her body is reputed to have been expertly embalmed.

cryoprotection is afforded by substances such as glycerol and sucrose. The perfusion pressures of the injected solutions are monitored by direct visualisation – through a small hole made in the skull observations are made to detect any swelling of the brain. Before the scalp is sewn over, a probe to measure the surface temperature of the brain is left *in situ*. The patient is then placed in two protective plastic bags and slowly cooled in a bath of silicone oil, over two to three days, down to a temperature of –77°C. The patient is then put in a pre-cooled sleeping-bag and gently placed in a special storage unit, likened to a large thermos flask, cooled by liquid nitrogen down to a temperature of −196°C. The body is then protected against 'fire, vandalism and seismic damage' to await the Brave New World.

Many of the practices that are now carried out on fee-paying clients of American cryonic organizations were first mooted by Robert Ettinger, a college physicist, in his book *The Prospect of Immortality*. It was Ettinger who identified the need for cryonic preservation, its likely methods and the inevitable difficulties – practical, social and ethical. Ettinger looked forward to a world free from death, in which everyone lived eternal and fulfilled lives. Not all of us would agree with Ettinger's utopia: 'I am convinced that in a few hundred years the words of Shakespeare, for example, will interest us no more than the grunting of swine in wallow … Not only will his work be far too weak in intellect, and written in too vague and puny a language, but the problems which concerned him will be, in the main, no more than historical curiosities. Neither greed, nor lust, nor ambition will in that society have any recognizable similarity to the qualities we know.'[14]

Ettinger cited a number of cases of revival after death and gave pride of place to a Soviet professor who had been involved in a road traffic accident in 1962. He sustained a fractured skull, brain injuries, nine broken ribs, a punctured chest, fractured pelvis, ruptured bladder, paralysis of his limbs and poor circulation and respiration. He 'died' four times and was resuscitated. In 1963 he was still alive and improving.

While such anecdotes testified to a dogged determination to cling to life, they did nothing to further the debate about the merits of cryonics. Today's zealots are just as prone to quoting portentous-sounding but irrelevant material in furtherance of their arguments concerning the scientific legitimacy of cryonics. The fact remains undisputed, even by cryonicists, that no human organ has yet been frozen down to the temperatures necessary for long-term preservation and subsequently recovered its normal function upon re-warming. Such recovery of function may well be achieved in the future, but will the technology exist to correct the additional injuries perpetrated on those organs by today's inadequate freezing methods? The cryonicists are in no doubt.

The question whether freezing and resuscitation will ever become a reality is not as interesting as debating some of the implications and consequences of successful cryonic preservation.

Recall the 500 million people embalmed in ancient Egypt, and remember that the sole purpose of mummification was ultimate rebirth. Suppose that, by some miracle, all the mummies had escaped the attentions of plunderers and were intact today. Further, suppose that twentieth-century medicine could revive those ancient Egyptians, cure their fatal diseases and grant them life anew. How many would we resuscitate? Would we seriously think of bringing back to life all half a billion? And if not, whom would we chose? Pharaohs, of course; a few priests; some token peasants. But what about the other 499,999,000? What about the vast majority of average citizens – such as you and me?

The official answers to the 'Who would be bothered?' question have a hollow ring. The first reason given as to why our descendants would want to revive us is their 'respect for human life and concern for the medical problems of the long dead lying mute and disease-ridden in a [future] elysium of perpetual health'. The second reason is even more limp: goodwill. The third and final reason is a cross between altruism and scientific machismo: 'Dramatically recovering patients who a century ago took this bet [to opt for cryonic resuscitation], and showing them the new world they won, might well be an interesting and appealing activity for a future proud of its achievements.'

Intimately bound up with 'Why bother?' is 'Where would we put them all?' Ettinger saw no problem. He calculated that the frozen population would increase by four billion every thirty years. He also guessed that it would be 300 years before civilization reaches 'immortality' level. That made a grand total of 40 billion to revive and relocate. 'There is ample room on our planet for forty billion people. Most of the land surface is thinly populated with vast areas of the Antarctic, the Arctic, the jungles of South America and Africa, and the deserts of Australia, Asia, Africa and the United States virtually empty.' And when these are full, Ettinger suggested honeycombing the Earth with vast underground complexes or setting up homes on some distant asteroid. With eternal wall-to-wall soaps or gameshows on a remote lump of rock orbiting beyond Mars, perhaps resuscitees would begin to look back to the 'good old days' when death came as a blessed release.

The problem of age was easily resolved. If a future technological society was able to bring you back to life, it would also be able to rejuvenate you to look as young as you wished with the physical features you had always wanted. The universe would consist entirely of Venuses aand Adonises. Good news indeed for the fat, the gauche and the disproportioned. But what an even greater boon it would be for those babies born with congenital malformations. All that parents would need to decide was whether such children were to live or be frozen. According to Ettinger, freezing 'a hideously deformed and defective child' would be an act of true mercy because of the laudable intention of future cure.

For parents of a child who has been frozen after death, it is postulated that the grieving process will be markedly attenuated, since, in some sense, the child is 'less than dead'. By similar reasoning it is argued that bereavement in general would become less traumatic emotionally, since death would have lost its sting.

Cryonicists argue that, ideally, people should be revived in the company of people they know – presumably in order to be able to talk about a common experienced past. But there can be no guarantee of synchronous resuscitation and more reason to predict that thawing of family members would not take place sequentially. Suppose a grandfather died at an advanced age of a cancer which had spread throughout the body, wreaking havoc on the function of every organ of the body. Suppose, further, that his grandson had died of a bullet wound in the heart in his mid twenties. It would be reasonable to suppose that the effects of a single bullet would be simpler to rectify than the multitudinous damage of disseminated cancer. Is the grandson to be revived before his grandfather? Is the natural sequence of the generations to be thereby reversed?

Similar familial complications can be envisaged if a widow remarried after her husband's death. What would happen when the time came for resuscitation of the woman and her two husbands? Ettinger stated rather dubiously that, 'The lover of her youth is likely to be the dearer', and his answer to this problem was simply to stagger resuscitation. The widow would be thawed first, followed by her second husband. They would then live together until such time as they could separate by mutual consent. Only then would the first husband be resuscitated. In the meantime the woman would have undergone a brain wash to expunge all memory of her second husband. And everyone would live happily everlastingly after.

One of the greatest and most fundamental of the ethical questions concerning successful cryonic resuscitation concerns the identity of the person brought back to life. Replacement surgery can substitute for original and diseased organs: a pump will circulate the blood, a bellows will take over respiration, and a sophisticated filter will serve as a kidney. But what about the brain, with its unique blend of personality, temperament and memory? How can a machine substitute for your ego, the very essence of what makes you unique, an individual and different from everyone else? It is a point reluctantly conceded by cryonicists: 'The only valid scientific uncertainty of cryonic suspension today is *possible* memory and identity loss due to imperfect brain preservation.' But the uncertainty is not reckoned to be very great, and dubious reassurance is given that long-term memory will be preserved and that the freezee's and thawee's identities will be the same. If this turns out not to be the case, the questions relating to family systems and generations will be of academic interest only, since the person resuscitated will be unaware of his own identity and be less than interested in the identity of his relatives.

The success of cryonic suspension and one's chances of ultimate revitalization could be profoundly affected by the mode of one's death. Ideally one should die of an accident that would preserve the body's basic structure and pose the fewest problems for the technicians of the future – a simple severance of the spinal cord, perhaps. Complicated, multi-organ pathology would probably ensure your suspension for many more centuries. The worst possible demise would be to be killed in a grossly mutilating accident such as an explosion or an air crash, or to be irrecoverable altogether, as in the jaws of a shark. Yet even in these circumstances cryonicists refuse to despair. They contend that the money that has been accumulating on your capital can be used to try to recover even the smallest bit of your anatomy – after all, a future technology that is able to grow a body from a cryonically preserved head will find it no more difficult to generate head and body from a fragment of skin or bone.

Similar considerations apply to suicide. If one merely wanted to end one's present existence, it would be logical to choose a method of suicide that maximized the chances of ultimately being brought back to life. If, on the other hand, the very idea of life, now or in the future, was

'The Inca Prince': the frozen
body of a child preserved for
centuries in a cave on Mount
Cerro del Plomo, Chile.

anathema, a violent end, perhaps by jumping in front of a train, might be
the method of choice.

And what of murderers and their victims? If one committed a 'clean'
homicide by shooting someone through the heart (with all the increased
expectation that the victim will be frozen and later brought back to life),
is one to be treated more leniently in court than if one did away with
one's victim by pulverizing him in a concrete-mixer? And if one *did* resort
to a violent murder which compromised the victim, cryonically
speaking, should the justice system similarly deny any chance of a
'second coming' by condemning such murderers to death in an equally
final fashion?

And will failure to freeze a relative lay one open to the charge of
intentional homicide?

If ever cryonics was shown to work, it would be seen as immortality for
the rich, since only the better-off would be able to divert the large sums
of money needed to provide for guaranteed storage at low temperatures
for perhaps hundreds, even thousands, of years. It would not be an
option for the poor and would be reminiscent of the posthumous
treatment afforded to paupers by the terms of the Anatomy Act. And
what if a well-off family suddenly suffered a change in their fortunes? Is
permanent death to be the penalty for default on payments?

If cryonics was shown definitely *not* to work, what about the huge
amounts of cash that would have been invested in a vain quest for life
everlasting? The stock answer to questions about money-back guarantees
is for a potential freezee to observe that, if by some mischance he
remained dead permanently, he would surely have no need for money.

This neatly eschews the uses to which others have put his money in the meantime.

Cryonics can evoke strong passions. Psycho-analytically, some see it merely as the substitution of repression by denial as a defence mechanism against those anxieties evoked by the prospect of death. Cryonicists often claim that at least they are doing something positive to combat death and not just passively accepting it as inevitable. Many see cryonics as an anti-religious movement with the expressed intention of permanently delaying 'salvation through death'. Others are drawn to the idea of cryonics but remain unconvinced and have a deep-rooted fear of becoming the victim of an elaborate confidence trick or the butt of posthumous ridicule.

Dora Kent died aged eighty-three, having told her son Saul to freeze her head. Saul respected his mother's wishes, and she was decapitated and the frozen head stored to be thawed in the future. At the present time, employees of an American cryonics organization are being taken to court and may be charged with murder, since the California coroner contends that the woman died as a direct consequence of the barbiturates injected into her in order to prepare the body for freezing. The coroner has demanded the head for an autopsy examination, but thawing and dissection would obviously seriously compromise Dora Kent's chances of living again. The case continues.

IV *The Fear of Being Forgotten*

1 WRITTEN ON STONE: THE KING AND THE COMMONER

On a thirteen-acre site, levelled to within a fraction of an inch, 2½ million blocks of limestone and granite, each with an average weight of 2½ tons, rise up in stepped tiers to a height of over 460 feet. A hundred thousand men worked in shifts for twenty years to complete this, still the most famous tomb in the world. Deep inside the structure there is a small chamber in which stands a highly polished granite sarcophagus. It is empty. Cheops no longer rests within his pyramid at Giza.

If Cheops' intention was to await eternal life safely cocooned in a mountain of stone, his empty grave attests to a misplaced optimism. If, on the other hand, he wished to have his name forever remembered as the king who conceived and built the only one of the seven Wonders of the Ancient World that still remains, he succeeded admirably. Because of his pyramid, Cheops is remembered 5,000 years after his death; the vast majority of humanity is long forgotten in fifty.

On 11 November 1920 King George V and Queen Mary, together with the Prince of Wales, the Duke of York and numerous other royals, both British and foreign, attended the funeral of a national hero. A hundred holders of the Victoria Cross lined the nave of Westminster Abbey. The grave, which contains French soil from the battlefield in which he fell, is covered by a slab of black Belgian marble. The inscription reads: 'They buried him among the kings because he had done good toward God and toward his House.' On a nearby pillar is pinned the Congressional Medal of Honour, the highest military honour of the United States of America. No name appears on the stone, despite the fact that he is buried in the most illustrious cemetery in Britain. Such is the memorial to the Unknown Warrior. The idea to commemorate an anonymous soldier came to the Revd David Railton in 1916, when he noticed a grave in a back garden in Armentières. It comprised a small wooden cross on which someone had pencilled, 'An Unknown British Soldier'.

What could possibly link Cheops and 'An Unknown British Soldier', a king and a commoner, individual and symbol, separated by class, country and five millennia? Both are dead and both are remembered still.[1]

The need to be remembered after death, and its corollary, the fear of being forgotten, is one of the most commonly expressed anxieties. Who among the living does not feel discomfort at the prospect of being unremembered a century from now? It will be as if we have never existed; and to most of us that realization is deeply disturbing. And yet, in human history, billions have departed this world, unlamented, unrecorded and unremembered. And countless billions more will follow. The lot of most of us is to be remembered by our grandchildren and be unknown to our great-grandchildren.

Through the centuries people have had recourse to many diverse strategies in order to increase the likelihood that they would be remembered by succeeding generations. Such have included burial near the pious and famous; burial close to living relatives; and construction of ostentatious or eccentric memorials.[2]

The narrow street of a Roman cemetery buried beneath St Peter's Basilica and facing the direction of the high altar. The cemetery contains the body of an early Christian, Aemelia Gorgonia, who had elected to be buried close to St Peter himself.

Many people have concluded that the length of time they will be remembered after their death is directly related to the calibre of those buried in the immediate vicinity. It was for this reason that many early Christians vied to be buried close to St Peter in Rome. In 1939, when work began in St Peter's Basilica to lower the floor behind the high altar, a Roman cemetery was discovered. Archaeologists believe that they have identified the bones of Peter himself. Aemelia Gorgonia, a Roman Christian, is known today simply because she contrived to be buried close to the saint, and her grave was discovered during the excavations.[3]

For reasons of sanitation, pre-Christian Romans were buried in mausoleums built on the sides of the roads leading away from the city. The nearer the city and the more imposing the memorial, the longer was the likelihood of being remembered. But with the advent of Christianity, more and more people expressed the wish to be interred within the sanctified confines of churches. This privilege was bestowed by a grateful Church upon Constantine the Great (c.274–337), the first Christian emperor: permission was granted for him to be buried in the vestibule of the Church of the Holy Apostles, which he himself had built. Thereby Constantine set a precedent which generations of lesser men and women would seek to copy. Princes, clerics and rich benefactors came to regard burial within the church as a right rather than a privilege, and some, not content with the vestibule or nave, would settle for nothing less than the chancel.

The Church tried hard to limit such burials, but abuse was widespread – to the extent that churches became packed with the bodies of the dead, with all the attendant risks to the health of the living. From time to time ecclesiastical edicts attempted to ease the overcrowding: one such declared that only bishops, abbots and 'laymen of the first distinction' were to be interred within churches. The interpretation of 'first distinction' was often left to be decided by the local clergy, and frequently became a value-judgement which could be influenced by a suitably large donation to church funds. The sums of money thus extorted were reckoned to be a small price to pay for the peace of mind which came with the knowledge that one's corpse would lie in a tomb, bedecked by a long eulogizing memorial, both sheltered from the ravages of the elements. Thus would the rich be longer remembered.

Those even richer could bequeath money in order to build a chapel within the church, dedicated only to their remembrance. In such chantry chapels and in return for a financial endowment, priests would be obliged to pray for the souls of the benefactors and their families. Philippe Ariès quotes from a will dated 1416: 'I desire and ordain that a chapel be founded ... on condition that two monks of the Abbey of

Saint-Florent ... shall say [masses] every day in perpetuity ... for the salvation and restoration of the souls of my very revered lord and husband and of my dearly beloved son.'[4]

BURIAL IN CHURCHYARDS

For those denied interment within a church, burial in the churchyard became the next best thing. Yet even here a hierarchy of sites soon became evident, and status could be judged by the position of a plot within the churchyard. The most favoured sites were to the east, as close as possible to the altar wall. In such a spot the deceased could be assured of the best view of the rising sun on the Day of Judgement. An added refinement was to be buried parallel to the long axis of the church, head to the west and feet to the east. People of lesser distinction were buried on the south side, while the north was considered the Devil's domain, suitable only for stillborns, bastards and strangers unfortunate enough to have died while passing through the parish.

Burial of stillborn babies in the north of the churchyard was regarded by parents as preferable to no burial at all. In the early Middle Ages, Augustinian teaching held that the fate of unbaptized children was everlasting limbo. Many parents tried to circumvent this cruel edict by taking the dead child to the shrine of a saint and spuriously claiming that their child had miraculously revived. A hurried baptism would then be arranged, often officiated at by a laymen, and when the baby subsequently 'died' a second time, the child would be eligible for a Christian burial. In the fifteenth century in Marseilles the parents of a stillborn infant who had been inadvertently buried in consecrated ground were ordered to exhume the body a year after burial. When a woman died in pregnancy, mother and child would sometimes share the same grave; at other times the foetus would be cut from the mother's womb and buried outside the graveyard.[5]

Suicides, if they were buried in consecrated ground at all, were often deposited in the north and, as an added sign of public opprobrium, laid north–south instead of east–west. Predictably there was bound to be someone who would find an advantage in being buried to the north of the church. Such was a Humberside man whose headstone read:

> And that I might longer undisturb'd abide
> I choos'd to be laid on this northern side.

During the Middle Ages pressure of space finally ousted the Devil from the north of the churchyard to make way for burial of locals.

In our own time an English churchyard is regarded as a haven of peace and tranquillity in a hectic world. The weathered and tilted tombstones amid wild flowers and stately yews engender a sense of restfulness and timelessness. The contrast with the sights and smells of an eighteenth-century churchyard could scarcely be more stark. In their insistence that burials take place outside the city walls, the pre-Christian Romans showed a better grasp of the potential health dangers of corpses than did succeeding generations. As we have seen, the innate logic of this form of disposal of the dead was lost in the Middle Ages as more and more people expected burial in 'God's Acre', as the land surrounding the church came to be known. In the eighteenth century, as towns and cities swelled in population, there developed a chronic shortage of space in churchyards.

The first solution to this problem was simply to pack the coffins more tightly together. Later coffins were stacked one upon the other often to the extent that the ground-level of some churchyards rose fully twenty feet above that of the church floor.

Another solution to the problem of lack of space was to grant only limited tenure to the occupier of a grave. Indeed, space became at such a premium that tenancy of a plot was sometimes measured in days, even hours, before the coffin was raised, removed and another put in its place. The vicar in Heptonstall, Yorkshire, even had recourse to reusing headstones, having them engraved on both sides.

With so many bodies crammed into small churchyards, it was little wonder that a hue and cry went up in protest from people living nearby. No one doubted that the putrefying bodies and vile stench posed a grave risk to health, and there was no shortage of anecdotes to attest to the illnesses – some with fatal outcomes – that were caused by such insanitary conditions. A crusade against the pernicious practice of burying the dead in cities and towns was mounted in 1839 by a surgeon, George Walker. In that year he wrote *Gatherings From the Graveyards: Particularly Those of London*, subtitled, *And a detail of dangerous and fatal results produced by the unwise and revolting custom of inhuming the dead in the midst of the living*. It is a glorious Victorian extravaganza replete with references to 'animal putrescency' and 'noxious effluvia'.

My pupil, Mr J H Sutton, entered the vaults of St — Church; a coffin, 'cruelly bloated', as one of the grave diggers expressed it, was chosen for the purpose of obtaining a portion of its gaseous contents. The body, placed upon the top of an immense number of others, had, by the date of the inscription on the plate, been buried upwards of eight years; the instant the small instrument employed had entered the coffin, a most horribly offensive gas issued forth in large quantities. Mr S, who unfortunately respired a portion of this vapour; he was instantly seized with a suffocating difficulty in breathing (as though he had respired an atmosphere impregnated with sulphur); he had giddiness, extreme trembling, and prostration of strength; in attempting to leave the vault he fell from debility; upon reaching the external air, he had nausea, subsequently vomiting, accompanied with frequent flatulent eructations, highly fetid, and having the same character as the gas inspired. He reached home with difficulty, and was confined to his bed during seven days.

It was clear that poor Mr Sutton had contracted a fever and was to consider himself lucky to have survived. Similar acute symptoms of fever overcame Benjamin Smith, a sexton in the church of Little Berkhamspstead, Hertfordshire, in 1835. Smith had lifted a stone which covered a vault in the aisle of the church in which, fifteen months before, a child's body had been deposited. The coffin was found floating in water and giving off such a vile smell that the sexton instantly became ill with nausea, diarrhoea, trembling and prostration.

Sutton and Smith were fortunate to have lived. Others were not so lucky. 'William Jackson, aged 29, a strong, robust man, was employed in digging a grave in the "Savoy"; he struck his spade into a coffin, from which an extremely disgusting odour arose; he reached his home, in Clement's Lane, with difficulty; complained to his wife that he had "had a turn; the steam which issued from the coffin had made him very ill". His wife stated that the cadaverous smell proceeding from his clothes affected her with trembling, and produced headache.' Jackson was ill for three days but, due to poverty, was obliged to return to work within the week to dig a grave in Drury Lane. Here, '... in this ground, long saturated with dead, it was impossible, without disturbing previous occupants, to select a grave; a recently buried coffin was struck into – the poor fellow was instantly rendered powerless, and dragged out by John Gray, to whom he was an assistant. Jackson died thirty six hours afterwards.' His death was attributed to cholera contracted from a previous victim.

The most celebrated case occurred in 1838 and became a *cause célèbre* in the attempt to forbid churchyard burials. *The Weekly Dispatch* of 9 September 1838 carried the story under the headline 'Two Men Suffocated in a Grave':

An inquest was held in Aldgate on the bodies of Thomas Oakes, the gravedigger belonging to Aldgate Church, and Edward Luddett, a fish dealer, at Billingsgate Market, who came to their deaths on that forenoon under the following circumstances: – Mr Edward Cheeper, the master of the workhouse, stated, that about eleven o'clock, while passing through Church Passage Aldgate, he heard the loud screams of a female in the churchyard, and he instantly hastened to the spot, and looking into the grave, about twenty feet deep, he saw the deceased gravedigger, Oakes, lying on his back apparently dead. A ladder was instantly procured, and the deceased young man, Luddett, who by this time, with several others, had been attracted to the spot, instantly volunteered to descend to the assistance of Oakes. *The instant he stooped* to raise the head of Oakes, he appeared as if struck by a Cannon ball, and fell back, and appeared instantly to expire.

Through a mixture of curiosity and philanthropy, Luddett had descended into a deep paupers' grave in which putrescent gases had replaced oxygen. Such graves were dug deep, in order to accommodate up to twenty bodies, and were left open until full. Little or no earth separated the coffins from each other.

Expanding on his thesis that insanitary churchyard burials caused illness and death to local inhabitants, Walker proceeded to cite the names of the worst offenders. The unluckiest, and unhealthiest, Londoners were those poor souls who lived in Clement's Lane, a narrow thoroughfare close to the Strand. Within a short distance were sited no fewer than four burial grounds (including St Clement Danes and the notorious Enon Chapel) and several slaughterhouses: '... the living here breathe on all sides an atmosphere impregnated with the odour of the dead.' The inhabitants were compelled to close their windows to keep out offensive smells, especially in summer. And walls were often seen reeking with fluids.

Walker directed especial venom at Enon Chapel on the west side of Clement's Lane. The building had opened for worship in 1823 and had given over its basement to the interment of the dead. It has been estimated that between ten and 12,000 bodies were placed in huge pits under the church. In hot weather, long black flies were commonly observed crawling out of the coffins in vast numbers. The children who attended Sunday School in the chapel nicknamed these insects 'body bugs'. Walker likened Enon to Golgotha and added, 'Can it be, thought I, that in the nineteenth century, in the very centre of the most magnificent city of the universe, such sad, very sad mementoes of ignorance, cupidity, and degraded morality, still exist?' It pained this patriot to answer his own question in the affirmative.

Let us return to consider the logistical problems of packing so many corpses into the cramped confines of the city churches and churchyards. One solution was to employ a variant of 'crop rotation', whereby fresh corpses were deposited on top of coffins long since rotted away by natural processes of decomposition. A burial cycle could be initiated, with ten- or twenty-year gaps between the first, second and subsequent burials in the same spot. Two factors mitigated against such a course of action: population and profit. The burgeoning death rate constantly outstripped the land available for burial, and the churches' need for income often meant that plots had to be vacated soon after burial for occupancy by the next temporary resident.

St Giles's burial ground is frequently cited as the source of the Great Plague of 1665. There in 1838, a reporter on the *Weekly Dispatch*

Angels Triumphant at Kensal Green Cemetery, London. This Corinthian temple, bedecked by Baroque angels, and erected in 1870 to the memory of Mary Gibson, is just one of a large variety of magnificent monuments which qualifies Kensal Green to be regarded as (arguably) London's most distinguished cemetery.

described how a newly interred coffin had been exposed and chopped away in order to make room for another. In another part of the burial ground a drunk was digging a grave. His progress had been stopped by his spade hitting the top of a child's coffin. Undaunted the digger hacked the coffin in two, thereby exposing a child wrapped in its shroud. In 1839 the *Morning Post* carried an equally disturbing report about burial practices. Mr Poole was a sharp-eyed railway employee who had contacted the police after observing two men and a boy exhuming bodies and hurling the bits 'in a most indecent manner, and indiscriminately, into a deep hole' in another part of the burial ground. Accompanied by Inspector M'Craw and Sergeants Parker and Shaw, Poole set out to investigate. They discovered a black-market in secondhand, hardly used funerary furniture: whole coffins, bits of coffin wood for sale as fuel, coffin plates and coffin nails. As soon as grieving relatives had departed, and on the orders of the undertaker, these men would exhume the bodies and dump them in a vast communal grave in a remote corner of the burial ground. In this pit Poole was able to discern arms, legs, heads and torsos in varying degrees of decomposition.

In June 1838 'J.M.', writing to *The Times*, addressed the same problem concerning the burial ground in Portugal Street. He had occasion to notice men carrying baskets full of bones from one area of the burial ground to another. With laudable constraint, since twelve of his 'nearest and dearest' relatives had been consigned to graves in Portugal Street, '... I felt that, perhaps, I might at the moment be viewing, in the baskets of skulls that passed before me, those of my own family thus brutally exhumed.'

LESSONS FROM ABROAD

Walker wrote in 1839 about London's insanitary graveyards, more than seventy years after the parliament of Paris had taken action against the dangers to health posed by rotting carrion. All the churchyards of the French capital were henceforth to be closed to burials for at least five years. Furthermore, eight cemeteries were to be established some distance away from the city, to serve the needs of eight metropolitan parishes. The new law was not universally popular, since richer families still regarded burial in church as a birthright. Fresh pleas were made to the nobility to abandon their pride and vanity for the greater good of their fellow citizens. The noblest Frenchman of them all, Louis XV, was persuaded to give the royal seal of approval when a large area of the forest of Satori, at Versailles, was designated a cemetery.

But mere closure of the city graveyards was not enough. In 1786 it was decided to move all the bodies out of the cemetery of the Innocents and transport them to catacombs hewn out of the quarries in the southern part of the city. It was an immense and awesome undertaking. On the night of 7 April a long procession of funeral carts, bearing the freshly cleaned bones of tens of thousands of people, plied its route by torchlight, to the chanting of priests. Identification of individual remains was clearly impossible, so it was decided to arrange the bones into rows of skulls, femurs, humeruses and so on. It is variously estimated that the catacombs contain the remains of between 3 and 6 million human beings.

In addition to the catacombs, four cemeteries were built in Paris in order to accommodate the dead: Père-Lachaise, Montmartre, Vaugirard and Montparnasse. The first, named after the confessor of Louis XIV, is probably the most celebrated burial ground in the world, though its beginnings were less than auspicious. If Napoleon had been buried there, as was his intention, instead of on St Helena, the businessmen who had invested money in the cemetery would have slept more easily. As it was, they were moved to mount a huge publicity campaign to try to persuade Parisians to be buried there. They even dug up the bones of famous Frenchmen and women who had been buried elsewhere and reinterred them at the cemetery – Molière, La Fontaine, Héloîse and Abèlard, and

A mechanical ramp by means of which coffins were transferred from the chapel above to the catacombs below – at Kensal Green Cemetery, London.

Beaumarchais. Ironically it was the burial of persons who had never lived that finally gained Père-Lachaise its popularity. The novelist Honoré de Balzac took to burying many of his fictional characters in Père-Lachaise. Every Sunday Parisians would come in droves and ask to see the tombs which Balzac had described in such great detail. Henceforth business boomed. (Within its walls now rest the illustrious dead of France, including Balzac, Hugo, Edith Piaf, Abélard and Héloïse, Colette, Beaumarchais and Proust. International representatives include Chopin, Oscar Wilde, Modigliani, Sarah Bernhardt and Jim Morrison of the Doors pop group.)

LAGGARDLY LONDON

When Paris led the way and New York followed close behind, London dragged its feet. In 1843, *The Builder* expressed its dismay: 'This London, the centre of civilization, this condensation of wisdom and intelligence, this huge wedge and conglomerate of pride, buries – no it does not bury – but stores and piles up 50,000 of its dead to putrefy, to rot, to give out exhalations, to darken the air with vapours, faugh!' Even as late as 1850 an anonymous poem entitled 'City Graves' appeared in *Household Words*:

> The toiler, at his work, can see
> The tombs of his mouldering kin;
> And the living without grow, day by day,
> More like the dead within.
>
> I saw from out the earth peep forth
> The white and glistening bones,
> With jagged ends of coffin planks,
> That e'en the worm disowns;
> And once a smooth round skull rolled on,
> Like a football on the stones.

The risks to health were not confined to the inhalation of pestilent vapours: sometimes the very water people drank was supplied by springs that tracked through graveyards. St George's in the East had a pump which provided drinking-water to the locality until, during a cholera scare, the Revd Harry Jones hung up a placard announcing 'Dead Men's Broth!' Charles Dickens, when he heard the pump being used to draw water, would conjure up images of the dead protesting, 'Let us lie here in peace; don't suck us up and drink us!'

In the first quarter of the nineteenth century, despite an ever-increasing population, the citizens of London continued to be buried either in churchyards or in privately owned burial grounds within the city limits. The calls for the establishment of cemeteries sited away from centres of population grew ever louder. The Rosary, the first English cemetery, was finally opened in 1819 – in Norwich. The Liverpool Necropolis followed six years later. It was not until 1830 that a barrister, George Carden, formed the London Cemetery Company to provide public interment for Londoners.[6]

In 1832 the company opened London's first public cemetery at Kensal Green. The first interment was Margaret Gregory on 31 January 1833. Here, at long last, the dead could be hygienically committed to the ground, in fifty-four acres of landscaped splendour, far away from the living.

Burial at Kensal Green was expensive, the cheapest grave costing 30 shillings, compared with the 12 shillings charged at Enon Chapel. But Enon could not match the classical grandeur of Kensal Green, with its hydraulic lift to lower the coffins from the Anglican chapel into the depths of the catacombs below. In the thirty-nine acres of consecrated ground awarded to members of the established Church and in the fifteen acres given over to 'Turks', Jews, Infidels, Heretics and "unbaptised folk"', the dead could rest, undisturbed in perpetuity, under any form of memorial they wished – Gothic spires and pinnacles, Doric- and Ionic-columned mausoleums or Egyptian obelisks.

From the very beginning Kensal Green was *the* place in which to be buried. This early success can be put down to the interment of one man – Augustus Frederick, Duke of Sussex (1773–1843). It was he, more than any other, who made the cemetery an acceptable place for the burial of the rich and famous. Augustus Frederick, the sixth son of King George III, was so appalled at the chaos that attended the interment of King William IV at Windsor in 1837 that he forthwith resolved to be buried at Kensal Green. A host of lesser royals followed, including George III's daughter Princess Sophia (1777–1848). Visitors to the cemetery can still peep through the windows of the Duke of Cambridge's mausoleum and gaze at his coffin, placed upon a shelf on the right-hand side. To the left, one on top of the other, rest the coffins of his wife and mistress. So fashionable did Kensal Green become that it can still boast the greatest number of royals buried outside Windsor and Westminster Abbey.

The variety of people buried in Kensal Green matches the variety of the architecture. Here were laid to rest Isambard Kingdom Brunel, the engineer; novelists Wilkie Collins, Thackeray and Trollope; and Blondin, who walked the tightrope across Niagara Falls. James Barry (1788–1865) was an army surgeon who became inspector general of hospitals; it was only at his death that the absence of a penis decreed that 'he' was, in fact, a woman who had successfully concealed her true gender throughout a long and active career in the forces!

Highgate on the Hill

If Kensal Green is London's most distinguished cemetery, Highgate is its most romantic. Overlooking the capital, the cemetery affords an unparalleled setting in which to while away eternity. Slowly the Friends of Highgate Cemetery are pushing back the overgrowth and repairing the crumbling masonry to reveal again the grandeur of this Victorian Valhalla.

Highgate Cemetery, founded in 1839 by the London Cemetery Company, was always meant to be enjoyed by the living, and very soon it became a favourite place for Victorians to go promenading on a Sunday afternoon. And as for the dead, so popular did the cemetery become – especially when the ban on churchyard burials finally came into force in 1852 – that more land was soon needed on the other side of Swain's Lane to accommodate all those wishing to be buried there. The west and east cemeteries were linked by a tunnel under the road (which is still in existence) through which the coffin was carried after it had been lowered on a hydraulic lift in the floor of the Anglican chapel. Although the monuments in Highgate are not of the variety or quality of those at Kensal Green, the Egyptian catacombs, built in a circle around an ancient cedar tree, stand today in magnificent, romantic decay.

Towering above the Egyptian catacombs is the vast mausoleum of Julius Beer, Victorian owner of *The Observer* newspaper. Like Kensal Green, Highgate catered predominantly for the post-mortem needs of Anglicans, and the area given over to the Dissenters was small and relatively unsalubrious. How then did Beer, a Jew, come to occupy the most favoured site in the whole of the cemetery? Wealth. Beer was able to buy the plot (for £800) and build his huge edifice (which was modelled imprecisely on the original mausoleum at Halicarnassus) many years before his actual death, for the enormous sum of £5,000. However, he was obliged to make a significant concession to Anglican sensitivities: his mausoleum had to be topped with a cross, the quintessentially Christian symbol.

The west cemetery has a profusion of petrified animals: George Wombwell made his money from importing wild animals (including the first boa constrictors ever to be seen in Britain, and a giraffe which cost him a fortune and which promptly broke its neck) and rests beneath a benign, sleeping lion. John Atcheler, horse-slaughterer to Queen Victoria, has a grave marked by a statue of a horse described by one early critic as a 'monstrosity', which today 'stands' legless and deaf, its four legs and its ears having been hacked off by vandals. Tom Sayers, bare-fisted pugilist, died a popular hero, with 100,000 mourners attending his funeral – his dog, given the place of honour at the head of Sayers' funeral cortège and wearing a black ruff around its neck, is commemorated in

Rows of coffins in decaying splendour in the catacombs of Kensal Green Cemetery, London. 'For there is good news yet to hear and fine things to be seen/ Before we go to Paradise by way of Kensal Green.' (G.K. Chesterton)

stone guarding his master's grave. Conspicious by the absence of dogs is the grave of George Cruft (1852–1938), founder of the world-famous dog show.

The most visited grave at Highgate is also the most grotesque. An outsize bust of Karl Marx looks severely down, extolling workers of all lands to unite and change the world. Something of Marx's private world is revealed by the fact that he, like the Duke of Cambridge at Kensal Green, shares his grave with both wife and mistress. The sombreness of Marx is offset somewhat by an in-joke of the Friends of Highgate Cemetery: on the other side of the path lies Herbert Spencer, the philosopher who coined the phrase 'survival of the fittest': it is fitting, therefore, that this corner of the cemetery is known as 'Marx and Spencer's'.

For feminists who may be indignant that men share their graves with their wives *and* mistresses, perhaps the imbalance is somewhat redressed by the female novelist George Eliot who was buried in Highgate next to her husband, John Cross, and opposite her lover, George Lewis. Another famous female novelist is also buried with her lover: Radclyffe Hall, author of *The Well of Loneliness*, shares her catacomb with Mabel

Veronica Batten. The love of these two women for one another had shocked Edwardian society. Batten died suddenly in 1916, Hall not until 1943, and it was the intention of her second lover, Una Troubridge, to join the other two women when she herself died. Unfortunately Troubridge died in Rome in 1963 and was buried in Italy.

Other notables resting in the rich Highgate clay include Michael Faraday, chemist and physicist; William Foyle, who founded what has become the world's largest bookshop; Mrs Henry Wood, the melodrama version of whose novel *East Lynne* contains the immortal line, 'Dead! – and never called me mother'; and Robert Liston, the surgeon-resurrectionist who amputated his patients' limbs and his assistants' digits with equal dexterity.

Highgate has witnessed three famous exhumations. The reader is reminded of Dante Rossetti's retrieval of poems which he had been rash enough to bury next to his wife's cheek; was guilt the reason he elected to be buried at All Saints, Birchington, in Kent? Karl Marx and his family were exhumed from their original burial plot to be reinterred at their present site to enable busloads of Chinese tourists to find him more easily. The third exhumation took place in 1907, amid a blaze of publicity whipped up by the yellow press.

Thomas Charles Druce, who owned a shop in Baker Street, had supposedly died in 1864 and was buried at Highgate. Fifteen years later, in 1879, when the fifth Duke of Portland died, Druce's family made the remarkable claim that Druce and the duke were one and the same man. They contended that the duke had led a double life – part aristocrat, part shopkeeper – and that he had been able to maintain this elaborate charade by using a tunnel which connected the shop in Baker Street to his residence in Cavendish Square. To add credence to their account, Druce's relatives pointed out that no one had ever seen Druce and the duke in the same place at the same time! When, finally, the duke tired of his double life, he conspired to 'kill off' his *alter ego* and to continue the rest of his life as a hermit at Welbeck Abbey, his country seat.

'The Portland millions' were at the bottom of this fantasy. In order to get their hands on the money, Druce's relatives claimed the duke as their father and themselves as his heirs. They demanded as exhumation to prove to the world that Druce's coffin was filled with lead weights. Incredibly the authorities agreed to their request, fully nineteen years after Druce's death. On a December morning the coffin was brought to the surface, its lid removed and the inner lead casing opened. Inside was the shrouded body of an old and bearded man who was identified from photographs as Thomas Charles Druce. The public immediately lost interest in the story, and consequently no one has ever thought to exhume the duke to see whether or not he was actually in residence.

Bunhill Fields

It is hard for those of us living in the 1990s to imagine the grisly horror of the overcrowded and insanitary burial grounds of Dickens' London, but there still remains one which affords us such a glimpse into the past: it is Bunhill Fields, the Dissenters' *Campo Santo*, the sole remaining burial ground within the present City of London. To stroll through Bunhill is to take a step back in time.

In 1549 the charnel chapel in St Paul's churchyard was pulled down, and one thousand cartloads of bones were transported and deposited on 'moorish ground' in Finsbury Field. 'Bunhill' is probably a corruption of 'Bone-hill'. Burials on the site did not commence until the mid-seventeenth century, but so popular did Bunhill become that by its closure in 1853 120,000 interments had taken place.

Bunhill Fields is like no other burial ground in London. Sedate chest tombs, tighly packed headstones and the virtual absence of angels, crosses, draped urns and broken columns set Bunhill apart. Its tombstones read like a *Who's Who* of English Nonconformism: George Fox, founder of The Society of Friends; William Blake, artist and poet; Daniel Defoe, author of *Robinson Crusoe*; John Bunyan, preacher and author of *Pilgrim's Progress*; Susannah Wesley, mother of John and Charles; Praise-God Barebones, who gave his name to the Barebones Parliament of 1653; and sundry descendants of Oliver Cromwell.

One famous inscription tells of the vicissitudes of Mary Page, who died in 1728 of a failing heart which necessitated fluid being drained from her abdomen:

Bunhill Fields burial-ground in 1866.

A section through Thomas Willson's pyramid cemetery, designed to be higher than St Paul's Cathedral, with alcoves to provide a last resting-place for 5,167,104 Londoners.

In 67 months she was tap'd 66 times,
Had taken away 240 gallons of water,
Without ever repining at her case,
Or ever fearing the operation.

My own favourite is an inscription which enshrines the Nonconformist sentiments concerning friendship, even unto the grave:

Mrs Elizabeth Raynor
Early allied in blood
To the illustrious House of Percy
Deemed it a still greater honour
To be the friend
And fellow worshipper of
Mr and Mrs Lindsey
And by her own desire
Was deposited in the same grave.

Friendship, pure, simple and eternal, with none of the undertones of Marx or the Duke of Cambridge. (A similar instance occurred in Godalming, Surrey, in 1875. William Bishop directed that his grave be made sufficiently large to receive two coffins, the second intended for his servant, in gratitude of 'her long, and, I hope and believe, faithful services to me').

What Might Have Been

Before leaving the subject of London's cemeteries, it is instructive to look at one idea that never got beyond the drawing-board. Thomas Willson took his inspiration from the Egyptian pyramids and set about designing a brick and granite-faced pyramid to accommodate 5 million bodies in niches arranged on ninety-four tiered levels. This vast construction was to be built on Primrose Hill, its base the size of Russell Square, its height 'considerably above that of St Paul's' and its volume larger than the Great Pyramid itself. Consisting of row upon row of small alcoves, in cross-section the pyramid would resemble a beehive. An observatory was planned for the top. The whole structure was to cost £2,500,000. Willson himself waxed lyrical: 'To toil up its singular passages to the summit will beguile the hours of the curious and impress feelings of solemn awe and admiration upon every beholder.' Modestly he added that his pyramid would be 'a *coup d'œil* of sepulchral magnificence unequalled in the world'. Others obviously took a different view, since Willson's dream never became reality.

BROOKWOOD CEMETERY AND THE NECROPOLIS RAILWAY

Despite the provision of large cemeteries for the burial of London's dead,

The London terminus of the Brookwood Necropolis Railway in the 1890s.

the burgeoning population of the capital meant that the demand for land continued to outstrip the supply. Burial companies were obliged to look further afield, even though they knew that the greater the distance a cemetery was from London the less the likelihood that it would be affordable by families of modest means. Another consequence of distance was that the deceased would be less likely to be visited regularly, and thereby more likely to be forgotten sooner by relatives. It became apparent to cemetery entrepreneurs that, if the poorer classes were to be tempted into being buried long distances from the centre of the city, transportation costs must be kept to a minimum.

The plan was deceptively simple: to find a large enough piece of land and turn it into London's sole necropolis, big enough to accommodate London's dead virtually indefinitely. The idea was regularly mooted but took on an added urgency following the cholera epidemic of 1848–9 which killed close on 15,000 Londoners. Two men, Sir Richard Broun and Mr Richard Sprye, resurrected the idea of a single necropolis, far enough out of London to pose no health danger to its citizens. Broun suggested a site at Woking in Surrey to which the dead and the bereaved would be transported by train. The idea did not win universal approval,

A coffin being loaded aboard the Brookwood Necropolis Railway at Westminster Bridge Road Station, c. 1905. The funeral party have just emerged from a private waiting-room.

No return. A third-class coffin ticket on the Brookwood Necropolis Railway.

and the Bishop of London found the proposal to have the dead from widely different social backgrounds all travelling *in the same train* 'offensive'. Finally the idea gained acceptance, and in 1854 Brookwood Cemetery, near Woking, was consecrated. The Necropolis Railway ran from Waterloo in London to the North Station at Brookwood – for Roman Catholics, Jews, Parsees and the Dissenting sects – and thence to the South Station, where the Anglican dead were unloaded. The railway continued to operate until the destruction of the London terminal in the Second World War. Today both the cemetery stations are long gone, only the platforms remaining as a mute reminder of a once flourishing trade.[7]

Considerations of social class pervaded everything about the Necropolis Railway. The train was divided into two religions (Anglican and others) and three classes – first, second and third. Such distinctions applied to both the living and the dead. Very wealthy funeral parties sometimes had the use of a specially coupled saloon carriage in order that they might grieve away from the intrusive gaze of *hoi polloi*. The different classes of coffins were distinguished by the quantity and ornamentation on the compartment doors and by the degree of deference shown by the necropolis staff when loading and unloading. In addition, rich relatives were allowed to watch the coffin being transferred from hearse to train. In the early days, when the train reached Brookwood, the engine was uncoupled and the compartments were then pulled the remaining distance by a team of black horses bedecked with black ostrich feathers.

A brochure produced by the Necropolis Company invited the bereaved, after the funeral service was over, to pause and admire the scenery, to be invigorated by the fresh country air, the shrubs and trees, and to contemplate 'the noble site of which their departed relative or friend had become a tenant'.

Normally, to travel by train when dead was expensive – indeed, in 1870 Miss Kitty Jenkyn Packe insisted that if she died away from home her coffin was to be disguised by enclosing it in a plain deal box and transporting it by train to Poole so as to cost 'no more than any other package of the same weight', since the charge for coffins was between sixpence and a shilling per mile.[8] With such considerations in mind and in order to attract customers, the London Necropolis Railway needed to offer cheap transportation. They decided on a charge of £1 for first-class corpses, 5 shillings for 'artisans' and 2s.6d. for paupers. Coffin tickets were issued only as singles. The corresponding charges for the mourners were 6 shillings, 3s.6d. and 2 shillings. These concessionary prices gave such good value for money that many London golfers, eager to avail themselves of the amenities of the Surrey courses, used to disguise themselves as bereaved relatives in order to save money on the regular commuter fare.

2   CREMATION

Realistically there are only three things you can do with a dead body: leave it, bury it or burn it. Burial is the disposal of choice for those who hanker after extended recall, since a fixed location serves as a focus at which relatives can gather and remember. Religious objections apart, the early opposition to cremation as a mode of disposal of the dead centred around the belief that to be reduced to ashes made it more unlikely that a person would be remembered than if the corpse disintegrated in a coffin. The increasing acceptance of cremation, especially in Britain, but latterly in the United States, owes much to revision of such illogical thinking.

Cremation has a long history, although experts are unclear whether human ashes discovered in prehistoric graves represent the mode of death or the method of disposal of the dead. In ancient Greece, cremation replaced burial as early as 1000 BC. Reduction to ashes greatly eased the logistical problems of transporting back to Greece soldiers who had died on far-flung battlefields. To the Greeks, fire symbolized purification and the release of the spirit from the confines of the body. Cremation was denied to suicides and those infants who had died before cutting their first set of teeth. Intriguingly, victims of lightning were always buried – perhaps the Greeks assumed that it was pointless for humans to cremate after the gods had incinerated.

To the ancient Romans, especially the rich upper classes, cremation was a common mode of disposal of the dead from pre-Christian times and into the second century AD. The explanation for the decline of cremation during the second century is largely unexplained, though some believe that inhumation became the preferred method of disposal because it was regarded as 'gentler' and more respectful. Certainly as early as AD 31 the Empress Poppaea, kicked to death whilst pregnant by her husband Nero, was, according to Tacitus, inhumed and not cremated. A hybrid of burial and cremation, *os resectum*, continued to be practised, whereby the finger of the dead person was cut off and buried while the rest of the body was burned. The ashes were then preserved in cinerary urns and placed in the niches of columbariums. [9]

The Jews buried their dead, reserving cremation for criminals. Saul and his sons are the only Old Testament examples of cremation, and this was resorted to only in order to prevent further mutilation of their bodies by the Philistines. The bones were subsequently buried. (1 Samuel 31: 12–13.)

The Christians followed the Jews in their abhorrence of cremation, regarding it as a pagan custom. A central tenet of Christianity was the resurrection of the body, and this belief could not be reconciled with cremation – though it must be emphasized that, for Christians, burial was a *symbolic* affirmation of resurrection and did not accord with the Egyptian belief that life in the other world depended on the *physical* preservation of the corpse. Ignorant of the symbolism, enemies of Christianity contrived to prevent the burial of Christian corpses and to burn them, so as to prevent resurrection. Christians themselves were not above using cremation as a bar to everlasting life: many years after his death in 1384, John Wycliffe, then regarded as a heretic, was exhumed and cremated and his ashes were thrown into the River Swift.

The rise of Christianity in Europe saw the further decline of cremation. A big disincentive was delivered by Charlemagne, in 789, when he decreed punishment by death for anyone found practising cremation. The renaissance of interest in cremation is usually given as being in the second half of the nineteenth century, although a famous case occurred in Italy in 1822. In that year Percy Shelley, the poet, drowned in the Mediterranean near Leghorn. When his body was washed ashore, the Tuscan quarantine laws, drafted to protect against imported plague, laid down that the body was to be burned on the beach. Shelley's corpse was temporarily buried beneath sand until the cremation could be carried out.

An account has been left to us in Edward Trelawny's *Recollections of the Last Days of Shelley and Byron*:

> I felt we were no better than a herd of wolves or a pack of wild dogs, in tearing out his battered and naked body from the pure yellow sand that lay so lightly over it, to drag him back to the light of day … Even Byron was silent and thoughtful. We were startled and drawn together by a dull hollow sound that followed the blow of a mattock; the iron had struck a skull, and the body was soon uncovered. Lime had been strewn on it; this, or decomposition, had the effect of staining it a dark and ghastly indigo colour. Byron asked me to preserve the skull for him; but remembering that he had formerly used one as a drinking cup, I was determined Shelley's should not be so profaned … After the fire was well kindled … oil and salt made the yellow flames glisten and quiver … The corpse fell open and the heart was laid bare. The frontal bone of the skull, where it had been struck with the mattock, fell off; and as the back of the head rested on the red-hot bottom bars of the furnace, the brains literally seethed, bubbled and boiled as in a cauldron, for a very long time. [10]

It is said that Byron's delicate constitution was so upset by the stench that he left early, begging friends, 'Let my carcase rot where it falls.' Shelley's ashes were buried in the Protestant cemetery in Rome, but the poet's heart, which had failed to burn, was plucked from the flames by Trelawny and subsequently returned to Britain for burial.

The most important impetus given to the renewed interest in cremation was the overcrowded burial grounds and insanitary conditions prevailing in nineteenth-century Europe. Better utilization of land to meet the needs of the living was a potent argument in favour of cremation. The major practical obstacle to cremation was the immense difficulty of achieving total incineration of a body in a reasonable time by methods deemed aesthetically acceptable. In the 1860s and seventies much energy was devoted to the design of furnaces by Professors Polli, Gorini and Brunetti in Italy and Siemans in Germany. In Britain an early advocate of cremation was Sir Henry Thompson, surgeon to Queen Victoria. He and like-minded people formed themselves into the Cremation Society of England in 1874, though loose talk of using cremated ashes as fertilizer or harnessing cremation gases for street lighting did little to further their cause. Amid great opposition from the clergy nationally, and from Surrey residents locally, Thompson and his associates built the first crematorium at Woking in 1878, just a few miles from Brookwood Cemetery. The furnace, designed by Professor Gorini, remained unlit for many years because the home secretary's permission was necessary before cremations could take place – and such permission was not forthcoming.

Despite hostility in high places, public opinion about cremation was shifting, albeit slowly. In 1882 a Captain Hanham requested permission to cremate his wife and mother. It was refused. Undeterred, he built a small crematorium on his estate and proceeded with the cremations. No action was taken against him. When he died in 1883, he was also cremated in his private crematorium.

The turning-point came in 1883, when a mad Welsh clergyman, Dr William Price of Llantrisant, who had fathered a child at the age of eighty-three, cremated this 5-month-old baby whom he had christened Jesus Christ Price. He immersed the body in a barrel of paraffin and set the pyre alight. The police, called by local villagers returning from chapel, quickly extinguished the flames, and the body was taken away for autopsy. Price was arrested and brought to trial at Cardiff. His acquittal was widely interpreted as affirmation that cremation was henceforth to be regarded as a legal and legitimate method of disposal of a corpse.

The founders of Woking crematorium were well pleased with the judge's decision, since prior to this time they had had to content themselves with experimental cremation of animals – in 1879 a horse was reduced to ashes in less than two hours, with minimal smoke and smell. The first human cremation at Woking was carried out in March 1885, that of Mrs Jeannette Caroline Pickersgill of Regent's Park, who had died, aged seventy-one, of 'broncho-pneumonia and asthema'. Many

A cut-away diagram to illustrate the working of an early crematorium.

famous people followed Mrs Pickersgill to Woking, including Sir Isaac Pitman, inventor of shorthand; Dr Barnardo, founder of homes for underprivileged children; and the Marquis of Queensbury, who formulated the rules of boxing. In 1934 an open-air cremation took place at Woking, when the body of Chamshere Jung, a Nepalese princess, was burned in accordance with Hindu religious rites.

The first cremation in modern times of a member of the British royal family was that of Princess Louise, a daughter of Queen Victoria, who died in 1943.

CREMATION IN BRITAIN TODAY

In Britain cremation has overtaken burial as the most popular form of disposal of the dead. Use is made of oil or gas-fired furnaces to reduce a body in about 1½ hours. The body water evaporates and the tissues are incinerated to ash and bone – roughly six pounds for an average-sized adult. The bone fragments are later pulverized by machine into a fine powder. At the beginning of the century a body was usually taken out of its coffin before being incinerated – today the body is cremated in the coffin, the ashes from the coffin, because of their lightness, passing up through the flue. Metal parts of the coffin can be raked out after incineration is complete, though more usually the 'brass' handles of a coffin destined for cremation are made of plastic and are therefore totally combustible. The ashes are collected in a container and can be stored in an urn in a columbarium or scattered, depending on the wishes of the deceased. Care is taken to ensure that ashes from different individuals are kept separate, and great vigilance is exercised with the bodies of children, where the quantity of ashes may be small.

CREMATION IN THE UNITED STATES

The USA has never had the land-shortage problems that have bedevilled the sanitary disposal of the dead in Europe. Ironically the first cremation in America predated that in Britain by seven years: in 1876 Dr Julius Lemoyne, a doctor in Washington, Pa., allowed people to use the crematorium he had constructed for his own disposal.

Many theories have been put forward to explain the American aversion to cremation. They include the erroneous notion that embalming procedures preserve the body indefinitely; that American funeral directors have a financial stake in elaborate burials and memorials; and that, in some way, cremation necessarily involves shortened recall by the bereaved.[11]

The increasing acceptance of cremation in the USA may be connected to the greater attention now being given to the 'memorialization' of ashes. It is no coincidence that the enthusiasm of American funeral directors for cremation is directly proportional to the amount of money set aside for memorialization. Commercial considerations, thinly disguised by talk of health hazards and posthumous indignity, forbid the scattering of ashes in many American states. The Interment Association of America has stated: 'The only proper disposition of cremated remains is inurnment in a niche, a vault, or an urn garden or in a recognized place for the interment of human dead.' There is little financial gain to be got from scattering ashes to the four winds or into the ocean. Funeral directors, who are apt to think in terms of dollars, also see no profit in encouraging such simple practices as scattering ashes into the earth, to be absorbed by the roots of a sapling. And if a tree, partly composed of the atoms of a loved one, is not a commercial proposition, how much less so is the idea of incorporating the atoms inside oneself?

There is a historical precedent for such an idea: Artemisia, the wife of Mausolus, sprinkled his ashes in wine and drank the mixture, thereby inextricably uniting her with her husband. By comparison, the Tibetan custom of casting the ashes into medallions appears almost orthodox.

SUTTEE: 'BURN ME, BURN MY WIFE'

In most cultures a man's status at death can be measured by the ostentatiousness of his funeral and the magnificence of his tomb. In India, before the early nineteenth century, the status of Hindu men might be gauged by the number of wives who accompanied them to the funeral pyre. In British India, in 1829, *suttee*, the name given to the barbarous practice of the immolation of wives, was decreed to be only 'culpable homicide', punishable by fine or imprisonment. Nothing so eloquently testified to the lowly social status of women than an expectation that they should not outlive their husbands. After death, to be forgotten in one's own right may be a painful prospect, but to be remembered only as the wife of one's husband is infinitely more ignominious.

There is considerable speculation about the origin of *suttee*. Some authorities claim that it emanated from a deliberate tampering with Hindu scriptures. The original version ran: '*Arochantu janayo yonim agre*' – 'Let the mothers advance to the altar first.' By a minor alteration the line becomes: '*Arochantu janayo yonim agneh*' – 'Let the mothers go into the womb of fire.' One anthropologist, Max Müller, dubbed this celebrated change of text 'perhaps the most flagrant instance of what can be done by an unscrupulous priesthood'.

Advocates of *suttee* were quick to point out that four of Krishna's wives and four of Vasudeva's wives joined their lords on the pyre. Despite such precedents, the practice was never universal, being concentrated mainly in the Ganges Valley, the Punjab and southern India. Numbers also varied, from one or two wives, through the sixty-four women who burned with Raja Ajit Singh in Jodhpur in 1780, to reports from Portuguese missionaries of the sacrifice of 11,000 women on the death of a south Indian raja. In 1818 the Maharaja of Jaipur, to dispel any notion of sexual bias, was accompanied by eighteen women and an equal number of men, including a barber sent to shave his lord in the next world. Variations on the custom included 'mother-*suttee*', whereby a mother mounted her son's pyre, and 'sister-*suttee*'.

The actual form of the ceremony was also variable: some widows would sit with their husband's head on their lap and then light the fire themselves; others were tied to their husbands; some would jump from a scaffold into the pyre after it had been lit (the scaffold could be tilted at the first sign of reluctance). Because it was bad luck to hear any sounds of pain, the assembled crowd would obligingly chant *fortissimo*.

Motivation for immolation was yet another variable. Some wives were so keen on dispatching themselves when they received news of their absent husband's death that they were incinerated long before his eventual safe return.

Any reluctance to commit *suttee* was seen as a slur on the family's honour, and such a disgrace could wound the pride of a bereaved son. In 1796, near Calcutta, a wife was duly fastened to the pile but in the darkness disentangled herself from her dead husband, crept from under the pile and hid in the bushes. As soon as her escape was detected, the relatives searched for and soon found her. Her son insisted that she mount the pyre, drown herself or hang herself in order to preserve the family name. She pleaded with him, but to no avail – he and the other relatives tied her hands and feet and threw her into the flames, where she quickly perished. Other reluctant wives were often plied with heavy doses of narcotics to lessen resistance and to induce a spurious acceptance.

Often there were secular rather than religious reasons for the continuance of *suttee*. By her death a mother ceased to be a financial burden on her son. But such base motives had to be rationalized and aggrandized by a culture that at that time regarded widowhood as sinful and which endeavoured to persuade surviving spouses that life without husbands was so desolate and miserable that burning to death was infinitely preferable.[12]

3   THE BUSINESS OF BEING REMEMBERED

It is the lot of most of us to be buried or burned and to have our remains interred in a municipal cemetery. In the fashion of the times, our lives will be condensed into a name, a date of birth, a date of death, and a number for the cemetery staff to identify the site in their registers. Chances are very high that our memorial will be similar to those on either side: made of the same material, of the same design and shape, with the same lettering. Only the names will be different. The striking conformity and monotony of the stones found in a modern cemetery are in stark contrast to the sheer variety of memorials to be seen and appreciated in any Victorian burial place. An even more poignant contrast is between the ordered precision of today's crematorium plaques and the comforting disorder of a British churchyard.

In parish churches the earliest tombs date back to the twelfth century and take the form of simple stone slabs, known as ledgers, laid over the corpses of church dignitaries. Inscriptions were in Latin. Table tombs were created when ledgers were raised up on legs. A chest tomb is a table tomb with its sides and ends filled in to provide extra surfaces for inscriptions and decoration. Many do not realize that chest tombs are hollow and that the corpse is interred underground – when such tombs suffer damage as a result of storm or vandalism, the curious are disappointed at not catching sight of coffins or skeletons.

The commonest of upright monuments is the simple inscribed tombstone, though variations include pedestal tombs, obelisks and miniature pyramids. Crosses were a comparative rarity before the second half of the nineteenth century. Monument and cross came together in King Edward I's remembrance of his beloved wife, Eleanor of Castile. When the queen died in Grantham in 1290, Edward broke off his campaign against the Scots in order to accompany the body back to London. The journey took thirteen days, and at every stop-over Edward vowed to erect a monumental cross in memory of his wife. Some say thirteen crosses once existed; others believe no more than nine were built. Only three 'Eleanor Crosses' remain – at Northampton, Geddington and Waltham Cross. A replica of the original now stands at Charing Cross, London, Eleanor's final stop before interment at Westminster Abbey.

The more unusual the memorial, the more likely the corpse beneath

A pyramid in an English country churchyard. The tomb of the eccentric John 'Mad Jack' Fuller (1757–1834) at Brightling, East Sussex. The surrounding countryside is peppered with other architectural follies built by Fuller.

will be remembered by subsequent generations. Who would remember Squire Fuller were it not for his memorial in Brightling, Sussex? Nothing quite prepares the visitor for the sight of a huge Egyptian pyramid rising up from an English churchyard. 'Mad' Jack Fuller made a deal with the local vicar: he would finance the building of a new church wall in exchange for permission to construct a twenty-five-foot pyramid in the churchyard. When he died in 1834 at the age of seventy-seven, Fuller was duly interred beneath his pyramid, built twenty-four years before in readiness to receive his corpse. Fanciful stories abound concerning the pyramid. Some suggested that Fuller – all twenty-two stone of him – was interred sitting at a table, dressed for dinner, wearing a top hat and quaffing claret. The floor was rumoured to be strewn with broken glass in order to keep the Devil at bay. Unfortunately the story is a fabrication: Fuller lies horizontally beneath the floor of the tomb – probably the only conventional thing this eccentric politician ever did!

Another truly memorable memorial is Sir Richard Burton's tent in the Catholic churchyard of St Mary Magdalen at Mortlake, south London. Burton (1821–90) was the archetypal Victorian adventurer: heavily disguised, he was the first white man to enter Mecca; in the Crimean War he commanded the Turkish cavalry; in 1856, with John Speke, he was unsuccessful in his attempt to discover the source of the Nile. When he died, in 1890, his wife, Lady Isobel (the same woman who went to such great lengths to make sure she was not buried alive and who, some maintain, accelerated her husband's death by refusing to give him medicines without a doctor being present – this, despite his plea, 'Quick Puss! Chloroform, ether ... or I am a dead man!'), applied to have him join Speke and Livingstone in Westminster Abbey. Permission was refused, probably because of Burton's translations of books about the sexual habits of primitives, including *The Perfumed Garden* and *Kama Sutra*. St Paul's Cathedral was no more forgiving. Eventually it was proposed to build an enormous stone tent in order to honour this remarkable man. Lady Burton was delighted and regularly held seances in the tent right up until her own death. The entrance to the tent was blocked up in 1951 after the monument was damaged by vandals. What is less well known is that at the rear of the tent is a ladder which gives access to a window in the roof, through which can be seen an interior bedecked with hanging camel bells, an altar and the gilt coffins of Burton and his wife.

Sometimes people are remembered not so much by eccentricity of design as by eccentricity of location. Sir Joshua Danvers (d.1753) lies in a chest tomb in the churchyard at Swithland, Leicestershire – or, to be more accurate, half of Sir Joshua lies within the churchyard and half without, since the church wall bisects his tomb. The explanation is quintessentially English: Sir Joshua wanted to be buried close to his beloved dog, and since dogs were not allowed to be interred in consecrated ground, a compromise was struck, whereby the hound was buried at his master's feet but safely outside the churchyard.

Yet another sure way to be remembered long after death is to be buried *other than horizontal and face up*. Ben Jonson (1572–1637) is remembered for more than his poetry. Tradition relates that he asked King Charles I to grant him a favour concerning his burial. 'Give me eighteen inches of square ground.' 'Where?' asked the king. 'In Westminster Abbey.' And so it was. Jonson was buried upright in the north aisle of the abbey. Cynical doubts about the accuracy of the story were dispelled in 1849, when a grave was being dug to receive Sir Robert Wilson. The loose earth of Jonson's grave 'rippled in like quicksand', and a clerk saw 'the two leg bones fixed bolt upright in the sand'.[13]

There are many accounts, usually apocryphal, about those who have been buried head down in order to be the right way up when all turns 'topsy turvy' on the Day of Judgement. Such a burial, of a French soldier, Major Labelliere, took place on Box Hill in Surrey. The story related about Richard Hull is definitely fantasy: it was said that he lay beneath a tower on Leith Hill, mounted on his horse, both horse and rider being upside down, patiently awaiting judgement.

Superstition also accounts for those who elect to be buried *within* the walls of a church. It was assumed that these individuals had entered into a pact with the Devil whereby he could claim their souls after death – 'Whether the body be buried in the church or out of it'. The obvious way to renege on the bargain was to be buried neither outside nor inside a church but to be shored up as part of the brickwork. Such a burial was that of William Eltrick in Wimbourne Minster, Dorset.[14]

WAXEN IMAGES

Sarah Hare will never be forgotten, despite the fact that she died in 1744. Her father decided that his daughter would be commemorated in wax. In Stow Bardolph Church, Norfolk, Mistress Hare, disarmingly life-like, stares sternly out of her mahogany case, dressed in her Sunday best. The day of the week is not unimportant, since it was believed that she died as a result of divine retribution, pricking her thumb while sewing on a Sunday – her waxen effigy testament of God's commandment to rest on the seventh day.

An effigy of an even more illustrious figure is to be seen in the undercroft at Westminster Abbey. There, magnificently regaled, stands King Charles II, proud and aloof. The face was modelled in wax shortly after his death. Keeping him company are King William III and his wife Queen Mary II; Mary's sister, Queen Anne; and sundry Stuart aristocrats. William, a mere five feet six inches tall, stands on a footstool in order not to appear too diminutive when set next to his five-foot-eleven-inch wife. Frances Stuart, Duchess of Richmond and Lennox, who died in 1702, looks splendid in the robes she wore to Queen Anne's coronation. Beside her perches an African grey parrot which lived with her for forty years and survived her by only a few days. This is the oldest stuffed bird in Britain.

Royal effigies made from wood date back as far as the fourteenth century, to the funeral of Edward II in 1327. The full-length effigy, usually attired in coronation regalia, was placed close to the monarch's coffin. When the coffin was buried, the effigy was exhibited for several weeks before being stored in the chantry chapel of the abbey. The earliest effigy still in existence is that of King Edward III, who died in 1377. Close study of the effigy reveals a drooping mouth on the left side and a flattened left cheek, evidence which suggests that the king's terminal speechlessness was caused by a stroke. The effigy of King Henry VII (died 1509) had a head modelled in plaster, and a body made of canvas and plaster moulded over hay. Henry's 'body' remained intact for nearly 450 years before its destruction in World War II; the head still survives. Perhaps the finest example of a wooden effigy is the head of Anne of Denmark, wife of King James VI/I, who died in 1619. The facial

The massive stone tent erected by Isabel Burton to commemorate her husband, Sir Richard, African explorer and translator of *The Arabian Nights*. St Mary Magdalen Churchyard, Mortlake, London.

detail, including a pimple on the left cheek, probably indicates that the head was modelled from the queen's death mask.

DEATH MASKS

The making of an effigy was a lengthy, painstaking and expensive business. Often, as in the case of Anne of Denmark, time could be saved by the judicious use of a death mask; sometimes the mask itself proved memorial enough. In the eighteenth and nineteenth centuries many famous persons (and a number of infamous ones too) had their facial features cast into death masks and thereby perpetuated their memory. The plaster cast, made as soon after death as possible before the features stiffened, could be used to generate any number of likenesses of the deceased.

Although the main purpose of such a mask was as a memorial, many nineteenth-ceuntury masks were made by phrenologists – pseudo-scientists who believed that one's personality, morality and intelligence could be gauged by examining the external contours of the skull. Phrenology, and post-mortem research into criminality, were the reasons why many of the infamous murderers of the nineteenth century, including William Burke, had death masks made of their features. Interestingly, William Hare, the 'one who got away' by turning King's

Evidence, had a *life* mask made during his trial, which is now in Edinburgh University.[15]

Death masks and life masks are made in the same way. To prevent painful adhesions of the plaster to the skin of the face, liberal amounts of oil are first applied. Tubes are inserted into the nostrils of sufficient length to allow them to project beyond the layers of plaster. Threads are laid across the face, and successive layers of plaster are built up and allowed to harden. Particular care is used when applying the plaster around the nose, mouth, eyes and forehead, with every effort being taken to faithfully record every wart and wrinkle. The mask is usually removed in three pieces, with the help of the silken threads previously laid against the face. To cast the back of the skull, the head, covered by a bathing-cap to protect the hair, is pushed back into a dish of plaster. Some people become frightened when the plaster begins to harden; others experience little or no discomfort – John Keats risked spoiling his life mask by his incessant giggling.

It is not always possible accurately to distinguish between a life mask and a death mask: in some lucky individuals the contentment of life is not dissimilar to the initial 'serenity' of death. This was certainly true of Mendelssohn, whose death mask '… assumed an almost glorified expression – so much he looked like one in sleep that some of his friends thought it could not be death'. In others, less fortunate, the death spasms remain recorded for posterity, as can be seen by the death masks made of Coleridge and Sheridan. The death mask of Sir Walter Scott clearly shows evidence of the stroke from which he died and also the autopsy scar where the top of the skull was sawn off in order to examine the brain. Besides Edinburgh, other important collections are in Princeton University, New Jersey; the Castle Museum, Norwich; and the Black Museum at Scotland Yard.

In our own century the features of those long dead have been conjured up by a mixture of consummate skill and modern technology. By such methods, using only the skull of the deceased, Prag and Neave have been able to construct the faces of people as diverse as Lindow Man (referred to in Part III, Chapter 2) and King Midas.

THE MASON'S ART

Before the emergence of an affluent middle class only the clergy and the nobility could afford elaborate burials and memorials. The poor were buried simply, one on top of the other. With increasing national prosperity came the urge to be remembered after death through splendid monuments attesting to the deceased's social status. The skills of monumental masons became highly regarded and much sought-after – right up to the era of mass production in the middle of the last century.

But having money enough to afford a monument did not guarantee remembrance: much thought had to be given to the durability of the materials used in monumental construction. Slate, for instance, is one of the most weather-resistant materials and, furthermore, it is easily worked to produce elaborate lettering and reliefs which are long-lasting and durable. Unfortunately slate is also regarded as sombre and austere and is little favoured outside Cornwall, Leicestershire, North Wales and the Lake District, areas served by nearby quarries. Most people opted to use local stones, some of which weathered very rapidly. In the Cotswolds, where the stone carves well but wears badly, inscriptions are often written on brass plaques which are then set into the monument. Contrary to expectation, marble does not wear well and is soon eroded by the wiles of the British climate. Granite is the opposite of marble – durable, very difficult to work and regarded by most as unaesthetic.

The two spectral poles in monumental materials are wood and metal. Besides durability, metal memorials lend themselves to shapes that are very difficult to achieve with stone. A major disadvantage of metal is the difficulty of adding further lettering once the design is cast – bolted on panels detract from the elegance of metal memorials.

CEMETERY SYMBOLISM

The pre-eminent Christian symbol is the cross, but in a monumental context the crucifix is a comparatively recent innovation. Prior to the Victorian era, pagan themes predominated, skulls and crossbones far outnumbering crosses. Elaborate and ornate memorials are remembered longer, albeit sometimes negatively, than plain and simple stones recording only name and age. A blueprint for remembrance is the construction of a grotesque and indestructible monument incorporating every conceivable funerary symbol, both pagan and Christian.

At Burton Lazars, Leicestershire, is a monument that would appear to have the lot: urns, orbs, snakes, angels, pyramids and obelisks. The dead man, William Squire, a local weaver, wished that any money left over, after the erection of his monument, be spent on the education of the village poor. In fact, the monument cost so much that the children of Burton Lazars continued uneducated.

At Hardenhuish in Wiltshire, the magnificent monument to David Ricardo MP represents the best of the classical style. Erected in 1823, it consists of four naked youths (even close inspection makes gender uncertain) striking mournful poses around a Corinthian column. This unashamedly pagan monument in its Christian setting ensures the remembrance of Ricardo in the minds of all who come and admire.

Some memorials attract attention in ways that were not intended by

the deceased. It is probably no coincidence that the Nightingale
memorial in Westminster Abbey is now hidden behind stacked chairs in
a part of the building not normally open to the public. The monument
shows Joseph Nightingale vainly trying to ward off the spectre of death
which is intent on claiming his young wife. Skeletal death, spear in
hand, rises up to carry off his prize. Its terrifying aspect has frightened
many generations. A tradition records that a robber, coming into the
abbey at moonlight, was so startled by the monument that he fled in
terror, leaving his crowbar on the pavement.

Remembrance can induce negative sentiments: two famous desecrated
tombs are to be found in Pere-Lachaise Cemetery in Paris. In a burial
ground full of stray cats and graffiti, the grave of Jim Morrison, American
pop musician and member of the group The Doors, is so regularly daubed
with multi-coloured spray paint that, for this very reason, it has become
one of the cemetery's most frequently visited plots. The famous memorial
to Oscar Wilde has also attracted the attention of vandals: close
inspection of Jacob Epstein's winged sphinx reveals that the creature has
had its genitals removed by hammer and chisel. Tradition has it that the
sight of such a large member so offended the sensitivities of two English
ladies that they resolved to remove the offending organ. Some say that it
is still used as a paperweight in the cemetery office.

A view inside the tent showing the coffins of Sir Richard and Lady Burton
amid a mixture of Christian and Islamic symbolism.

PEOPLE WHO PLANNED THEIR OWN FUNERALS

Some consider that their death and dispatch are too important an event to leave to the wiles of others. Charles V (1500–1558), Holy Roman Emperor, rehearsed his funeral many times before participating in the real thing. He ordered that his tomb be erected in a monastery chapel and had his servants march in procession, each with a black taper in his hand. Charles followed behind dressed in a shroud. As the service began and the hymns struck up, the emperor would lie in the coffin, joining in the prayers offered up for his immortal soul. The priests would sprinkle holy water over him as he wept with emotion. The ceremony over, the congregation would silently file out and shut the doors behind them. A little while later Charles would rise from his coffin and make for his bed.

Another famous man who had strong views about his funeral was the Victorian novelist Charles Dickens (1812–70). In his will he directed that he 'Be buried in an inexpensive, unostentatious, and strictly private manner; that no public announcement be made of the time or place of my burial; that at the utmost not more than three plain mourning coaches be employed; and that those who attend my funeral wear no scarf, cloak, black bow, long hat-band, or other such revolting absurdity. I direct that my name be inscribed in plain English letters on my tomb, without the addition of Mr or Esquire. I conjure my friends on no account to make me the subject of any monument, memorial, or testamonial whatever.' Perhaps the great man was a trifle naïve to suppose that a proud country would be content with such a low-key farewell to one of its most illustrious writers. In the event, Charles Dickens found his house of clay in the soil below Westminster Abbey.

An American president tried for a simple funeral – with much the same success as Dickens. Franklin Delano Roosevelt (1884–1945) detailed his wishes in a four-page document, written in 1937: a simple service to be held in the East Room of the White House; that he should not lie in state; that a gun carriage and not a hearse be used; that his casket (coffin) be of a simple design and made of dark wood; that he was not to be embalmed or hermetically sealed; and that his grave be not lined with bricks, cement or stones. FDR's mistake was to place his instructions in a private safe, where they were discovered a few days after his funeral. In the event Roosevelt *was* embalmed, *was* placed in a hermetically sealed coffin made of fine bronze-coloured copper and then *was* conveyed in a Cadillac hearse to a cement-lined vault. At least he did not lie in state.

LAST WORDS

It need not always be the case that one's final words on earth are those that adorn a tombstone or memorial plaque. Last words can be delivered verbally, rather than cast physically, and need not necessarily be ephemeral as a consequence. Much depends upon the import given to them by those gathered around to listen. Death-bed piety and patriotism are common, but not infrequently famous examples of last words are characterized by humour, self-effacement, inaptness or incongruity.

Memorable last words can crown a famous life or call attention to an otherwise undistinguished one. One of the problems with last words is that, apart from suicides and those condemned to death by others, none of us knows when the end will come. Many will simply deny the imminence of death; others, recognizing the paramount need for economical use of time, will choose to put mundane matters before more portentous reflections on the nature of death or the existence of an afterlife. Sadly, such husbandry, even when voiced by the famous or infamous, is seldom memorable. Further, there is more than a little suspicion that many of the last words attributed to eminent men and women have been altered, exaggerated or simply invented by others, often to show the deceased in a better or worse light. In reality, most of us will die too exhausted to be bothered with anything more memorable than a groan or a goodbye. For those who take the trouble to compose and rehearse a parting speech, it is likely that fate, capricious to the last, will contrive that there is no one within earshot to hear and record it – or understand it: when Albert Einstein died, in 1955, his last words were spoken in his native German, a language that none of his friends could understand, as he died in the United States.

Two examples which call into question the accuracy and authenticity of last words concern a politician and a king.

William Pitt (1759–1806) became prime minister at the age of twenty-four. Accounts of his last words vary from the patriotic to the alimentary. Most report the statesman as having said, 'Oh, my country! How I love my country!', sentiments befitting such an eminent statesman. Yet a later prime minister, Benjamin Disraeli, has Pitt saying, 'I think I could eat one of Bellamy's veal pies.' A similar diversity of sentiment is displayed by the varying accounts of the final words of King George V (1865–1936). Most of the king's biographers have him inquiring, 'How is the Empire?' But there is another version: when the king was taken ill in 1929 he convalesced at Bognor, a seaside resort in Sussex; when, in his final illness, his doctor tried to revive his spirits by saying, 'We'll soon have you back in Bognor, Sire,' the king's reply was pithy: 'Bugger Bognor!'

Three very different versions of Christ's last words have come down to us. St Mark has Jesus saying, 'My God, my God, why hast thou forsaken me?' St Luke's version is, 'Father, into thy hands I commend my spirit.' St John's is the simplest: 'It is finished.'

Many have attempted to categorize the wide variety of final words. Probably the largest number can be subsumed under the rubric 'The End Is Nigh.' They are rarely noteworthy and include such lame efforts as Lord Byron (1824), 'Now I shall go to sleep'; Carl Maria von Weber, musician (1826), 'Now let me sleep'; Laurence Sterne, author of *Tristram Shandy* (1768), 'Now it has come'; Felix Mendelssohn, composer (1847), 'Weary, very weary'; and Franz Schubert, composer (1828), 'Here, here is my end'; to the simple 'Goodbye' of William Hudson, the American author who died in 1922.

It is to be expected that some would die ill at ease, others happy and accepting. When Oliver Goldsmith (1774), author of *The Vicar of Wakefield*, was asked whether his mind was at ease, he answered, 'No, it is not.' Gerard Manley Hopkins (1889), poet and scholar, exited with very different emotions: 'I am so happy, so happy.' William Hunter, doctor and embalmer, died weary but happy in 1783: 'If I had the strength to hold a pen, I would write how easy and pleasant it is to die.' Boredom is a much less predictable sentiment. W. Somerset Maugham,

The wax effigy of Sarah Hare stares out of her glass case in the church of Stow Bardolph in Norfolk. She died when, wantonly sewing on a Sunday, she pricked her finger.

the British novelist who died in 1965, commented dryly, 'Dying is a very dull, dreary affair. And my advice to you is to have nothing whatever to do with it.' Lytton Strachey (1932) was even more direct: 'If this is dying, I don't think much of it.'

Religious last words run the whole gamut from 'Jesus.' (Joan of Arc, 1431), through 'Jesus! Mary!' (Earl of Arundel, 1580), to 'Jesus, Mary and Joseph!' (Elizabeth Seton, 1821). There are abundant quotations from the scriptures, the most popular being variations upon, 'Into Thy hands, O Lord, I commit my spirit' (Christopher Columbus, 1506). The Roman Emperor Vespasian (AD 79) commented, 'Dear me, I must be turning into a god.' The thesis that a religious faith can make dying easier is attested to by Joseph Addison, the British essayist (1719): 'See in what peace a Christian can die.' But Voltaire (1778), philosopher and aetheist, observed goodnaturedly as he watched the flickering of a candle. 'The flames already?'

Predictably patriotism figures largely in the last words of kings, politicians and soldiers. King George V (1936) worried about the British Empire; Pitt the Younger (1806) about England; Pierre Laval (1945) about France; Napoleon (1821) about France, his army and Josephine – in that order; while von Ribbentrop, the Nazi war criminal, went to his death in 1946 asking God to save Germany.

Perhaps the most memorable last words are those that are examples of wry humour in the face of death. Anna Pavlova (1931), the ballerina best remembered for her role as the dying swan, asked those around her to 'Get my swan costume ready.' The comedian Stan Laurel (1965) struck up a terminal banter with his nurse:

'I'd rather be skiing than doing this.'

'Do you ski, Mr Laurel?'

'No, but I'd rather be doing that than this.'

This is reminiscent of W.C. Fields, the film comedian, who died in 1946. He commented, 'On the whole, I'd rather be in Philadelphia,' recalling his aversion to that city.

Humour in last words may be intentional or unintentional, true or apocryphal and from expected or unexpected sources. Oscar Wilde (1900) observed, 'Either this wallpaper goes, or I do.' Another nineteenth-century humorist, Thomas Hood (1845), watched the application of a mustard plaster to his foot: 'There's very little meat for the mustard.' Joel Harris, the American humorist, died in 1908 just after saying, 'I am about the extent of a tenth of a gnat's eyebrow better.'

Unexpected sources of deadly humour include Kathleen Ferrier, opera singer (1953): 'Now I'll have *eine kleine pause*'; Henry Fox, first Baron Holland (1774): 'If Mr Selwyn calls again, show him up. If I am alive I shall be delighted to see him, and if I am dead he would like to see me.'

An example of unintentional humour was provided by the death of

General Sedgewick, American civil war commander (1864), who, peering over a parapet was heard to observe, 'They couldn't hit an elephant at this dist ...'

Condemned prisoners frequently have a chance to practise their timing. Neville Heath, hanged in 1946, asked for a last whiskey: 'You might make that a double'; William Palmer, the Victorian poisoner, hanged in 1856, stepped onto the gallows and asked, 'Are you sure it's safe?'; Ned Kelly, the Australian outlaw, hanged 1880: 'Such is life'; and James Rodgers, an American criminal shot in 1960, when asked if he had any last requests replied, 'A bulletproof vest.' Cherokee Bill, a hoodlum hanged in 1896, was asked if he had anything to say: 'No. I came here to die, not make a speech.'

And is deliberate humour or deep philosophy to be gleaned from the last deathbed conversation of Gertrude Stein, the American writer (1946) who is best remembered for, 'A rose is a rose is a rose'? Stein asked, 'What is the answer?' When no answer was given, she laughed and said, 'In that case, what is the question?'

The most arresting last words are those that conjure up images of childhood behaviour. Sir William Ostler (1919), the most eminent physician of his day, said to his doctor, 'Nighty-night, a-darling.' But, for me, the most poignant by far are the last words of Horace Williams, the American philosopher: when a nurse asked him his name, he replied in a child-like voice, 'Horace Williams.'[16]

USES OF THE DEAD TO THE LIVING: HARVESTING CADAVERS

From the discussion of the diagnosis of death, in the chapter on premature burial, it is clear that many of the earlier uncertainties can be obviated by the concept of 'brain death' – when the electrical activity of the brain ceases, a person is deemed dead, regardless of whether the heart is still beating or the lungs are still respiring. Succinctly put: anyone whose brain is dead, is truly dead. But it follows that such 'corpses' may be kept warm, respiring, pulsating, evacuating and excreting purely by mechanical means. Such cadavers, nourished and groomed, could be kept 'alive' for years, possibly decades. Such living dead would certainly not be forgotten!

What purpose could this artificial prolongation of life possibly serve? Many see it as a means by which the dead can continue to be of use to the living. The subject was comprehensively covered by Willard Gaylin in 1974.[17] He started from the premise that, given the choice, most of us, at death, would elect to donate our organs to help prolong the life of another. (Gaylin wryly observes that this idea needs some qualification: Harvard Medical School has a surfeit of donors while cadavers at Boston

University are always at a premium. In New England, evidently, the kudos of getting into Harvard extends even to the dissecting table). He envisages the brain-dead (neo-morts,) pulsating and respiring in specialized wards, (bioemporia). The uses to which neo-morts can be put are directly proportional to the power of the imagination: '...they can be used to allow junior doctors to practice liver biopsies, lumbar punctures or surgical procedures ... the efficacy and side effects of new drugs could be tested: cancers could be induced and subsequently treated ... antibodies could be produced by the injection of poisons, bacteria and viruses ... organs and tissues could be continually harvested – especially blood products, bone marrow, and skin for grafting.'[18] It is arguable whether this altruism would appeal to most people, but what is certain is that such a gesture would combine the need to be remembered with the wish to do some good for others.

Utilitarian Postscript

In Père-Lachaise cemetery is an example of the use of the dead to the living. It is the bronze statue of a naked young woman. The statue is discoloured with age – except the breasts, which are highly polished from the caresses of generations of male palms.

This wax effigy of King Charles II (1630–85) stood near the place of his burial in Westminster Abbey until 1723. He is wearing a black velvet Garter hat with a plume of ostrich and heron feathers. Today the effigy can be seen in the Undercroft Museum in the Abbey.

V The Fear of an Ignominious Death

1 REGAL ENDS

A good death does honour to a whole life.

Petrarch (1304–74)

Research has consistently shown that, were we able to choose, the majority of us would opt for a pain-free death, preferably at home, in the company of family and friends who would then make sure we were interred with dignity. Such is the popular conception of a 'good death'. In the Middle Ages many treatises were written about the art of dying well, *ars moriendi*. Sudden death, *mors improvisa*, was considered undignified. Although 'kings (and queens) were expected to die with special dignity and composure', it is surprising how relatively few of them actually managed to achieve this goal.[1] King Charles II's death was neither sudden nor dignified: he 'took an unconscionable time a-dying', the principal player in a tragedy which frequently bordered on a farce.

The Final Days of King Charles II

The restoration of the monarchy in 1660 replaced the austerity of Oliver Cromwell with the hedonism of that most flamboyant of Stuart kings, Charles II (1630–85). Not everybody welcomed Charles's return, and many heartily disapproved of his life-style of gluttony, drunkenness and infidelity and would predict retribution on this dissolute king. John Evelyn, the diarist, on the day before Charles's fatal illness, writes of, 'Inexpressible luxury and profaneness ... total forgetfulness of God ... the King sitting and toying with his concubines ... a French boy singing love songs ...' Evelyn goes on to record dryly: 'Six days after, all was in the dust.' On the night before his fatal illness, the king, talking about his

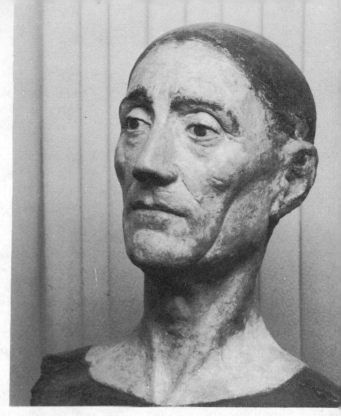

The plaster head of King Henry VII (1457–1509) was proven to be a death mask when, in 1950, it was discovered that one eyebrow showed clotting of the hair by the grease used in taking the mould. Only the head remains – the rest of the effigy was destroyed in World War II.

new palace being built in Winchester, had remarked, 'I shall be most happy this week, for my building will be covered in lead.' Within a week Charles lay dead in a leaden coffin.

When the king finally retired to bed, his attendants settled down to sleep in an ante-room, together with a dozen spaniels and numerous clocks which chimed every quarter of an hour throughout the night. When Charles woke on the Monday (2 February), he went as usual, to his private closet. A groom noticed that the king was deathly pale, and he rushed off to report to Ailesbury. Ailesbury immediately called for Chiffins, First Page of the Backstairs, and the only man allowed to enter Charles's private closet. Eventually the king was persuaded out of the closet. He remained pale and mute. It was obvious to all that something was very wrong but everyone was at a loss as to what to do. Suddenly Charles had a violent convulsion and with a cry fell into the arms of Ailesbury.

The first decision was whether to bleed the king. If, as was suspected, he had suffered an apoplectic fit, the orthodoxy of the times prescribed immediate blood-letting. Sixteen ounces of blood were taken from Charles's right arm. Attendants held the king's mouth forcibly open to prevent him from biting his tongue should the convulsions recur. The blood-letting had an immediate beneficial effect, and soon the physicians were plying the king with other remedies popular at the time. More blood was removed by means of deep scarification; a strong antimonial emetic was given to induce vomiting, followed by zinc sulphate; a powerful purge was administered; the king's head was shaved and blistering preparations were applied to the scalp. Even red-hot cautery was got ready.

It was then that Charles was moved into the bed from which he never again arose. Doctors were summoned, and subsequently there were rarely fewer than twelve physicians in attendance. Charles's death is one of the best recorded in history, since there were always doctors, clergymen, ambassadors and relatives milling around his bed, many of whom left detailed descriptions of the scene.[2]

Soon the king was out of immediate danger and was able to tell the assembled dignitaries that when he awoke he had felt unwell and had gone to the closet to get some 'King's Drops', a volatile extract of bone. The doctors then began to confer on the best way to proceed. It was an unwritten rule that their decisions should appear unanimous, presumably so that the onus for mistakes should be borne by a group and not by an individual. It was agreed that they should try to relieve the pressures of the humours around the brain. To that end they administered white hellebore roots to encourage sneezing. A preparation of cowslip flowers and sal ammoniac was given to 'strengthen' the brain, and in order to relieve the scalding of the urine produced by blistering, a draught containing mallow roots, sweet almond kernels, melon seeds and barley water was given to the king. A gargle made from the inner bark of elm was administered to soothe the throat, which was inflamed as a result of the forcible separation of the teeth during the convulsions. A plaster of pitch and pigeon dung was applied to the royal feet.

By Tuesday the omens were looking more propitious. In order to try to prevent further convulsions a julep of 'Black cherry water' was made out of flowers of lime, lilies of the valley, spirit of lavender and prepared pearls – mixed with white sugar candy to improve the taste. Alas, all to no avail. On the Wednesday evening the king suffered another violent fit, which produced a deep air of pessimism as regards his chances of eventual recovery. 'Spirit of human skull' was given 'a sure harbinger of impending dissolution'. Peruvian bark (crude quinine) in syrup of cloves was given on the Thursday morning but the king's condition was now deteriorating rapidly, and rumours began to circulate that he was already dead.

Bishop Ken of Bath and Wells absolved Charles of all his sins, but when he offered the sacrament, the king answered that there was time enough to think of that. At five o'clock on the Thursday afternoon Barillon, the French ambassador, had a meeting with the Duchess of Portsmouth, one of Charles's most famous mistresses and life-long spy for Louis XIV. She told the ambassador that Charles was a secret Catholic and that they must conspire together to think of a way to get a priest to the death-bed to give him the sacrament. James, Duke of York, was first to check with his brother that these were his wishes, and when this was done the three would lay their plans to admit a Catholic priest under the very noses of the prelates of the Church of England. It was finally agreed that James would ask all but two of the spectators to retire to an ante-room, whilst those who remained were placed far enough back so as not to be able to hear what was going on.

One difficulty that was overlooked was the problem of finding a priest who could speak English! The queen's priest spoke only Portuguese, and James's only Italian. By pure good fortune there was a Scots priest, John Hudleston, in the Queen's household – indeed, he was the very priest who had saved Charles's life after the Battle of Worcester. After the withdrawal of the doctors, clergy and politicians, Hudleston, disguised in a wig and cassock, gained entry into the king's bedroom by a back staircase. Charles immediately recognized him: 'You that saved my body has now come to save my soul.' The absolution and sacrament took three-quarters of an hour, the presence of two duped Protestant earls successfully allaying the growing suspicions of those who waited in the ante-room.

Even with Charles prepared now for his death, the doctors still felt moved to try for a miracle. Cardiac tonics, such as Sir Walter Raleigh's cordial, were given (comprising, in part, seeds, herbs and spices brought from South America and mixed with coral, pearl, 'oyle of Vitreoll', hartshorn, ambergris, musk and sugar), followed by Goa stone in a draught of broth, more quinine bark, yet more sal ammoniac and finally Oriental bezoar stone, a sort of gallstone from the stomach of the eastern goat, widely used as an antidote to poison. Charles submitted to this medicinal onslaught with resignation and good humour, apologizing to the company for taking so long to die. He continued politely to refuse Bishop Ken's urgings to take the sacrament.

At six o'clock on the Friday morning, 6 February, the king had the curtains drawn back to enable him to watch the sunrise for the last time. He asked that the eight-day clock be wound. At 7 a.m. he became suddenly breathless and was bled to twelve ounces and given further cardiac tonics. Mercifully he died just before noon. 'He was buried at night, without any manner of pomp, and soon forgotten, after all his vanity.' His effigy can still be seen in the Undercroft Museum in Westminster Abbey.

'Thus reposes one of the most popular and the least deserving of monarchs.'[3]

IGNOMINIOUS ROYAL PRECEDENTS

There are few greater ignominies that can be perpetrated upon the corpse of a king than to cast it into the sea in an effort to lighten a ship's load. King Henry IV (1367–1413), first Lancastrian king of England, elected

Dr Samuel Johnson: portrait painted by James Barry (*c.* 1777) and death mask.

to be buried at Canterbury and was transported from London down the Thames to Feversham. *En route* the wind freshened and the ship got into difficulties. It was then that the crew jettisoned their royal cargo.

Alas, the story proves to be complete fabrication. In 1832 Henry's tomb at Canterbury was opened and '... to the astonishment of all present, the face of the deceased king was seen in complete preservation.'[4]

Despite the farcical antics going on around him, Charles II did have the good fortune to die in bed. Such a death would never have found favour with the Spartans, who looked upon death in battle as the fulfilment of a hero's life. But even this warrior race shared an intense fear of the indignities that the victor might perpetrate upon their lifeless bodies. Although King Richard III (1452–85) died bravely on Bosworth Field, gross indignity was to follow.

Early on it became clear that many on Richard's side had little stomach for the fight, and many important noblemen were conspicuously biding their time waiting to see which way the battle would go before committing their forces to either Richard or Henry Tudor (later Henry VII). After his horse was killed under him, Richard, ignoring advice to flee the field and return to fight another day, decided that he would lead a direct attack on the usurper. Courageously he launched himself at Henry and his bodyguard but was soon surrounded and killed, 'fighting manfully in the thickest press of his enemies'.

On this gallant showing and considering his rank, it might have been expected that Richard's corpse would have been treated with respect by the victor. Such was not to be the case. Henry had the body subjected to the grossest indignity. The corpse was stripped naked and bundled across the back of a horse: 'And Richard late king as gloriously as he in the morning departed from that town [Leicester], so as irreverently was he that afternoon, brought into that town, for his body despoiled to the skin, and nought being left about him, so much as would cover his privy member, he was trussed behind a pursuivant called Norroy as a hog or other vile beast, and all to besprung with mire and filth.'[5] Thus was the body taken to the church of the Grey Friars, where it was exposed to public view for two days. Richard was buried in an unmarked grave, the body being tipped out of a coffin that later served as a horse trough and which was finally broken up and used to construct the cellar steps at the White Horse Inn. (After the dissolution of the monasteries, the corpse was exhumed and thrown into the River Soar.)

THE DEATH OF GLORIANA

Death for Elizabeth I, 'the Virgin Queen', came in 1603, in her seventieth year and the forty-fifth year of her reign. She was a wise and resolute monarch, well loved by her people; she was also cantankerous and stubborn – and never more so than in her final days, when events frequently took on the aspect of some bizarre surrealist comedy rather than the dignified demise of a queen of England.

Some date Elizabeth's declining health to the execution of the Earl of Essex in 1601. One account, almost certainly apocryphal, has Elizabeth visiting the death-bed of her friend Lady Nottingham, who confessed that Essex, whilst in the Tower awaiting execution, had sent the queen the ring she had given him some years before. Elizabeth had promised Essex that delivery of this ring would grant him instant pardon for any crime. Lady Nottingham told her sovereign that her husband had held onto the ring, thereby ensuring Essex's death. Elizabeth was reported to be beside herself with anger, rushed from the room and thenceforth seemed to lose the will to live.

With death imminent, Elizabeth ensconced herself on a pile of cushions on the floor of a room at Richmond Palace and refused to budge, her finger firmly stuck in her mouth, her eyes constantly staring into the distance. Robert Cecil, her secretary, had the temerity to try to get her to go to bed: 'Madame, to content the people, you *must* go to bed.' '*Must*? The word "must" is not to be used to princes.' In the face of such obstinacy the Queen's ladies-in-waiting joined her on the floor. At one point Elizabeth decided to stand up – indeed, she stood, supported on either side, for fully fifteen hours before she was finally persuaded into her bed.

It was time for her to make peace with her God. Archbishop Whitgift was summoned, but even this solemnity was punctuated by macabre humour. 'After he had continued long in prayer, till the old man's knees were weary, he blessed her, and meant to rise and leave her.' But the queen signalled him to stay kneeling. 'He did so for a long half hour after, and then thought to leave her.' Again the queen made signs to have the old man stay where he was. 'He did so for half an hour more.' Finally the archbishop was released and so also was the spirit of the queen: 'Hir Majestie departed this lyfe, mildly like a lambe, easily like a ripe apple from the tree.'[6]

Elizabeth left instructions that she was not to be embalmed or disembowelled. The body was transferred from Richmond to Whitehall, where it lay in state watched over by the ladies of the Court. There was a final indignity, related by Elizabeth Southwell, one of Elizabeth's maids-of-honour: '[The Queen's] body burst with such a crack that it splitted the wood, lead and cere-cloth: whereupon the next day she was fain to be new trimmed up.'[7] Gaseous decomposition could explain this phenomenon; others chose to believe it was a Popish falsehood invented to discredit the Protestant monarch.

HANOVERIAN DEATH

Here lies Fred,
Who was alive and is dead;
Had it been his father,
I had much rather;
Had it been his brother,
Still better than another;
Had it been his sister,
No one would have missed her;
Had it been the whole generation,
Still better for the nation;
But since 'tis only Fred,
Who was alive and is dead,
There's no more to be said.

This scurrilous, anonymous verse was penned to commemorate the unlamented death of Frederick, Prince of Wales, son of King George II, and to give vent to popular feelings about the Hanoverians in general. Frederick's death in 1751, when he was forty-four years old, was doubly ignominious for an heir to the throne of Great Britain: firstly, it was widely rumoured that death was due to the delayed effects of his having

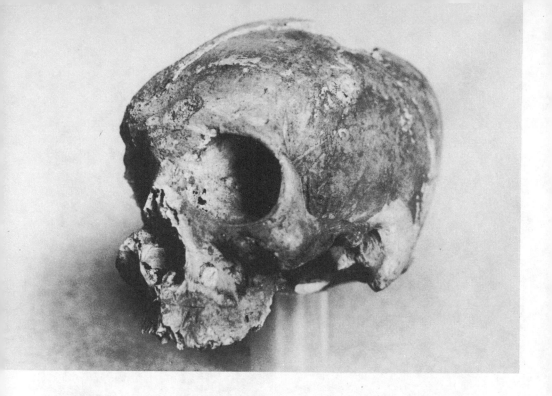

The skull of King Midas, ruler of Gordion in Central Turkey, from 738 to 696 BC. Discovered in 1957, the skull lay forgotten in a box in Ankara until 1988.

been hit with a tennis ball; secondly, the mode of exit was far from regal – 'He complained of a sudden pain and an offensive smell, and immediately threw himself backwards and died.'[8] An ignoble life was ended by an ignoble death.

Britain grew great in spite of George II (1683–1760), a man known more for his infidelities than for his kingship. His long-suffering queen, Caroline of Anspach, predeceased him by twenty-three years and made an undignified exit, dying of 'Mortification of ye Bowels', exacerbated by a surfeit of royal pride. Despite suffering dreadfully painful bouts of colic, Caroline refused to take to her bed for fear of annoying her irascible husband. Eventually, with increasing pains and vomiting, she was persuaded to seek treatment. Her family gathered around her, Princess Caroline weeping copiously between nose-bleeds. George II visited his sick wife and alternated between tearful sympathy and carping criticisms. ('How can you stare like that?' the king said at one point, 'You look like a calf that has just had its throat cut.') A famous death-bed exchange had the queen encouraging George to marry again after her death. The sobbing monarch replied, 'No – I shall have mistresses.' 'Ah! my God!' exclaimed Caroline, 'That won't stop you.'

Caroline was dying from late complications of an umbilical hernia

The face of King Midas, the
king who was able to turn all
he touched to gold, recon-
structed after 2,700 years by
Dr John Prag and Richard
Neave.

caused during the birth of her youngest daughter, fourteen years
previously, which, out of embarrassment, she had refused to have
treated. Even now the royal surgeon was summoned only when her
bowels finally ruptured, expelling their contents into the abdominal
cavity. Despite these dire circumstances, Caroline displayed the sense of
humour for which she was justly famous: the sight of Ranby, her surgeon,
bending over her abdomen, his wig set alight by a candle flame, sent the
queen into such paroxysms of laughter that she begged him stay his
scalpel until she had recovered her composure. For twelve days her agony
continued, prompting a cruel couplet from Alexander Pope:

> Here lies wrapt in forty thousand towels
> The only proof that Caroline had bowels.

But even *in extremis* there were compensations. Her son, Frederick,
the same 'Poor Fred' who was later to die so unappreciated and who had
once lampooned his parents as 'King Guinea's' and 'Queen Tripe', was
refused admittance to tender his goodbyes. Initially Caroline had
wondered whether she would be 'fool enough to let him come and give

him the pleasure of seeing my last breath go out of my body', but ultimately she decided against the idea. 'At least,' she said of her son, 'I shall have one comfort in having my eyes eternally closed – I shall never see that monster again.' When told that she would soon find peace, the exhausted queen answered, in French, 'So much the better.'[9]

The widower loudly lamented his loss. One morning he called for a portrait of Caroline to be propped on a chair at the foot of his bed. For two hours he gazed on the features of the dead queen. But mere likenesses in oils failed to expiate his grief. For almost a month Caroline lay unburied in her coffin at St James's Palace, visited frequently by her inconsolable husband. Even after she had been deposited in the vaults of Westminster Abbey, the king could not bear to parted from her – as was attested to in a letter written by Lord Wentworth: 'Saturday night, between one and two o'clock, the King waked out of a dream very uneasy, and ordered the vault, where the Queen is, to be broken open immediately, and have the coffin also opened; and went in a hackney chair through the Horse Guards to Westminster Abbey, and back again to bed.'[10]

Horace Walpole describes George II's own undignified demise thus: 'He went to his bed well last night; rose at six this morning as usual, looked, I suppose, if all his money was in his purse, and called for his chocolate. A little after seven, he went into the water closet – the German valet de chambre heard a noise louder than royal wind, listened, heard something like a groan, ran in, and found the hero of Oudenarde and Dettingen on the floor, with a gash on his right temple, by falling againt a bureau – he tried to speak, could not, and expired.'[11] The indignity of George II's death in the lavatory was in sharp contrast to a little-known instruction he left concerning his placement in the abbey vaults. He commanded that his coffin be laid next to that of his wife and that the adjacent panels were to be removed, in order that their bones might lie together. And so it was done for this, the last sovereign to be buried in Westminster Abbey.

DEATH BY TORTURE

There can be few more ignoble deaths than to be tortured by one's enemies, especially if they are in the employ of one's spouse. Such was the fate of King Edward II (1284–1327), the first English Prince of Wales. Living forever in the shadow of his illustrious father, Edward was roundly loathed by his French wife Isabella. She and Mortimer, her lover, eventually had the hapless Edward imprisoned in Berkeley Castle. There are many vivid and generally specious accounts of the king's death, but many think the most vivid and specious to be that by Geoffrey le Baker, written nearly a quarter of a century later. Baker cites a cryptic message sent by the Bishop of Hereford to Edward's gaolers: '*Edwardum occidere nolite timere bonum est.*' There are two meanings, depending on where the comma is placed – either, 'Do not fear to kill Edward, it is a good thing' or, 'Do not kill Edward, it is good to be afraid.' To be murdered is indignity enough, but to be murdered as a result of bad grammar represents Fate at its most capricious.

Baker's explicit account adds further details of the indignities suffered by the king:

> The brutes ... at night on 22 September, having suddenly seized him lying in bed and having pressed him down and suffocated him with great pillows and a weight heavier than fifteen robust men, with a plumber's iron heated red hot, through a horn applied leading to the privy parts of the bowels, they burned out the respiratory organs past the intestines, fearing lest, a wound having been found on the royal body ... his tormentors would be bound to answer for an obvious offence and pay the penalty for it ... The cry of the dying wakened many of Berkeley and certain ones of the castle, as they asserted, to compassion and prayers for the holy fleeting soul.

Another description has Edward dying 'with a hoote broche putte thro the secret place posterialle'.[12]

Although scholars now doubt the accuracy of Baker's chronicle, it is intriguing to note that the funeral of Edward II was the first to use a wooden effigy of the deceased instead of displaying the corpse itself.

THE DIGNIFIED DEATH OF A REGICIDE

Robert François Damiens (1714–57) was a French soldier who attempted to assassinate King Louis XV by stabbing him as he entered his carriage at Versailles. A detailed account of the torture and death of Damiens has come down to us, clearly showing that dignity is not the prerogative of royal victims.

> The sulphur was lit, but the flame was so poor that only the top skin of the hand was burnt, and that only slightly. Then the executioner, his sleeves rolled up, took the steel pincers, which had been especially made for the occasion, and which were about a foot and a half long, and pulled first at the calf of the right leg, then at the thigh, and from there at the two fleshy parts of the right arm, then at the breasts. Though a strong, sturdy fellow, this executioner found it so difficult to tear away the pieces of flesh that he set about the same spot two or three times, twisting the pincers as he did so, and what he took away formed at each part a wound about the size of a six-pound crown piece.

The executioner filled these holes with molten lead, as Damiens cried out, 'Pardon, my God! Pardon, Lord!' From time to time he would raise his head and look over his tortured body. Ropes were then tied to his limbs.

> The horses tugged hard, each pulling straight on a limb, each horse held by an executioner. After a quarter of an hour, and after several attempts, the direction of pull of the horses were changed: those at the arms were made to pull towards the head, those at the thighs towards the arms. The arms then broke at the joints. He raised his head and looked at himself. Two more horses had to be added to those harnessed to the thighs, which made six horses in all. Without success. Monsieur Le Breton ordered renewed efforts to be made, but the horses gave up and one of them harnessed to the thighs fell to the ground.

Damiens was heard to say, 'Kiss me, gentlemen,' and to ask the priest to say a mass for his soul. 'After two or three attempts [to pull the body apart], the executioner, Samson, and the other man who had used the pincers, drew out knives and cut through the thighs.' At last the horses were able to tear away the legs, first the right, then the left. Next the upper limbs were cut through to the bone and joints in order to facilitate the severance of the arms.

'When the four limbs had been pulled away, the confessors came to speak to him; but his executioner told them that he was dead, though the truth was that I saw the man move, his lower jaw moving from side to side as if he were talking. One of the executioners said that he was still alive when his trunk was thrown on the stake.' The torso and limbs were reduced to ashes and thrown to the four winds.[13]

A DIGNIFIED DEATH ON THE SCAFFOLD

Tragedy and misfortune, usually of their own making, dogged the Stuart dynasty. In vain did the Stuart monarchs try to emulate their illustrious Tudor predecessors. It was the arrogance and conceit of King Charles I – (1600–1649) that alienated the majority of his subjects and contributed to his defeat at the hands of Oliver Cromwell and the Roundheads. After two years of imprisonment this uncompromising king was eventually brought to trial in 1648 and sentenced to death by 'the severing of his head from his body'. The first and only English king ever to be murdered by his people approached his death with a dignity that eclipsed the ignominious manner of his dispatch.

After his trial Charles was taken from Whitehall to St James's Palace, so as not to be disturbed by the banging and hammering of men constructing the scaffold. With him went William Juxon, Bishop of London. Gypsy, his greyhound, and Rogue, his spaniel, were left behind. Most of the king's family had fled to safety on the Continent, but two of his children, Elizabeth, aged thirteen, and Henry, aged eight, were brought from custody for a final farewell meeting with their father.

This meeting was poignantly recorded by Elizabeth: 'What the King said to me on the 29th of January, 1648–9, the last time I had the happiness to see him.' The document attests to the tenderness of a father, and the dignity of a king about to die: 'He told me he was glad I was come ... He wished me not to grieve and torment myself for him, for that would be a glorious death that he would die ... He told me he had forgiven all his enemies, and hoped God would forgive them also; and commanded us, and the rest of my brothers and sisters, to forgive them.'

30 January 1649 was a bitterly cold day. Charles had slept only four hours. On rising he asked for an extra shirt, '... by reason the season is so sharp as probably may make me to shake, which some Observers will imagine proceeds from fear. I would have no such Imputation.' When Colonel Hacker knocked on the door Charles was ready. He walked briskly across St James's Park, appearing cheerful and talking to those on either side of him. At Whitehall Juxon celebrated Holy Communion, after which Charles said that he was 'prepared for all I am to undergo'. There followed an inordinate delay of four hours during which reluctant commissioners were pressured to add their signatures to the death warrant. Although Charles wished the sacrament to be his last food on

Two headstones in the same churchyard:
(a) An enduring inscription in slate

earth, he was eventually induced to eat a little and to drink some claret, in case hunger should invoke faintness.

Finally, at about two o'clock, Hacker escorted the king to the scaffold, which was draped chest-high in black, obscuring the view of the vast crowd – except those who looked down upon the scene from vantage-points in neighbouring buildings. The two executioners, Richard Brandon and his assistant Ralph Jones, looked grotesque, dressed as sailors and wearing huge false wigs. As an added indignity the block was a mere eight inches high, and staples had been fixed in order to tie down a struggling monarch.

Charles's studied calm faltered momentarily when someone brushed against the axe. Fearing that this would blunt its edge, he exclaimed, 'Take heed of the axe! Hurt not the axe that may hurt me!' Quickly regaining his composure, the king tried to address the crowd, but it was hopeless, his voice being drowned out by the noise of the onlookers. With supreme dignity Charles said, 'I go from a corruptible to an incorruptible crown, where no disturbances can take place.' The king then turned to Brandon and told the executioner not to strike until he signalled by stretching out his hands. When Brandon tried to tuck away some of the king's hair, Charles, fearing that the strike was imminent,

(b) Remembrance compromised by soft stone.

lost his composure for the second time: 'Stay for the sign!' His prayers completed, the king slowly stretched out his arms. A single blow detached the head from the body. The crowd were transfixed and a groan went up – '… such a groan as I never heard before, and desire I may never hear again'.[14]

The further indignity of a furtive burial at Windsor, and the refusal by the authorities to permit the use of the Book of Common Prayer, did nothing to take away from the majesty with which this vain and arrogant king went to meet his Maker. In the words of Andrew Marvell, poet, republican and no lover of Charles I:

> He nothing common did or mean
> Upon that memorable scene.

MARY, QUEEN OF SCOTS

Charles I had followed in the footsteps of his grandmother, Mary Stuart, Queen of Scots (1542–87). Perhaps her dignified end inspired his.

In 1587, after Mary had been nearly twenty years in prison, Elizabeth I was finally persuaded to execute her. The sentence was carried out in the great hall of Fotheringhay Castle before an audience of 300 knights and gentlemen. Mary entered the hall, her tall, majestic figure dressed in a black robe and white veil, a gold crucifix hanging from her neck. She mounted the scaffold and sat down to listen to her death sentence being proclaimed by Lord Shrewsbury. She appeared perfectly composed and looked around, smiling at those she recognized. The dean of Peterborough, officiating on behalf of the Church of England, was told, 'I am a Catholic and shall die a Catholic. Your prayers will avail me little.' There then followed a contest not without humour, as Mary and the dean vied with each other in the volume and intensity of their prayers, until the exasperated dean gave up in despair.

When she had finished praying, Mary was helped to disrobe. The black cloak was shed to reveal crimson undergarments. Standing on the black scaffold, she was crimson from head to feet. Slowly she knelt and, still smiling, wished her ladies, 'Adieu! Au revoir.'

What followed evokes chills even today. The first blow missed the neck and cut into the back of the head.

Mary remained perfectly still and was heard to whisper 'Sweet Jesus.' The second stroke severed the neck except for a small sinew which was cut by using the axe as a saw. The executioner held up the severed head, grasping it by the hair. At that instant the head separated from an unsuspected wig and fell to the floor. The audience gasped at the gruesome spectacle of a bald, wrinkled, care-worn old woman. It was claimed that her lips still moved and continued to do so for a quarter of an hour after death. As the executioner was about to remove Mary's stockings, her little Skye terrier scurried from under her discarded robe. After '… being put from hence [the dog] went and laid himself down betwixt her head and body, and being besmeared with her blood, was caused to be washed'.

A NOBLE ROYAL DEATH

Many illustrious men and at least one notable woman have received the appellation 'great', but in only one case has the description become irrevocably blended with the name itself, in Charlemagne (742–814). And as he lived, so did he die: noble, courageous and God-fearing.

Charlemagne, Charles le Magne, King of the French and Holy Roman Emperor, was in his beloved Aix-la-Chapelle (Aachen) when he first felt a severe pain in his chest. He could not be persuaded to take any of his doctors' remedies and, believing that abstinence would ultimately cure him, refused all food. When he realized that he was not going to recover, Charlemagne called for the Archbishop of Cologne to administer the Holy Sacrament. Though weak, he made the sign of the cross, joined his hands together in prayer and said, 'Into thy hands, O Lord, I commend my spirit.' The dead emperor was buried, with much pomp, in the church of St Mary at Aix, his seven-foot frame magnificently clad in royal robes (this, despite being the son of Pepin the Short!).

In 997 the Emperor Otto III had Charlemagne's tomb at Aix opened: 'Charles the Great was seated upright like a living person in a chair. He was crowned with a golden diadem; his hands were covered with gloves through which the nails had grown; in his right hand he held a sceptre, his sword was by his side, and on his knees was a manuscript of the Gospels. We paid our homage in the act of kneeling. All the limbs were in perfect preservation, but a small portion of the bridge of the nose was missing; this was replaced by gold.' Before he left, Otto removed one of Charlemagne's teeth as a memento.

The tomb was opened again by Emperor Frederick Barbarossa, in the twelfth century, when Charlemagne's bones were placed in a silver chest. In the nineteenth century Empress Josephine visited Aix and was presented with Charlemagne's scapula (shoulder blade) in which was set a piece of the true cross enclosed in a crystal as large as a turkey egg, attached to a gold chain which had once hung round the emperor's neck.[15]

THE DEATH OF VICTORIA

The procession of English and Scottish kings and queens offers up few examples of dignified death and burial. Perhaps this is because medieval kings frequently met violent ends – by torture, murder, death in battle or execution; or when they did die natural deaths, lurid descriptions of their terminal agonies have come down to us. In such a pageant of ignominy and commonplace, the paradigm for a noble death was given by a queen who conspired to die in the manner in which she had endeavoured to live. Queen Victoria (1819–1901) died with regal dignity, going down 'like a great three-decker ship'.

Victoria died at Osborne House on the Isle of Wight, surrounded by many members of her large family – including her son Bertie, later King Edward VII, and her grandson the German kaiser. The queen lapsed in and out of unconsciousness but retained her mental functions to the last. When awake she would ask to have her Pomeranian, Turi, up on the bed beside her. Her children would come and go and at each visit would announce themselves to Victoria, who had long since been virtually blind. Finally the kaiser's presence was revealed: 'Your Majesty, your grandson is here; he has come to see you as you are so ill.' The queen smiled and understood. To everyone's relief the kaiser behaved impeccably. Sinking by slow degrees, Victoria seemed free of pain, her expression calm and dignified 'like that of an old Roman'. She would apologize for the trouble she was causing and would address the dressers as 'my poor girls'.

At about 6.30 p.m. on 22 January the family were summoned for a final time by Sir James Reid, the royal physician. The queen was supported in bed by Reid on the one side and the kaiser on the other. Victoria turned her eyes and gazed at The Entombment of Christ, hanging over the fireplace. And thus she died.

2   THE INGREDIENTS OF ARS MORIENDI

Michel de Montaigne, the sixteenth-century French essayist, said, 'There is no subject I wish more to learn about than people's deaths.' Much of our interest in famous lives concerns the nature of their deaths. Ignominious death, rarely an absolute concept, can take many forms and may depend on factors as diverse as timing, mode and location.

Few men were more terrified of death than Samuel Johnson (1709–84), critic, poet and compiler of the famous dictionary. He spoke about death often, and once declared that he would give one of his legs 'for a year more of life'. He would wonder about when and in what manner his end would come and how he would conduct himself. In 1783 Johnson suffered a stroke and was aware that death was close. In 1784, in deep melancholy, he wrote to a friend, 'It is vain to look round and round for that help which cannot be had. Yet we hope and hope, and fancy that he who has lived today may live tomorrow.'

Throughout his middle and later life Johnson had always sought reassurances, often spuriously given, that he was in good health and looking well. With death approaching fast, uncharacteristically he asked his doctor for a direct answer to a question: 'Tell me plainly, can I recover?' The doctor replied that only a miracle could save him. 'Then I will take no more physic – not even opiates; for I have prayed that I may render up my soul to God, unclouded.' With resigned composure he received the Holy Sacrament.

LIFE'S SPAN AND DEATH'S TIMING

Johnson died in ripe old age, in his own bed, in full possession of his faculties and at peace with his Maker. History is replete with those less fortunate. The biblical yardstick of lifespan is 'three score years and ten', and anyone who reaches this arbitrary figure is deemed, in cricketing parlance, to have had 'a good innings'. But an innings can be judged both quantitively and qualitatively. Longevity alone may be deemed ignominious if it is associated with senility; it may also be the means by which a commoner is interred in Westminster Abbey.

Thomas Parr of Winnington, Shropshire, was 152 years old when he died in the seventeenth century. He married at eighty and was compelled

A sombre, melancholy evocation of Death in Lawnswood Cemetery,
Leeds

to do penance for adultery at the age of 105. Seven years later he married
a second time, 'to the stated satisfaction of his new wife'. Forty years later
he finally succumbed to rich food, strong drink and the sulphurous air of
London. No less a man than William Harvey performed the autopsy.

A qualitatively productive life would appear to have prepared David
Hume for death. The Scottish philosopher died in 1776, aged sixty-five.
Though he had had a long life by eighteenth-century standards, it was
also a remarkably fulfilled life and enabled Hume to approach his death

with dignity and wry good humour. Just before his death he talked to fellow Scot, Adam Smith. Since reading Lucian's *Dialogues of the Dead* Hume had mused about what excuses he might offer Charon, boatman to the other world, for not wishing to come on board. He could find none: he had no house to finish, he had no daughter to provide for, he had no enemies upon whom he wished to revenge himself: 'I have done everything of consequence which I ever meant to do, and I could at no time expect to leave my relations and friends in a better situation than that in which I am now likely to leave them: I therefore have all reason to die content.'

In issues of ignominy, timing is often of greater importance than chronological age. At 5.20 a.m. on Friday, 29 September 1978 a nun served coffee in bed to Albino Luciani. She found Luciani, Pope John Paul I, Vicar of Christ on Earth, dead. It was an instance when the ignominy of murder was reckoned to be less embarrassing than the ignominy of a pope, elected just over a month before, having died from natural causes. Assassination theories proliferated (the most persuasive arguing that John Paul had had his drinks laced with digitalis) in order to minimize talk of God's having intervened personally to force a new election. Recently evidence has accumulated to show that the pontiff suffered from chronic ill-health which did not equip him, physically or mentally, for the arduous task of leader of the Catholic Church. One wonder's how many devout Catholics would have wished a less ignominious death for this pious priest, preferring him to have died Cardinal Luciani rather than Pope John Paul I.[16]

Timing also played an important part in the passing of King George V (1865–1936). The announcement of his impending demise was recorded in the famous bulletin, 'The life of the King is moving peacefully to its close', written on the back of a menu by his doctor, Lord Dawson. In 1968 it was revealed by Dawson's biographer, Francis Watson, that the doctor had taken it upon himself to accelerate death with a lethal mixture of morphine and cocaine injected into the king's jugular vein. Dawson had resorted to euthanasia not for the comfort of the king – since he was already comatose – but so as not further to exhaust the assembled onlookers. A second reason was also given: Dawson wished the announcement of George's death to appear in the morning papers; laggardliness on the king's part ran the risk of the news appearing less 'appropriately' in the 'evening journals'.

As we have seen, timing is a two-edged sword and can lend itself to ignoble or dignified death. A soldier killed in action after peace has been declared dies a death tinged with pathos and ignominy. A movie star whose fame owed more to good looks than acting ability may prefer early death to a lingering middle and old age.

THE MODE OF DEATH

Mayor Cermak of Chicago, Anton von Webern, the composer, and Thomas 'Stonewall' Jackson, Confederate general in the American Civil War, share a common ignominious end: they were all shot by mistake.

Joseph Zangara shot at and missed Franklin Delano Roosevelt and felled Cermak instead.

Webern, one of the most important composers of the twentieth century, died in 1945 near Salzburg. He and his wife had gone to stay with one of their daughters and her husband, Benno Mattel. Mattel, who was mixed up in the black market, was visited by two American soldiers sent to incriminate and arrest him. During their business Webern stepped out into the unlit corridor in order to smoke a cigar. He bumped into one of the soldiers, who, imagining himself attacked, turned and shot him three times in the stomach.

Jackson's death was the most ignominious of the three, since he was accidently shot by his own men. In May 1863 this brilliant soldier routed a much larger Union force at Chancellorsville. After the battle Jackson was riding at dusk on the outskirts of his camp when he was shot three times, once in the left arm, by a sentry who mistook him for the enemy. The arm was subsequently amputated but Jackson died of post-operative complications. Such an ignoble death is rendered all the more capricious by the intended compliment of General Robert E. Lee: 'You are better off than I am, for while you have lost your left, I have lost my right arm.'

Many of us have a particular horror of certain modes of death, and death by drowning, lightning, fire and murder fall into this abhorred category. Two – murder and drowning – combined to bring about the death of the duke of Clarence, brother of King Edward IV (1442–83). Clarence was imprisoned in the Tower of London and died 'by being plunged into a jar of sweet wine' – drowned in 'a butt of malmsey'. 'Mad' King Ludwig II of Bavaria (1845–86), patron of the composer Richard Wagner, committed suicide by drowning in Starnberg Lake, taking with him Dr Bernhard von Gudden, his unwilling psychiatrist.

There appears to be something vaguely ridiculous about being killed by lightning, a sentiment expressed by Pope in his 'Epitaph on the Stanton-Harcourt Lovers':

Here lie two poor Lovers, who had the mishap
Though very chaste people, to die of a clap

And how much more ridiculous was the death of Marcus of Arethusa, who was smeared with honey, hoisted up in a basket and stung to death by bees?

Death by burning at the stake was for centuries the method of getting rid of heretics. But while burning is calculated to inflict maximum pain and humiliation on the victim, ignominy frequently has less to do with the mode of dispatch and more to do with an attitude of mind. The reign of Mary Tudor, 1553–8, posed a threat to England's fledgling Protestantism. The vigour with which the Catholic Queen persecuted 'heretics' earned for her the sobriquet 'Bloody' Mary. It is often debated how much Mary was personally responsible, but what is not in doubt is that in the last three years of her reign 300 people were burned at the stake. Many of Mary's victims featured in Foxe's *Book of Martyrs*. Three such martyrs were Hugh Latimer, Nicholas Ridley and Thomas Cranmer.

Latimer and Ridley died on the same pyre, opposite Balliol College, Oxford, in October 1555. Latimer, Bishop of Worcester under Henry VIII, and Ridley, Bishop of London, refused to embrace Catholicism and perished as a consequence. An ignominious death by fire was eclipsed by the dignity with which these two churchmen met their end. Ridley comforted his companion: 'Be of good heart, brother, for God will either assuage the fury of the flame or strengthen us to abide it.' God chose the second option. As the faggots were lit, it became Latimer's turn to encourage Ridley: 'Be of good comfort, Master Ridley, and play the man. We shall this day light such a candle, by God's grace, in England, as I trust shall never be put out.' Ridley replied (in Latin): 'Into your hands, O Lord, I commend my spirit; Lord, receive my spirit.' Latimer seemed to embrace the flames and quickly died. Ridley was not as fortunate, and was heard to cry out, 'I cannot burn.' His brother-in-law made desperate

The tomb of William Squire, an eighteenth-century weaver, in Burton Lazars, Leicestershire. Famous as 'the tomb that has everything', it has guaranteed that Squire is remembered long after his death.

but ineffectual efforts to stoke the flames and hasten his end. Finally the flames ignited the small bags of gunpowder which had been tied around his neck, and Ridley was released from his agonies.

In the next year Thomas Cranmer, former Archbishop of Canterbury, followed Latimer and Ridley to the stake. Cranmer had risen to power and influence as a supporter of Henry VIII's efforts to rid himself of Catherine of Aragon and marry Anne Boleyn. When Edward VI died, he was reluctantly persuaded to throw his weight behind Lady Jane Grey's candidature for queen of England. For this miscalculation and upon Mary's accession, he was imprisoned. Pressure was brought to bear to induce him to disavow Protestantism, and Cranmer signed a succession of humiliating recantations. In March 1556, when he was publicly to declare his previous heresies before an audience gathered in front of St Mary's Church, Oxford, instead he recanted his recantations '... as things written with my hand contrary to the truth which I thought in my heart'. He vowed that the offending and 'unworthy right hand' should burn first, and when tied to the stake he stretched out his hand and plunged it deep into the flames.

King Charles I was murdered by commoners. Rasputin, the 'Mad Monk', was murdered by a prince. And like Damiens, Grigori Rasputin (?1864–1916) proved difficult to dispatch. In 1905 Rasputin was introduced to the Russian imperial family and almost immediately won the confidence of Tsarina Alexandra because of the beneficial effects he seemed to exert upon the course of the haemophilia suffered by her son Alexis. Such power was bound to invoke envy, and Rasputin's life was constantly threatened. In 1916, with the Tsar away and Rasputin in virtual control of the country and the war against Germany going badly, an assasination plot was hatched by Prince Felix Yussoupov and four conspirators to rid Russia of this meddlesome monk. Yussoupov was once described as 'the most beautiful young man in Europe'. He loved to dress up in female clothes and flirt with soldiers. In Paris, dressed as a woman, he was once admired by Britain's King Edward VII.

The plan was to ply Rasputin with chocolate cake and wine, both containing cyanide 'sufficient to kill several men instantly'. With the rest of the gang upstairs, Yussoupov and Rasputin met in the basement of the prince's residence. Greedily Rasputin tucked into the cake and consumed vast amounts of the poisoned madeira. Yussoupov waited for the monk to drop down dead, but Rasputin continued to eat and drink. After 2½ hours the prince suddenly lost his nerve and his patience, rushed upstairs and returned with a loaded revolver. He shot Rasputin in the chest. The monk fell to the floor, and a doctor, one of the conspirators, pronounced him dead. But the diagnosis was premature: Rasputin suddenly opened his eyes and lunged at Yussoupov, who ran upstairs, terrified. Behind the prince, clambering on all fours, came Rasputin, roaring his fury and hatred. In the courtyard Rasputin yelled 'Felix! Felix! I will tell everything to the Tsarina!' before he was brought down by two more bullets. The prince then battered his head with a rubber cosh. The body was dragged back into the basement, its arms and legs bound tightly with rope. Later that night Rasputin was dumped into the freezing waters of the Neva. Some versions of the story have the 'corpse' bursting free of his bonds before finally drowning. An autopsy demonstrated water in the lungs, suggesting that Rasputin was indeed alive when he entered the river.

Yussoupov's punishment was to be exiled where he recounted his story in a series of newspaper articles in *The Sunday Chronicle*.

IGNOMINY OF PLACE

Sixty-nine-year-old Jean, Cardinal Danielou, died in a flat on the Rue Dulong, Paris, in May 1974. Danielou was Jesuist theologian, ecclesiastical scholar and strong advocate of clerical celibacy, and his death caused a national sensation simply because of *where*, not *how*, he died. The flat, owned by a Madame Santoni, was in the Etoile, deep in the red-light district of the city, and among the crowd that gathered to gaze upon the body of the dead cleric were women 'well known to the police of the 17th arrondissement as prostitutes'. Madame Santoni, aged twenty-four, plied her trade as a procuress while her husband languished in gaol for living off immoral earnings.

The official version had the cardinal going about his pastoral duties proselytizing sinners, and declared that the large wad of notes he carried was to pay off a blackmailer of one of his parishioners. The situation was not helped by the discovery, six months later, of the dead body of Monsignor Roger Tort, aged fifty-seven, the Catholic bishop of Montauban, whose body was found in 'an establishment used solely for prostitution'.

The posthumous reputations of film stars may be positively enhanced by death in lascivious locations. John Garfield died in 1952, in bed, but not alone. A Hollywood wit suggested the epitaph, 'Died in the saddle.' Or even statesmen: bachelor President Felix Faure expired in 1899 in the Elysée Palace in the arms of one Madame Steinheil. This story is a titbit of history well known to most French schoolchildren.

3   SUICIDE: TO CHOOSE HOW AND WHEN TO DIE

People commit suicide for a variety of reasons, but in a large number of cases it is a deliberate decision taken to avoid the indignity of old age, senility or pain – whether physical or emotional.[17] The association between mental illness and suicide is difficult to gauge: some people would contend that suicide is proof positive of mental imbalance, regardless of whether a psychiatrist has diagnosed a formal mental illness. It was Cyril Joad (1891–1953) who wryly observed that in England you must not commit suicide, on pain of being regarded as a criminal if you fail and a lunatic if you succeed.[18]

Attitudes to suicide have varied markedly in different times, countries and religions. Many hold that a person has an unalienable right to take his or her own life; others, equally as strongly, contend that life is a gift from God and only He decides when it shall be given up. The word 'suicide' is a relatively new one. In England, prior to the seventeenth century, the words 'self-homicide' or 'self-murder' were commonly used. Edward Philipps in his *New World of Words*, published in 1662, commenting on the use of the word, leaves us in no doubt about his feelings: '... *suicide*, a word which I would have preferred to be derived from *sus*, a sow, rather than from the pronoun *sui* ... as if it were a swinish part for a man to kill himself.'

A BRIEF HISTORY OF SUICIDE

It was once asserted that suicide was a disease of civilization and that members of primitive societies did not kill themselves. Nineteenth-century psychiatrists were fond of stating that native tribes were not capable of the profound emotions necessary to move one to commit suicide – conveniently ignoring the many thousands of Negro slaves shipped to the New World who killed themselves in abject despair and in the hope that their souls might return to their native Africa. The truth is much more complicated: in some parts of the world suicide is virtually unknown, while in others it is a relatively common occurrence.

In classical Greece and Rome, suicide was an accepted means of

A dramatic depiction of Death pitilessly claiming his victim. Roubiliac's monument to Lady Elizabeth Nightingale in Westminster Abbey, 1761.

hastening reunion with one's ancestors. This was the time of 'the honour suicide', a description which subsumed at least three major motives for ending one's own life: the warrior who wished to escape his enemies; the woman who wished to safeguard her chastity; and the person who wanted to die with dignity rather than suffer the ignominy of disease or senility. The ancient Greeks and Romans looked tolerantly upon suicide, and anyone who was moved to take their own life was not regarded as a criminal. Indeed, three philosophical schools – Cynics, Stoics and Epicureans – actively encouraged the practice. Stoics taught that it was a man's right to live in dignity and that he was at liberty to seek escape from anything that might compromise such dignity, be that disease, senility or being compelled to live under a political tyranny.

The philosophy was encapsulated by Epictetus: 'Be not more timid than boys at play. As they, when they cease to take pleasure in their games, declare they will no longer play, so do you when all things begin to pall upon you, retire; but if you stay, do not complain.' Seneca was more cryptic: 'Do you seek the way to freedom? You may find it in every vein of your body.' His views on old age would readily find echoes today: 'I will not relinquish old age if it leaves my better part intact. But if it begins to shake my mind, if it destroys its faculties one by one, if it leaves me not life but breath, I will depart from the putrid or tottering edifice.'

Even though many eminent Greeks and Romans committed suicide, often for reasons of political expediency or to escape the vicissitudes of disease or old age, it must be remembered that three of the greatest philosophers, Pythagoras, Aristotle and Plato, railed against a practice that they regarded as cowardly and undignified. According to them, man owed it to himself and his country to endure suffering and not to flee prematurely from it.

Nowhere in the New Testament is suicide explicitly condemned. Indeed, some have argued that the majority of the early Christian martyrs were suicides, since they knew that open profession of their faith would incur capital punishment, and yet did so. Jesus Christ's death has been viewed by some as such.

It was not until the fourth century, and the invective of St Augustine, that the Christian Church began to denounce suicide as sinful and inspired by the Devil. The suicide's crime was to have destroyed God's creation. Indeed, Judas Iscariot's more heinous sin was not to betray Christ but to hang himself afterwards. Early in its history, the Church's opprobrium towards suicides was compromised by its need to excuse the 'voluntary' suicides of the martyrs , of those devout Christians who accelerated their death by self-deprivation and asceticism, and of women who killed themselves to protect their virginity or chastity. By the end of the fifth century the attitude of the Christian Church had hardened to such an extent that not even the martyr, ascetic or virgin could claim absolution. At the Council of Braga in 563 it was decided that *all* suicides were to be punished, unless they were proven insane. Such punishment took two forms: indignities perpetrated on the corpse itself, and forfeiture of the deceased's property. The indignities varied from place to place, each community having its local customs set down for the burial of suicides. In Danzig, for instance, the corpse was not allowed to leave the room through the door but through the window; in some parts of England the body was not allowed to enter the churchyard through the gate but over the wall.

It was common for the Church to deny the suicide burial in consecrated ground, and the custom grew up of interment at night at a crossroads with a stake driven through the heart. The last person to suffer such degradation was a man named Griffiths who was buried at the junction of Grosvenor Place and the King's Road, Chelsea, in 1823. Such bizarre practices are thought by some to have had their origins in primitive beliefs and taboos, and to have been aimed at pre-empting the vengeance of the suicide's ghost – because it was assumed that, since society had driven a man to suicide, his ghost would return to seek retribution and punishment for those responsible for his death. This need for society to protect itself explains many of the diverse indignities perpetrated upon the corpse: the complete annihilation of the body in order to render the ghost harmless; the amputation of a suicide's hand, on the assumption that one-handed ghosts were less formidable; the stake driven through the heart to prevent the ghost from 'walking'; and burial at a crossroads to confuse the ghost about direction.

In France some unfortunate suicides were dragged head down through the streets, while in Metz the bodies were bundled into barrels and floated down the Moselle to be carried out to sea.

With all these disincentives, it is hardly surprising that suicide was formerly considered to have been rare in the Middle Ages. More recent authors have suggested that the true incidence was a great deal higher than formerly acknowledged, and that medieval suicide was often concealed by relatives in order that the deceased might receive a Christian burial. Certainly many cases are recorded of people who committed suicide in order to avoid the protracted agonies of dying of plague.[19]

A readier acceptance of suicide came with the Renaissance and its increasing interest in the melancholic disposition. With the pursuit of knowledge came uncertainty, and with uncertainty came the realization of the shortness of life and the endlessness of eternity. Suicide became the thinking man's solution to the 'slings and arrows of outrageous fortune'. Hamlet was the epitome of a Renaissance man. Apologists for suicide began to appear: Robert Burton, whose gloomy masterpiece *Anatomy of Melancholy* appeared in 1621; and John Donne, Dean of St

Paul's Cathedral, whose *Biothanatos. A Declaration of that Paradoxe, or Thesis, That Self-homicide is not so naturally Sinne, that it may never be otherwise*, published posthumously in 1644, became the first defence of suicide in English. Another such was *Pelecanicidium*, written by Sir William Denney in 1653, which took its title from the notion that pelicans end their lives by committing suicide.[20] Interest in the subject may be gauged by the fact that Burton's prose far outsold Shakespeare's poetry in the seventeenth century. Yet it was Shakespeare, speaking through Hamlet, who encapsulated the dilemma of the times in Hamlet's soliloquy 'To be or not to be, that is the question.' So popular an issue did suicide become that no fewer than fourteen of Shakespeare's characters exited in this manner.[21]

The result of such speculations was the emergence of a more humane attitude and a greater tolerance shown to suicides, especially among the intelligentsia. But the Church remained obdurate, except when granting dispensations to aristocratic suicides in order to allow them a Christian burial. Such social discrimination is well illustrated in *Hamlet*: Ophelia, despite committing suicide, is allowed religious obsequies in death because of her station in life.

Fresh arguments for a man's innate liberty to take his own life were voiced in the 'Age of Enlightenment', with David Hume's famous *Essay on Suicide*, published in 1789. Although the French have always thought the English particularly prone to suicide ('*Anglomane*', 'English madness', was a penchant generally ascribed to the weather), many of their philosophers argued as vehemently as their English counterparts against ecclesiastical orthodoxy. Montesquieu, Voltaire and Rousseau aligned themselves with the pro-suicide faction and defended self-destruction.

Two famous eighteenth-century British suicides caused a national sensation and brought the whole subject into the public arena. Thomas Creech took his own life in 1700, and Richard Smith and his wife decided to commit suicide in 1732.

Creech (1659–1700) had long decided on suicide and wrote in the margin of his translation of Lucretius, 'NB. I must remember to hang myself when I have finished my commentary.' He did indeed hang himself, but not for another twenty years, during which time he translated the works of Horace. (Voltaire, who believed that one was less likely to commit suicide if one had enough to do, maintained that Creech would have lived longer had he been translating Ovid.) Although he was officially deemed insane, Creech's death had a profound effect on the way in which suicide came to be regarded by the educated melancholic.

Richard Smith was a bookbinder who was imprisoned for debt together with his wife and 2-year-old daughter. They decided on a permanent end to their problems: they killed their daughter as she slept and then hanged themselves, having written a long suicide note which detailed the reasons for their actions – as well as a request for their landlord to look after the dog and cat. People endlessly debated the pros and cons, especially how despair borne of poverty could be reconciled with a caring God. The Smiths wrote:

> …We apprehend the taking of our child's life away to be a circumstance for which we shall be generally condemned; but for our own parts we are perfectly easy on that head. We are satisfied that it is less cruelty to take the child with us, even supposing a state of annihilation as some dream of, than to leave her friendless in the world, exposed to ignorance and misery … And as we know the wonderful God to be Almighty, so we cannot help believing that he is also good – not implaccable, not like such wretches as men are, not taking delight in the misery of his creatures; for which reason we resign up our breath to him without any terrible apprehensions, submitting ourselves to those ways which in his goodness he shall please to appoint after death … [We] leave the disposal of our bodies to the wisdom of the coroner and his jury, the thing being indifferent to us where our bodies are laid …[22]

Although outwardly the Church remained adamant in its continued condemnation of suicide, religious and legal attitudes began to soften in the eighteenth and nineteenth centuries. In 1823 Parliament decided to do away with crossroads burial and permit suicides to be interred in graveyards. Such burials were frequently confined to 'suicides' corner and were conducted at night, between the hours of nine and midnight, without religious ceremony. It took another half a century before forfeiture of a suicide's property and lands was finally abolished and for the corpse not to be automatically given over to the medical schools for dissection. In acts passed in 1879 and 1882 suicide ceased to be legally regarded as homicide, and day-time burial was finally allowed.

In the 'Age of Romanticism', suicide became fashionable, and young men throughout Europe flocked to end their lives in the manner of Thomas Chatterton or Goethe's Werther. (Both these famous suicides will be considered in more detail later.)

The twentieth century has seen the rise and rise of the depressive and societal suicide, of which type Richard Smith and his wife were eighteenth-century precedents. Emil Durkheim has suggested that the prevalence of suicide within a society varies inversely with its sense of cohesion. It follows that during those times when society pulls together (as in times of war), suicide rates fall; when society fractures and individuals compete rather than co-operate, suicide rates will rise. In a society which equates happiness and fulfilment with wealth and beauty, it is little wonder that the poor and the ugly so frequently have recourse to suicide. And yet the notion of making death meaningful continues to have a powerful draw on the imagination.

Jacob Epstein's memorial to Oscar Wilde in Père-Lachaise Cemetery, Paris. The story goes that two English women were so affronted at the overly-endowed winged sphinx that they neutered the creature to save feminine sensibilities.

Cesare Pavese (1908–50), conceding that death is inevitable and unpredictable, asks, 'Why not seek death of one's own free will, asserting one's right to choose, giving it some significance instead of passively letting it happen? Why not?' Pavese answers his own questions: 'In short, because one thinks – and I speak for myself – that there is plenty of time. So the day of natural death comes, and we have missed the great opportunity of performing, *for a specific reason*, the most important act in life.'[23]

VARIETIES OF SUICIDE

Honour Suicides

While the following varieties of suicide are claimed to be neither comprehensive nor mutually exclusive, honour suicide is a rubric which subsumes many sub-categories of suicide, including suicides of the vanquished in battle, heroic and altruistic suicide, and suicide to protect virginity or chastity. Some political suicides are committed because of impending dishonour.

Greek mythology provides us with an archetypal honour suicide. When Jocasta discovered that she had inadvertently married her son Oedipus, the man who had innocently killed her husband Laius (who was also Oedipus's own father), such were her shame and grief that she hanged herself.

Suicides of the vanquished were not uncommon: Hannibal (247–182 BC), the Carthaginian general and the man who took elephants across the Alps, swallowed poison rather than surrender to Rome; Boadicea (or Boudicca), first-century British warrior-queen of the Iceni, also took poison after her defeat by Suetonius Paulinus (and, incidentally, is reputed to be buried under Platform 10 at Liverpool Street Station, London); twentieth-century Nazis are represented by Hitler and Himmler, the latter committing suicide by breaking the capsule of cyanide that he always carried between his teeth.

In Japan the honour suicide was mainly recourse to committing hara-kiri, the ancient practice of self-disembowelment. There were two types of hara-kiri: compulsory and voluntary. When a nobleman was found to have broken the laws or to have been disloyal, the usual punishment was to commit hara-kiri using a jewelled dagger sent for that very purpose by the mikado (emperor). In an elaborate and dignified ceremony, the suicide would kneel on a red felt carpet raised a few feet above the ground in order to afford the audience a good view. Dressed for the occasion, the victim would take the mikado's dagger and plunge it up to the hilt into his left side, just below the waist. Slowly the blade would be moved to the right inside the abdomen, being first turned and then drawn upwards. Added honour was bestowed on the suicide if he managed to inflict the fatal wound without flinching. When it was clear that the dagger had pierced the stomach, a friend of the victim would put the man out of his agony by swiftly decapitating him. The practice of hara-kiri was once so common that Montesquieu could comment wryly that the Japanese 'rip open their bellies for the least fancy'. Compulsory hara-kiri was made illegal in 1868, but the voluntary type has never been completely eliminated from Japanese culture and continues to be a method of dispatch even in our own time – especially to avoid disgrace or humiliation.

Perhaps the most celebrated 'vanquished honour' suicide was Marcus Procius Cato (95–46 BC). He was a man who inspired respect rather than affection from his fellow Romans. A brave soldier, he fled to Greece and then to Libya when Julius Caesar crossed the Rubicon in 49 BC. Refusing to compromise his high principles by living under the rule of a tyrant, Cato decided upon suicide. After having ensured the safety of his men, he ate supper with his son, after which he retired to bed to read *Phaedo*, Plato's treatise on the soul. At dawn, after a short sleep, he drew his sword and plunged the blade into his chest. Cato's alleged last words, 'And now I am master of myself', epitomize the sentiment of men who hold that to choose the moment and mode of one's own death is an inviolable human right.

Even had Cato been captured by Caesar, it is likely that the victor would have given to the vanquished the opportunity to commit suicide. It represented honour in defeat. (Indeed, Caesar might have spared Cato altogether, since he is reputed to have said, 'Cato, I grudge you your death as you have grudged me the preservation of your life.')

Seneca (5 BC–65 AD), the Roman philosopher and statesman, illustrates the *genre*. After he had fallen out of favour with his former pupil, Nero, word reached him that the emperor wished him dead. With admirable stoicism the old man mused that it was no more than one might have expected from someone who had already killed his mother and brother. With his villa surrounded by Nero's soldiers, Seneca prepared to die. He embraced his wife Paulina and urged her not to give way to grief. She determined that they should die together as proof of their love for one another. Consequently both had the veins in their arms opened. Unfortunately, probably due to Seneca's sluggish circulation, his blood merely trickled from the open vessels. He asked that the blood vessels in his legs be opened. He also requested that Paulina be moved to another room to spare her witnessing his suffering. In another attempt to accelerate his end, Seneca swallowed a cup of hemlock, the poison that had despatched Socrates nearly 500 years before. With the philosopher *in extremis*, his slaves and attendants had recourse to a bath of hot water to quicken the loss of blood. Finally he died and, according to his wishes, was cremated. Nero, who had no use for martyrs, ordered that Paulina's wounds be dressed and the blood loss staunched.

Two other Roman wives succeeded where Paulina failed. Portia, after Brutus's suicide at Philippi, took her own life by swallowing red-hot coals. When Caecina Paetus was condemned to death by the Emperor Claudius, his wife Arria, seeing her husband hesitate, took the dagger and stabbed herself. Handing him the weapon, she said, 'Paetus, it doesn't hurt.'

An example of the 'chastity suicide' is Sophronia, who was unfortunate enough to have been admired by Emperor Maxentius. When Sophronia's husband consented to her being given over to satisfy the emperor's sexual appetite, and Maxentius arrived to claim his prize, Sophronia asked for a few minutes to prepare herself. Straightaway she plunged a dagger into her breast. St Augustine excused Sophronia, who had later been canonized for her action, by saying that she, and a small number of other woman, had had a special dispensation from God. But pagan women had no such excuse, and St Augustine had harsh words to say about Lucrece, the most famous chastity suicide of all. The rapist, Sextus, son of Tarquinius Superbus, was merely banished for his crime. According to St Augustine, it was Lucrece who committed the greater crime, since chastity is an attitude of the mind and not a state of the

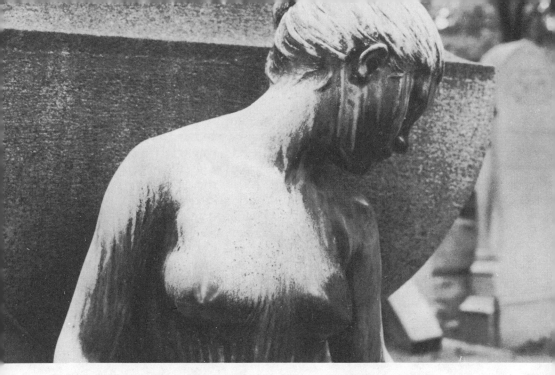

A gift to the living from the dead: the highly polished breasts of this tarnished bronze nude testify to the pleasure given to generations of male palms by a deceased benefactor buried in Père-Lachaise Cemetery, Paris.

body. 'Lucrece, so celebrated and lauded, slew the innocent, chaste, outraged Lucrece.'

Although suicide to safeguard chastity was condemned by the Church, mutilation for the same purpose was not. In 870 Ebba, a Yorkshire abbess, and all the nuns in her convent, when besieged by the Danes, cut off their upper lips and noses rather than endanger their virtue.

Imitative Suicide

According to the poet Byron, no one who has ever handled an open razor has not, at some time, had the fleeting temptation to draw the blade across the throat. A similar phenomenon occurs when perfectly sane people edge towards a precipice and imagine what it would be like to throw themselves over.

Sometimes it needs only one person to slit his throat or jump from a high building for a host of imitative suicides to follow. Favoured places to commit suicide include the London Monument (from which Elizabeth Moyes threw herself in 1839 and thereby started a fashion), St Peter's Basilica in Rome, the Campanile in Venice and the Kegon Waterfall near Tokyo. The column at the Place Vendôme in Paris had to be closed to the public in 1881 because of the numbers of people hurling themselves down. New Yorkers have the pick of hundreds of skyscraper buildings.

In February 1933 Kiyoko Matsumoto, a 19-year-old schoolgirl, plunged to her death by jumping into the open mouth of the volcano of Mihara-Yama on the island of Oshima, Japan. Her suicide caused a sensation and prompted thousands of imitators. In the remainder of 1933 another 143 followed Miss Matsumoto into the crater, and on one day alone there were six successful suicides and twenty-five unsuccessful attempts. In the next year the volcano claimed another 167. So great was public interest that boatloads of tourists flocked to the island. Visitors could dine at the coastal restaurants, take a camel ride to the top of Mihara-Yama and, on a good day, witness a suicide or two. 1,208 people attempted suicide in two years before a barrier was errected around the crater and it was made a criminal offence to purchase a one-way ticket to Oshima.

Plutarch tells of an epidemic of frenzied women in Miletos who committed suicide by hanging themselves. The 'plague' seemed to be of 'an unearthly character and beyond human remedy' until one of the city worthies hit upon a powerful disincentive: 'The body of every young woman who hangs herself is to be dragged naked through the streets by the same rope as which she committed the deed.' The same expedient was used centuries later, when a similar epidemic broke out in Marseilles: the body of every woman guilty of 'self-murder' was to be publicly exposed. The prospect of posthumous indignity brought the imitative suicides to an abrupt end.

And just to show that imitation is not solely a female prerogative, the story is told of a French soldier who hanged himself at the Invalides in 1792. Twelve others quickly followed his example by suspending themselves from the same hook. It was not until someone had the brilliant idea of removing the hook that the epidemic ceased.

Eccentric and Exhibitionist Suicide

There is only one way to be born and a thousand ways to die.
Serbian proverb

'Eccentricity in suicide' may be applied either to the motive or to the method. Perhaps the most famous example of the former is Zeno (342–279 BC), founder of Stoic philosophy, who was so disgusted by falling and stubbing his toe that he hobbled home and promptly hanged himself.

A great deal more forethought and planning went into a double suicide in Paris in the last century. Two young men decided to dine out in grand style, no expense spared. The best food on the menu was accompanied by superior champagne and followed by cognac – and the bill. The youths had attracted attention throughout their meal by their loud and raucous laughter. The bill caused them to break into even louder guffaws. They called for the owner.

> ... the elder of the two informed him that the dinner was excellent, which was the more fortunate, as it was decidedly the last that either of them should ever eat; that for his bill he must of necessity excuse the payment as neither of them possessed a single sou; that upon no other occasion would they have thus violated the customary etiquette between guest and landlord; but that finding this world with its toils and its troubles, unworthy of them, they had determined once more to enjoy a repast and then take their leave of existence! For the first part of this resolution, he declared that it had, thanks to the cook and his cellar, been achieved nobly; that for the last, it would soon follow, for the *café noir*, besides the little glass of his admirable cognac, had been medicated with that which would speedily settle all their accounts for them.[24]

There was little the restaurateur could do except inform the police. Alas, by the time the *gendarmes* arrived at their lodgings, the poison had taken effect.

Although a young Polish woman may well have been insane, the method she chose to end her life could only be considered bizarre and eccentric: unhappy in love, over a period of five months she swallowed four spoons, three knives, nineteen coins, twenty nails, seven window-bolts, a brass cross, 101 pins, a stone, three pieces of glass and two rosary beads.

In the nineteenth century a Parisian lady procured her end by applying a hundred leeches to her body, and a man threw himself into the bear pit at the Jardin du Roi.

Another mentally unstable person who chose an eccentric method to attempt suicide was Matthew Lovat, an eighteenth-century Italian shoemaker. His mental condition first showed itself when he castrated himself as a young man. The ridicule that this aroused in his native village of Casale forced him to move to Venice. A year later he tried to crucify himself in the street but was stopped when he attempted to nail his left foot to a wooden cross. He returned to Casale and began work making a second cross, which he attached to a rope suspended from the ceiling of his third-floor room.

With the cross laid flat on the floor, Lovat stripped off save for a handkerchief girding his loins. He donned a crown of thorns. Slipping his feet into a specially made bracket, he proceeded to hammer a nail through his feet into the wood of the cross. He tied his body securely to the shaft of the cross to prevent him slipping off and imitated Christ's spear wound by cutting himself with a knife. Next, using his free hands, he edged the cross towards the window ledge, until it overbalanced and fell vertically out into the street. Thus suspended, Lovat used his left hand to nail his right into the cross; predictably he found it impossible to nail his left, despite the fact that he had previously pierced the palm with a nail. Equally predictably, his actions did not go unnoticed by passers-by, who rushed to his rescue.

The self-crucifixion of Matthew Lovat. Redrawn by Robin Boutell from F. Winston's *Anatomy of Suicide* (London, 1840).

Lovat's third attempt at suicide was successful but more orthodox. He starved himself to death in a lunatic asylum.

The twentieth century saw a new variant of eccentric suicide. The vast wastage of human life during the First World War prompted many young intellectuals to question the values of the older generation. This total rejection of traditional precepts spawned the Dada movement, whose members regarded art and life as equally meaningless and worthless and who looked upon suicide as merely an expression of art in a morally bankrupt world. Jacques Vaché was an eccentric dandy who used to idle away many hours arranging and rearranging the photographs and flowers on his bedside table. Vaché believed life to be futile and maintained, like the Stoics before him, that he would choose when he was to die. He added that to die alone was boring and that he intended to die in the company of friends. In 1919 at the age of twenty-three, he and two friends died together. The 'triple suicide' was not what it appeared, since he had neglected to tell his friends about the lethal dose of opium he had prepared. To Vaché, such a suicide and double murder would add immeasurably to the significance of this supreme Dada gesture.

In 1970 Christine Hubbock ended her life in a sensational and public way. She was an American television newsreader who shot herself in the head in the middle of a programme: 'And now, in keeping with Channel 40's policy of always bringing you the latest in blood and guts, in living colour, you're about to see another first – an attempted suicide.'

'You'll Be Sorry' Suicides

Many turn to suicide in order to punish those they leave behind. Besides the naming of individuals, much of the invective in a suicide note is directed towards the society that the suicide holds responsible for driving him to his death. Such a suicide was Thomas Chatterton (1752–70).

Brought up in penury by his widowed mother in Bristol, in his early teens Chatterton became apprenticed to an scrivener. The preparation of legal documents probably gave him the idea of concocting medieval poetry, which he wrote on parchment in an ancient hand, complete with Chaucer-like spelling. At the age of seventeen Chatterton sent 'The Ryse of Peyncteynge yn Englande, wroten by T. Rowleie 1469, for Mastre Canynge' to Horace Walpole, claiming to have discovered it in the muniment room of St Mary Redcliffe. Walpole was so completely deceived by the Rowley poems that Chatterton was promted to send more. Inevitably it was not long before the poems were shown to be fakes, and Chatterton felt the full force of Walpole's fury at having been so duped.

Wounded by his fall from grace and outraged by snubs and

condescension from people he considered his intellectual inferiors, Chatterton's thoughts turned to suicide. He wrote a suicide note but, whether intentionally or otherwise, left it where his master would be likely to find it. A second intended suicide attempt was prevented by the discovery of a Last Will and Testament containing vitriolic attacks upon the philistinism of Bristol worthies. It was a classic example of the 'You'll be sorry when I'm dead' *genre* and proved too much for Chatterton's master, who dismissed him immediately.

Chatterton moved to London to seek the fame and fortune he felt he so richly deserved. For a time his circumstances improved and he was able to make a modest income from his writing. He found a champion in William Bingley, editor of *North Briton*, a prestigious weekly publication. Bingley agreed to make over an entire issue to Chatterton's work, but Fate had not written such recognition of his genius into Chatterton's life-script. As the presses were about to roll, Bingley contracted rheumatic fever and died. Chatterton's chance was gone and his embryonic career developed no further.

His ambition ruthlessly thwarted, Chatterton was found by his landlady, lying dead on his bed, his features horribly contorted by the effects of arsenic. Torn manuscripts littered the floor of the dingy garret. He died three months short of his eighteenth birthday and was buried in a pauper's grave.

The disproportionate importance of Chatterton, precocious and disregarded genius, lay in the example he set for the Romantic poets who were to succeed him. His life came to represent the association of genius and youth, the very antithesis of mediocrity and middle-age. Frustrated poets and artists bade farewell to an unappreciative world by emulating Chatterton. In France would-be novelists and painters flocked to join Suicide Clubs, believing that to die by one's own hand would ensure lasting fame. De Vigny's *Chatterton* was held responsible for a doubling of the suicide rate in France in the 1830s.

Romantic Suicide

Suicide for love is the very stuff of romantic fiction and has a long pedigree. The story of Hero and Leander can be regarded as typical of someone who committed suicide because they could not contemplate life without a loved one. Leander fell in love with Hero and, guided by a light, would swim the Hellespont every night to be with her. One night a storm blew out the light, and Leander was drowned. Hero, bereft, threw herself into the sea in order to die with her lover.

A real-life double suicide occurred in France. Faldoni was a handsome young man who fell in love with a beautiful young woman in Lyons. Her

The Death of Chatterton by Henry Wallis (1856).

parents refused consent for their betrothal. In deep despair the man suffered an injury whilst fencing, which his doctors told him would prove fatal. He arranged to meet his lover in an empty church. She arrived with two pistols. Embracing for the last time they prepared to die together. A rose-coloured ribbon was tied around each trigger. Simultaneously each pulled the ribbon which fired the gun at the other. They fell together. Rousseau was inspired to write a laudatory epitaph for the 'lovers of Lyons'.

The truth about the deaths of Archduke Rudolph and Baroness Marie Vetsera was hushed up by Rudolph's father, Emperor Francis Joseph of Austria. Rudolph (1858–89) was the heir to the Habsburg empire but rebelled against the stiff ceremonial of the Austrian Court, preferring the company of artists and liberals, much to the disapproval of his father. In 1881 Rudolph married Stephanie, daughter of the King of the Belgians, but the match was not a happy one. Over the years Rudolph took many mistresses, including Marie Vetsera, a beautiful young woman still in her teens. Whether he cared for Marie more than his other women is not known with certainty. What is sure is that the couple were found dead at the imperial hunting lodge at Mayerling, just outside Vienna. Rudolph had shot his mistress and then committed suicide. Was it a homicide-suicide, prompted by a love without a future, or, more likely, was Marie the willing dupe of a disillusioned man suffering the hereditary nervous constitution of the Habsburgs? The suicide notes give little clue.

Rudolph wrote to his wife telling her that henceforward she would be free from the torment of his presence. Marie wrote to a friend, expressing thanks, asking forgiveness and suggesting suicide: 'If life becomes hard for you, and I fear it will after what we have done, follow us. It is the best thing you can do.'

Love-suicides became fashionable in the last quarter of the eighteenth century, due, in no small measure, to a young man with the unlikely name of Jerusalem who shot himself as a consequence of an unhappy romance with a married woman. Johann Goethe (1749–1832) dramatized the event in his *Sorrows of Young Werther*, a novel which became a sensation and influenced European attitudes towards suicide for decades. Werther, a sensitive and melancholy artist, is hopelessly in love with Charlotte, a girl engaged to marry another. Ultimately he shoots himself, a martyr to unrequited love. A Werther epidemic broke out across Europe, with pilgrims visiting Jerusalem's grave. Young men dressed Werther-like in blue tail-coats and yellow waistcoats appeared to desire to die in like manner. 'One "new Werther" shot himself with particular *éclat*: having carefully shaved, plaited his pigtail, put on fresh clothes, opened *Werther* at page 218 and laid it on the table, he opened the door, revolver in hand, to attract an audience and, having looked around to make sure they were paying sufficient attention, raised the weapon to his right eye and pulled the trigger.'[25]

Thackeray debunked this fashionable mode of suicide in a well-known satirical verse:

> Charlotte, having seen his body
> Borne before her on a shutter,
> Like a well-conducted person
> Went on cutting bread and butter.

Suicide Pacts and Mass Suicide

The suicide of Heinrich von Kleist, the German poet and dramatist, and Henriette Vogel, in November 1811, had more to do with theatre than love. For years he had asked his cousin Marie to join him in a suicide pact but she had refused. He eventually persuaded Henriette, who was terminally ill with cancer, to agree. He shot her and then turned the gun on himself.

Here is part of the letter he wrote to Marie: 'I assure you, I love you so, you are so exceedingly dear and precious to me, that I can hardly say that I love this dear, this divine friend more than you. The decision that she came to in her soul, to die with me, drew me, I cannot tell you with what inexpressible and irresistible force, to her breast.'

In 1983 Arthur Koestler, writer and journalist, discovered that he was

Mass suicide at Jonestown, Guyana, in 1978, when 400 American followers of the Revd Jim Jones drank cocktails of fruit juice and cyanide.

suffering from Parkinson's disease and a slow-killing variety of leukaemia. He had long been an advocate of euthanasia and decided that he would end his life with an overdose of barbiturates. Koestler, aged seventy-seven, was found sitting in an armchair, a glass of brandy in his hand. In order not to frighten the maid, he had left a note saying: 'Don't go in. Call the police.' Koestler made his motives plain in his last letter:

> Should this attempt fail and I survive it in a physically or mentally impaired state in which I can no longer control what is done to me, I hereby request that I be allowed to die in my own home and not be resuscitated or kept alive by artificial means ... I wish my friends to know that I am leaving their company in a peaceful frame of mind, with some timid hopes for a de-personalised afterlife beyond the confines of space, time and matter and beyond the limits of our comprehension. What makes it nevertheless hard to take this final step is the reflection of the pain it is bound to inflict on my few surviving friends, and above all my wife Cynthia.[26]

He need not have worried about Cynthia, twenty years his junior and in good health. She was found seated opposite her husband, a large whisky on the table beside her.

Death by choice can be a decision taken by a community as a whole or by many members of a community acting individually but more or less simultaneously. Examples of the latter type occur when large numbers of people commit suicide rather than suffer the slow and painful indignity of death by plague: the Black Death in the fourteenth century and later cholera epidemics claimed many uninfected victims who commonly shot themselves or threw themselves out of windows.

To a Jew, human life is sacred. Consequently Jewish suicide was extremely rare. There are only four suicides mentioned in the Old Testament: those of Samson; Saul, who fell upon his sword rather than become the prisoner of the Philistines; Abimelech, wounded by a stone thrown by a woman, killed himself so it might not be said he was slain by a woman; and Ahithophel, who committed suicide in a fit of pique when his advise to Absalom was ignored. Jewish suicides were buried in the clothes they had on when they died, without religious rites and after sunset. Those who died in suspicious circumstances were nearly always given the benefit of the doubt: persons found hanged or impaled on their swords were generally deemed to have been murdered and were given an orthodox burial.

The long history of anti-Semitism is peppered with examples of mass suicide, where Jews have killed themselves rather than face a slow death at the hands of their enemies. The mass suicide of 500 Jews at York in 1190 is an early example. The population set upon the Jewish community, who fled for protection to the castle. A siege ensued and for many days mob fury was whipped up by a fanatical white-robed hermit. Inside the garrison a rabbi exhorted his flock not to allow themselves to be taken alive. Most took his counsel, the men cutting the throats of their wives and children and then killing each other. The few who surrendered bargained to save their lives by offering to be baptized – alas, a forlorn hope.

The inhabitants of the Indian town of Chittor resorted to mass suicide before a conquering army on no fewer than three occasions. In 1303 Ala-ud-din Khilji, the Pathan king of Delhi, besieged the fort in order to capture the beautiful Padmini, who was married to Bhim Singh. When defeat was inevitable, Bhim Singh led his men out to certain death, while Padmini and the women committed *jauhar*, ritual suicide, by throwing themselves onto a funeral pyre. In 1535, when Badadur Shah, Sultan of Gujarat, was victorious, it is said that 32,000 Chittor warriors left the town to meet their deaths, and 13,000 women committed *jauhar*. Finally when, in 1568, the Moghul Emperor Akbar took the town, mass suicide was enacted for the third and final time.

In November 1978 163 women, 138 men and 82 children took their own lives. They were mostly émigré Californians, members of a fanatical sect founded by the Revd Jim Jones, a self-styled Marxist social philosopher. Regarded as a messiah by some and a 'con man' by most, Jones had organized the mass suicide at the People's Temple following the assassination of an American congressman and a television cameraman who he believed had come to expose him as a fraud. Those who were not prepared to drink the home-brewed cocktail of fruit juice and cyanide were either shot or fled into the jungle. The lunacy of Jonestown had included bizarre sexual practices and the punishment of small children by pushing their heads below the water in a deep, dark well. Jones himself, suffering from terminal cancer, died from a bullet in the head – as did his wife, son and mistress.

The 'Ultimate Revenge' Suicide

One famous nineteenth-century suicide could equally as well be categorized as being of the love, spectacular or Chatterton-like 'You'll be sorry' *genre*. A Frenchman who had been betrayed by his mistress planned his suicide in minute detail. Before killing himself he called his servant and gave orders that after his death a candle should be made from his fat and carried, lighted, to his mistress. To accompany it he wrote a note saying that, just as he had burned for her in life, so would he after his death. Proof of his passion she would find in the light by which she read his letter – a flame fed by his miserable body!

AFTERWORD: FEAR OF PLANNING ONE'S OWN FUNERAL

Jessica Mitford, in her best-seller *The American Way of Death*, was one of the first authors to expose the wiles of funeral directors, who focus much forethought and psychology on ways of extracting money from the bereaved.

Take, for instance, the problem of choosing a coffin. It is replete with a veritable maelstrom of psychodynamic forces including depression, injustice, guilt and snobbery – all available to be tapped to the financial advantage of an unscrupulous undertaker. It would be grossly naïve, and poor psychology, for an undertaker to arrange the coffins sequentially in order of price, with the cheapest at one end and the dearest at the other. How much more subtle to have the coffins arranged into four price ranges, two above the average price and two below. The grieving relative is first shown a coffin priced above average, and his reactions are closely studied. Should the buyer recoil at such an expense, he is immediately shown a coffin well below the average price. The contrast in quality is striking and usually has the effect of shaming the buyer into protesting that he did not mean to go *that* low. On the rebound there is a high probability that the relative will opt for a coffin above the average price and only a fraction below the price of the first coffin he was shown.

Other sales strategies, common on both sides of the Atlantic, talk openly of 'average' families and how much they spend on coffins, in the sure expectation that most of us regard ourselves as *above* the average. If the undertaker is obliged to show cheaper models, he will try to foster a sense of guilt by talking about '*savings*'. The seemingly haphazard promenade through the casket room has, in reality, been preplanned with the precision of an army manoeuvre.

The analogy with warfare is, however, less than apt, since the notion of combat usually presupposes an adversary who can anticipate moves made by the other side and attempt effective counter-measures. Such is not the case in the funeral parlour, where the odds are stacked heavily in favour of the undertaker. Few of the bereaved know how much to spend and most are so upset that their everyday sense of 'value for money' is severely compromised. Although it is claimed that a funeral is the third largest expense (after a house and a car), virtually no one attempts to

To plan one's own funeral is
to confront one's own
mortality. A painting by
Anton Wiertz (1806–65).

apply comparative criteria to the services available from local
undertakers. It is virtually unknown for the bereaved to 'shop around' for
bargains, and even rarer for a corpse to be transferred from the care of
one undertaker to that of another. And how many bereaved relatives
ever return to complain about the service they have received?

It is ironic that the management of one's funeral, representing as it
does the ultimate rite of passage, is given over unquestioningly to
strangers who rarely deviate from the commonplace. And yet it is surely
unreasonable to wish to add to the pain of your bereaved relatives the
burden of arranging a tasteful funeral at a reasonable cost. The answer is
obvious: to take over the pre-mortem management of one's own funeral.

To plan one's own funeral is to confront one's own mortality, and it is
for this reason that funeral directors need have no fear of going out of
business. Most of us, like Dr Johnson, think that it is difficult to believe
that someone who is alive today will not be alive tomorrow. Morbid
apprehension of death, or else an unrealistic optimism about one's own
chances of immortality, is usually sufficient to postpone all thoughts about
one's funeral until the time for meaningful planning has passed. Nevertheless, there is an ever-growing number of people who wish to blunt the
commercial excesses, predictability and bad taste of modern funerals and
take an active part in organizing this, the ultimate of earthly ceremonies.

Let us stick with the example of buying a container in which to deposit
a dead body. There are a number of ways of purchasing a coffin – or
'casket' as it is called in funerary parlance. Perhaps the simplest way is to
state a price range for this item in your will, including, not without
irony, a factor to take into account the rising cost of living. Another
expedient may be to purchase 'prior to need': in many Oriental countries

coffins (and shrouds) are given as wedding gifts. Sarah Bernhardt chose and bought her own coffin and is said to have kept it in her bedroom and to have been photographed lying in it.

Those who are economically constrained, or else environmentally aware, might care to investigate eco-friendly, bio-degradable, oak-simulated, reinforced cardboard coffins. The idea is not new, since 'earth-to-earth' coffins, characterized by rapid degradation, had a brief vogue in the nineteenth century, when Seymour Haden contended that when a body was enclosed in an air-tight coffin it putrefied and remained thus for decades, whereas if it was exposed to the earth it would resolve itself into its constituent elements within five years.

The only difference between pre-morbid purchase of a coffin and the planning of one's entire funeral and obsequies is one of degree. After all, royalty and the aristocracy have always taken an active part in the planning of their own funerals, and there is no reason why this jealously guarded prerogative should not be the right of everyone. We must rid ourselves of the idea that such pre-arrangement is somehow immodest or self-aggrandizing. Indeed, two famous people already referred to in this book, Charles Dickens and President Roosevelt, planned their own funerals with modesty and humility.

While the majority of royals preplanned elaborate and costly funerals for themselves, such was not invariably the case. A modest ceremony was requested by Queen Adelaide, the widow of King William IV. She wished a simple funeral with minimum fuss, and Queen Victoria made sure that her wishes were respected. Adelaide wrote:

I die in all humanity, knowing well that we are all alike before the Throne of God, and I request therefore that my mortal remains be conveyed to the grave without any pomp or state. They are to be moved to St George's Chapel, Windsor, where I request to have as private and quiet a funeral as possible. I particularly desire not to be laid out in state, and the funeral to take place by daylight; no procession; the coffin to be carried by sailors to the Chapel. All those of my friends and relations, to a limited number, who wish to attend may do so … I request not to be dissected, nor embalmed; I desire to give as little trouble as possible.

Queen Victoria had some very set and very secret ideas for what should happen at her own funeral – so secret, in fact, that only Mrs Tuck, her dresser, was in the know. And so intriguing. The queen had a lengthy list of items she wished placed in her coffin: a dressing-gown which had belonged to Prince Albert; one of Albert's cloaks sewn by Princess Alice; a plaster cast of his hand, and numerous photographs, as well as rings, chains, bracelets, lockets, shawls and handkerchiefs. Over all these was placed a quilted cushion in the shape of a coffin, in order to conceal them from members of her family. Most intriguing and endearing of all, the queen had instructed that a photograph of John Brown, her devoted attendant and 'true friend' for thirty-four years, and a lock of his hair were to be placed in her left hand – they were hidden from view by a posy of flowers from Queen Alexandra.

We can only guess at the reason why Victoria wished to keep her memorabilia secret. What is much more important is the idea of taking 'precious' objects with us into the grave. It is a highly personal choice which others cannot readily make on our behalf – always assuming that the idea of mementoes ever occurs to our relatives. A list is all that is needed.

In the final quarter of the twentieth century eccentricity in life is severely censured, and eccentricity in death is poorly tolerated. In the age of mass-produced commodities it is inevitable that the hallmarks of modern funerals should be their predictability and anonymity. There is a dire need to foster a greater diversity in a sea of conformity and commonplace.

But huge obstacles are raised by those with a vested interest in the status quo. Few Americans, for instance, know that there is no legal requirement to be embalmed. Fewer still realize that there is no obligation to have a coffin at all! It is perfectly legal to transport a body directly to a cemetery – unfortunately the cemetery officials will probably refuse to accept any corpse which has not been delivered by a funeral director, and even less likely to accept an uncoffined body.

Undeterred, growing numbers of people are trying to prearrange their funerals with undertakers. The motives usually devolve around questions of aesthetics and cost. The funeral director is not usually sympathetic to either of these motives but is moved by the anticipated income to be made from like-minded people. Even when pre-arranged funeral agreements are entered into, there are often a large number of 'get-out' clauses which tend to add post-mortem 'legitimate' extras to the undertakers' bills.[1]

There are some fundamental decisions to be made concerning one's own funeral, and these generally include a wish to have a religious ceremony or not, to be embalmed or not, to be buried or cremated, the location of one's grave or the manner of disposal of one's ashes, and a number of less important matters such as whether to have flowers – cut or in wreaths – or donations to charity.[2] Most of these preferences will have been gleaned by the bereaved from long acquaintance with the deceased when alive. It is less likely that relatives will know one's wishes regarding the making of a death mask to be hung on the wall, or the casting of a hand or foot to decorate the mantelpiece.

Funeral photographs, common in Victorian times, are now exceedingly rare, and yet funerals are unique in bringing together widely scattered family members from both extremes of the generational spectrum. If it is made clear beforehand that it is one's wish, an official photographer can be invited to take discreet photographs of relatives as well as oneself. In the days before photography, John Donne (1573–1631), poet and Dean of St Paul's Cathedral, arranged to be sketched just before his death. In preparation, he undressed and donned his winding sheet, knotted at the head and feet. 'With his eyes shut, and with so much of the sheet turned aside as might show his lean, pale and death-like face' – so was he engraved for posterity.

The funeral service has become a time-limited and perfunctory affair, and it is difficult to see how this can be changed in any substantial way. Any lengthening of one's own service may encroach on the time allotted to the next corpse to be processed. I have been to funerals at which a delay caused by rush-hour traffic has meant that one has 'lost one's slot', and in a like manner to the stacking of aircraft, the cortége has been sent away to tour the neighbourhood and return at a later time. All ceremonies these days are pervaded with a sense of urgency in order to increase efficiency and through-put. With such time constraints the actual form of the service often becomes irrelevant.

Of course, there is no obligation to have a religious ceremony at all. The form and order of the service are a matter for the relatives, who when the deceased has expressed no preference, will generally go along with a conventional religious format which includes recorded music and a reading from the Bible. When there is uncertainty regarding the

Funerals offer unique opportunities for family photographs. A lapsed tradition in need of a renaissance.

John Donne (1573–1631), poet and Dean of St Paul's Cathedral. This portrait was commissioned by Donne shortly before his death. To add realism he donned a winding-sheet knotted at the head and feet, shut his eyes and 'turned aside as might show his lean, pale and death-like face'. From an engraving by W. Sketton.

deceased's wishes, there is a reluctance to challenge this format with any singing of favourite folk- or pop-songs or readings from well-loved books or poems – least of all, jokes. There is an even greater reluctance on everyone's part to stand up and substitute for the priest, even when it is clear that the priest and the deceased have never met. A written request by the deceased that his brother or best friend 'say a few words' may be all that is needed to break down the barrier of self-consciousness. If one thinks that relatives will make a hash of one's eulogy, it is probably best to write it oneself – just as it is becoming increasingly acceptable to write one's own death notice for the newspaper, and an obituary for one's trade or professional journal.

The conformity that undertakers attempt to impose on a funeral is as nothing compared with the conformity the church and local authorities impose on where one can be buried and by what means one may be remembered. Most of us will be buried in municipal cemeteries or, if cremated, have our ashes either urned and buried or scattered (the Church prefers 'strewn') in the wind. The scope for individuality in cemeteries is severely restricted by the rules and regulations which govern the form of memorial which is permitted. Such constraints account for row upon row of identical masonry, glazing the eye and numbing the imagination. The ornate, the vulgar and the ostentatious have given way to the merely monotonous. Only the epitaphs, when permitted, give variety in this sea of sameness: the more contrived the poem and the less it scans, the more welcome it becomes.

In crematorium gardens, with memorial tablets all the same size and each flush with the clipped grass, one yearns for 'Rest in peace', 'Gone but not forgotten' or even 'Asleep'. Instead, only name, dates and number. To escape this post-mortem *ennui*, it is important to locate burial grounds that still permit personal expression and then negotiate one's admission. Theoretically one can be buried in one's own back garden, provided one does not constitute a health risk and the neighbours offer no objection. In reality the council will almost invariably refuse permission on health grounds. Oh, to be an owner of a large tract of land and be able to construct whatever tasteless memorial or ribald rhyme one wishes![3]

One advantage that cremation has over burial is that one can do a greater number of legal things with ashes than with corpses. No one will object to one's ashes being dug into the garden to feed a rose bush or sapling. Less commonly nowadays ashes are placed in marble urns and deposited in columbaria or simply taken home. Some couples wish their ashes mixed in a single urn which is then sealed. Another bonus of having cremation ashes is the fact that different portions can be put to widely

Commemorative plaques in a crematorium: characterized by conformity, utility and brevity.

different uses: some can be stored in an urn, another handful might be incorporated into a magnolia tree, while a pinch may be kept in a locket.

There is a desperate need for eccentricity in funerals. One such eccentric was James O'Kelly of New York, who at the turn of this century invented penny-in-the-slot machines. His proposed invention for burial in the stratosphere can only be described as bizarre. It was called the Navohi and comprised an elliptical structure similar to a large egg-shell. Inside was gas under pressure, surrounding a coffin which was placed upright, resting on a rubber cushion. An intricate mechanism allowed acid to seep over the body, producing copious quantities of gas which escaped through a valve into the cavity of the Navohi. As the coffin grew lighter, a system of levers fired the combustible mixture. When air rushed in to replace the burning gases, the Navohi was supposed to speed like a rocket into the sky, as earth-bound relatives waved their final goodbyes.

The great difference between a funeral service and a memorial service is that the latter usually takes place when the acute pain of bereavement is beginning to pass off. A memorial service for oneself can be made a highly personal affair – at a place of one's own choosing, with great flexibility with regard to time and, most important of all, with only invited and welcome guests. Many people make special provision in their wills for money to be set aside in order to provide food and drink to be eaten and drunk in their memory. Some memorial occasions happen within a few weeks or months of death; others are planned to coincide with important anniversaries. Here, then, is the opportunity to request all those pieces of music, readings and family videos that were denied to one at the funeral service. The funeral photographers can be invited back to snap this happier occasion. Some people put so much planning into their memorial gatherings that they become acutely depressed at the thought that they will not be there to share in the festivities. It is here that modern technology can come to the fore: a guest appearance on video can easily be arranged.

Another use suggested for video is to record oneself reading one's will. It is suggested that written wills are too impersonal and that a video can capture on film a host of non-verbal gestures, smiles and grimaces. Another suggestion is even more intriguing: a computer programme could be devised which would be 'interactive', whereby a bequest would be dependent upon the prospective recipient's keying in the correct answers to questions appearing on the screen.

In 1739 Samuel Baldwin, a truly English eccentric, made arrangements for his burial at sea, near the Needles rocks, off the Isle of Wight. This odd choice of disposal was chosen in order to disappoint his wife, who had repeatedly assured him in their many quarrels that she would revenge her conjugal sufferings by dancing on his grave. Long live eccentric death!

Illustration by Charles Dana Gibson, from a German postcard (c. 1908).

REFERENCES

The following have proved invaluable as source material:

Fulton, Robert, *Death, Grief and Bereavement: A Bibliography. 1845–1975* (Arno Press, New York, 1977)

Simpson, Michael, *Dying, Death and Grief: A Critically Annotated Bibliography and Source Book* (Plenum Press, New York and London, 1982)

Shneidman, Edwin (ed.), *Death: Current Perspectives* (Mayfield Publishing Company, third edition, 1985). Besides Shneidman himself, there are authoritative extracts from, among a host of others, Arnold Toynbee, Philippe Ariès, C.S. Lewis, Lily Pincus and Bertrand Russell.

I FEAR OF PREMATURE BURIAL

1 For most of his life Edgar Allan Poe walked an emotional tightrope, fearful of falling into the abyss of insanity. His death in 1849 was not due to catalepsy but was the result of a combination of circumstances, including the death of his wife in 1847, bouts of profound depression and alcoholism. Paranoid and suffering from delirium tremens, Poe was found insensible on a Baltimore street unable to recall how he had got there. He died in hospital, crying out, 'Lord, help my poor soul!' Those interested in Poe are recommended to read *Edgar Allan Poe* by David Sinclair (Dent, 1977).

2 Spurious and irrelevant scholarship is highlighted by a cynical reviewer in *The Quarterly Review*, Volume 85, June and Sepember 1849, when talking about life remaining after being guillotined: 'One [author] mentions a man, or to speak more correctly, the *head* of a man, who turned his eyes whichever way they called him; and having thus digested the camel without difficulty, he [the author] grows scrupulous about the gnat, and cannot be confident whether the name of the person was Tillier or de Tillier.

3 See Chapter 20 in *Akenfield* by Ronald Blythe (Penguin, 1972)

4 The extent of the European preoccupation with premature burial can be gauged by the plethora of references cited by Tebb and Vollum in the bibliography of their book *Premature Burial and How It May Be Prevented* (Swan Sonnenschein, 1905). There are seven pages of French and German sources as well as a list of twenty-nine French nineteenth-century theses on apparent death, diagnosis of death and the horrors of premature burial.

5 The British edition of Winslow's *Uncertainty of the Signs of Death* was published in 1746. The author's philosophy about corroboration of facts can be summarized thus: 'But though we should grant, that narratives of Accidents which happened so long ago, are purely spurious, yet surely we must yield a ready assent to the testimonies of persons whose candour and veracity we have no reason to suspect.'

6 Being buried alive is also the subject of the most celebrated of Poe's *Tales of Mystery and Imagination*: 'The Fall of the House of Usher'.

7 Montague Summers, *The Vampire: His Kith and Kin*, (Kegan Paul, Trench, Trubner & Co Ltd, 1928)

8 P. Brouardel, *Death and Sudden Death* (Bailliere, Tindall & Cox, 1902)

9 Franz Hartmann, *Premature Burial: An Examination into the Occult Causes of Apparent Death, Trance and Catalepsy* (1895). After a two-year search there would appear to be not a single copy available in Great Britain; copies exist in the USA.

10 The review appears in *The British Medical Journal*, 29 February 1896, p. 540.

11 *Lancet*, 22 May 1858, p. 519.
12 William Tebb and Edward Perry Vollum, *Premature Burial and How it May Be Prevented* (Swan Sonnenschein, 1905). Tebb was a 'Member of the Geographical Society', while Vollum was a colonel and medical inspector of the United States Army.
13 W. Tebb and E. Vollum, op. cit.
14 G. Eric Mackay, 'Premature Burials', *Popular Science Monthly*, Vol. 16 (1880), pp. 389–97.
15 Julia de Fontenelle, *Récherches Médico-légales sur l'Incertitude des Signes de la Mort* (1834)
16 David Walsh, *Premature Burial: Fact or Fiction* (1897)
17 For a wonderfully humorous review of premature burial in general and of de Fontenelle's book in particular, see the *Quarterly Review*, Vol. 85 (1849), pp. 346–99.
18 *Quarterly Review*, op. cit.
19 W. Tebb and E. Vollum, op. cit.
20 G. Eric Mackay, op. cit.
21 W. Tebb and E. Vollum, op. cit.
22 W. Tebb and E. Vollum, op. cit.
23 See the correspondence generated in *Notes and Queries*, Sixth Series, Vol. (July–December 1881).
24 *Quarterly Review*, op. cit.
25 David Walsh, op. cit.
26 Quoted from Robert Kastenbaum and Ruth Aisenberg, *The Psychology of Death* (Duckworth, 1974), chapter on 'Thanatomimesis'.
27 P. Brouardel, op. cit.
28 Quoted from Barbara Jones's *Design for Death* (André Deutsch, 1967). Prescribed reading.
29 N.M. Shrock, 'On the signs that distinguish real from apparent death', *Transylvanian Journal of Medicine* Vol. 13 (1835), pp. 210–20. Try also: M.R. Fletcher, *One Thousand Buried Alive by Their Best Friends* (Boston, 1890)
30 P. Brouardel, op. cit.
31 Today's medical technology can keep people 'alive' long after all realistic hope of recovery has gone. I am reminded of the famous case of Claus von Bülow, who was accused of having murdered his heiress wife 'Sunny' with an overdose of insulin. At the time of his acquittal in 1985, his wife had been unconscious for five years on a life-support system. She was still comatose in 1987, when the financial niceties were finally settled. The reader is referred to the section on 'Harvesting of the Dead' in Chapter 4.
32 From Harriet Martineau's will in Somerset House.

II THE FEAR OF POSTHUMOUS INDIGNITY

The following books have served as my main sources of information concerning the activities of the resurrectionists:
Adams, Norman, *Dead and Buried?* (Impulse Books, 1972)
Bailey, James Blake, *The Diary of a Resurrectionist to which are added an account of the Resurrectionist Men in London* (1896)
Ball, James Moores, *The Sack-'Em-Up Men* (Oliver & Boyd, 1928)
Cohen, Daniel, *The Body Snatchers* (Lippincott, Philadelphia and New York, 1975)
Cole, Hubert, *Things for the Surgeon* (Heinemann, 1964)
Turner, Cecil Howard, *The Inhumanists* (Alexander Ouseley Ltd, 1932)
Contemporary accounts have been consulted using indexes of *The Times* newspaper.
The social background to body-snatching and the events leading up to the introduction of the Anatomy Bill of 1832 are painstakingly documented by Ruth Richardson in her epic book *Death, Dissection and the Destitute* (Routledge & Kegan Paul, London and New York, 1987). This fascinating book is highly recommended.

1 Perhaps the closest anyone came to being 'curst' by Shakespeare was an American, Delia Bacon. So convinced was this Victorian lady that Francis Bacon had written the plays of Shakespeare and that the proof lay in a bundle of paper which she was

sure had been buried with Shakespeare, that in 1856 she came close to persuading the vicar of Stratford to open up the tomb. Another popular candidate for the authorship of Shakespeare's plays is Christopher Marlowe. In 1969 William Honey 'deciphered' the anagram thus:

> Good ffrend who wishes for Shakespeare
> To dig the dust: entombed heae:
> Playes by the men, verses hys sonnets
> And Christopher Marlowe's bones.

Thus, according to Honey, it is Marlowe and not Shakespeare who is buried at Stratford. Is anyone going to risk the curse to find out? In 1956 a petition was granted to open up the Walsingham tomb in St Nicholas' Church, Chistlehurst, to search for documents to prove that Marlowe was not murdered at Deptford in 1593, was not interred at Chistlehurst and had lived on to fruitful middle age, penning works later ascribed to Shakespeare. The tomb was duly opened but no documents were found.

2 The description appearing in the *Lancet* (March 1828) was taken from a doctor's eyewitness account and described in detail the ignorance and incompetence of the surgeon. It also gives, in harrowing detail, the way in which the patient was bound on his back in a crouching position, with his hands tied to the soles of his feet, and his knees to his shoulders. Bransby Cooper later published his own version of events. Such overt medical accountability seems to be a thing of the past.

3 For an account of the search of Bellingham's skull in the basement of St Bartholomew's Hospital, see John Thornton and S. Zivanovic's 'The Skull of John Bellingham', *The Practitioner*, Vol. 212 (1974), pp. 107–14.

4 James Blake Bailey, op. cit.

5 Jessie Dobson, 'The College Criminals, 4. William Corder', *Annals of the Royal College of Surgeons*, Vol. 11 (1952), pp. 249–55. The other criminals written about by Dobson, and whose remains are in the college, are Jonathan Wild, Eugene Aram and John Thurtell.

6 James Blake Bailey, op. cit.

7 Francis Clerihew, 'My First Resurrection', *Aberdeen Magazine*, spring 1831.

8 James Blake Bailey, op. cit.

9 Cited in Hubert Cole, op. cit. (no source identified).

10 Hubert Cole, op. cit.

11 James Blake Bailey, op. cit.

12 O'Brien suffered from a tumour of the pituitary, a small gland situated in a bony pouch in the skull. If Hunter had only sawn off the top of the skull and looked inside, he would immediately have noticed the grossly enlarged pouch and thereby have further enhanced his reputation by being the first to elucidate the cause of giantism (acromegaly).

13 Richard Smith's death-bed regret at not having acquired Cotter's skeleton is recounted by George Pycroft in *Land and Water*, 16 October 1875.

14 Most of the information about Cotter is contained in G. Frankcom and J.H. Musgrave's book *The Irish Giant* (Duckworth, 1976). Earlier correspondence about giants in general and Cotter in particular can be found in copies of *Land and Water* throughout the summer and autumn of 1875.

15 James Blake Bailey, op. cit.

16 Southwood Smith's article appeared in the *Westminster Review*, 1824, pp. 59–97.

17 James Blake Bailey, op. cit.

18 Ruth Richardson, op. cit.

19 This highly individual list of advantages of the Anatomy Bill was compiled by James Moores Ball in *The Sack-'Em-Up Men*, op. cit.

20 The source for this anecdote and many more is William Tegg's *The Last Act: Being the Funeral Rites of Nations and Individuals* (1876).

21 See also K. Pearson and G. Morant, 'The Wilkinson Head of Cromwell', *Biometrika*, Vol. 26 (1934), pp. 269–378. Many conflicting accounts have been given over the centuries regarding the fate of Cromwell's corpse. One version of events has

Cromwell's daughter Mary, Countess Fauconberg, bribing the guards at Tyburn to secure her father's headless corpse in order to have it interred in a secret location at her home in Newburgh. In another account Cromwell's remains were switched at burial, on his own orders, and interred in the vaults of St Nicholas' Church, Chiswick Mall.

22 Henry Halford's own account of the opening of Charles I's tomb is appended to his *Essays and Orations* (1842, third edition). The main body of this book concerns the mode of death of 'some illustrious persons of antiquity' as well as 'eminent persons of modern times'.

23 Christopher Hibbert and Ben Weinreb (eds), *The London Encyclopaedia* (Macmillan, 1983). (No source identified.)

24 The source of information on the search for James VIII's final resting-place is Arthur Penrhyn (Dean) Stanley's spell-binding book *Historical Memorials of Westminster Abbey* (1869)

25 Philippe Ariès, *The Hour of Our Death* (Allen Lane, 1981)

26 Paul Barber, *Vampires, Burial and Death* (Yale University Press, 1988).

III THE FEAR OF BODILY DISINTEGRATION

The most interesting volume by far about mummies worldwide is Cockburn and Cockburn's *Mummies, Disease and Ancient Culture* (Cambridge University Press, 1980). Not a dull page in the book! Another valued source is Ange-Pierre Leca's *The Cult of the Immortal*, translated by Louise Asmal (Souvenir Press, 1979).

1 The matter is more fully discussed by F. Filce Leek, 'The problem of brain removal during embalming by the ancient Egyptians', *Journal of Egyptian Archaeology*, Vol. 55 (1969), pp. 112–16.

2 The natron controversy is well aired, with illustrations of the effects produced by each method, in A.R. David's *The Manchester Museum Mummy Project* (Manchester Museum, 1979). It also documents the painstaking unwrapping of an Egyptian mummy.

3 For Peruvian mummies, see Simone and Roger Waisbard's *Masks, Mummies and Magicians* (Oliver & Boyd, 1965). For Peruvian mummies, Canary Island mummies and sundry others, see Warren Dawson's 'Contributions to the History of Mummification' *Proceedings of the Royal Society of Medicine* (1927) pp. 832–54.

4 Louise M. Robbins, 'A Woodland "Mummy" From Salts Cave, Kentucky', *American Antiquity*, Vol. 36, No. 2 (1971), pp. 200–206.

5 See P.V. Glob's *The Bog People* (Faber & Faber, 1969). Also highly recommended is Don Brothwell's *The Bog People and the Archaeology of People* (British Museum Publications, 1988).

6 Jessie Dobson, 'Some Eighteenth Century Experiments in Embalming', *Journal of the History of Medicine*, pp. 431–41 (October 1953)

7 Jessie Dobson, op. cit.

8 For a comprehensive account, see Charles Bradford's *Heart Burial* (George Allen & Unwin, 1933). As the author notes, 'An ampler description would be "On the ancient custom of the division of the human body at death, and the separate disposal of its parts, as illustrated by cases associated with the London Postal area." '

9 For an uncritical account, see Joan Carroll Cruz's *The Incorruptibles* (Tan Books, Illinois, USA, 1977)

10 A more realistic approach to Xavier is contained in William Ireland's *The Blot on the Brain* (1886, reprinted by Books for Libraries Press, New York, 1972).

11 Jessica Mitford, *The American Way of Death* (Simon & Schuster, New York, 1963).

12 For modern embalming techniques (and many other gems), see C.J. Polson and T.K. Marshall's *The Disposal of the Dead* (English Universities Press, 1975, third edition).

13 The Alcor Life Extension Foundation is based in Riverside, California, and publishes a monthly magazine called simply *Cryonics*. There are a number of other such organizations, usually Californian. Robert Nelson's *We Froze the First Man* (Dell, 1968) is unintentionally amusing. The biologists' view is ably and forcibly put by

David Pegg, for example in 'Mechanisms of Freezing Damage', *SEB Symposium, No. 41, Temperature and Animal Cells* (1987).

14 Robert C.W. Ettinger, *The Prospect of Immortality* (Sidgwick and Jackson, 1965)

IV THE FEAR OF BEING FORGOTTEN

1 It might be thought that anyone who built on the scale of Cheops could not fail to be remembered in perpetuity. Maybe so, but things did not go according to plan, for Ozymandias, when a traveller to Egypt, read the inscription on 'two vast and trunkless legs of stone' buried in the desert:

> 'My name is Ozymandias, king of kings
> Look on my works, ye Mighty, and despair!'
> Nothing beside remains. Round the decay
> Of that colossal wreck, boundless and bare
> The lone and level sands stretch far away.

Shelley, 'Ozymandias'

Nevertheless, this reference testifies to our remembrance.

2 There are a large number of good books on churches, churchyards and burial grounds, and I cannot hope to list them all. One of the best is Mrs Basil Holmes's *The London Burial Grounds: Notes on Their History from the Earliest Times to the Present Day* (1896). More recently there are Harvey Hackman's *Wates's Book of London Churchyards* (Collins, 1981); Brian Bailey's *Churchyards of England and Wales* (Robert Hale, 1987); and Charles Cox and Charles Ford's *The Parish Churches of England* (Batsford, 1935). Another invaluable reference source is Douglas Greenwood's *Who's Buried Where in England* (Constable, 1982). Less comprehensive is Conrad Bailey's *Famous London Graves* (Harrap, 1975). Also highly recommended is James Stevens Curl's *The Victorian Celebration of Death* (David & Charles, 1971).

3 For a full description of the fascinating search for and identification of the apostle's bones, see John Evangelist Walsh's *The Bones of St Peter* (Gollancz, 1982).

4 The French have always taken a lively interest in death – much more so than the British, and many of the most authoritative works come from France, including Philippe Ariès, op. cit. See also works by Michel Vovelle.

5 A more recent quarrel about burial of an unbaptized 2-year-old is recorded in Ronald Fletcher's *The Akenham Burial Case* (Wildwood House, 1974).

6 See the encyclopaedic volume by Hugh Mellor, *London Cemeteries: An Illustrated Guide and Gazetteer* (Gregg International, 1985, second edition).

7 See John Clarke's comprehensive *The Brookwood Necropolis Railway* (Oakwood Press, 1983; a second, enlarged edition has just been published).

8 William Tegg, op. cit.

9 See J.M.C. Toynbee's *Death and Burial in the Roman World* (Thames & Hudson, 1971).

10 Edward Trelawny, *Recollections of the Last Days of Shelley and Byron* (1858).

11 For an exposé of American funeral practices, see Jessica Mitford's classic *The American Way of Death* (Simon & Schuster, New York, 1963). An earlier volume, in similar vein, is Leroy Bowman's *The American Funeral* (Public Affairs Press, Washington, DC, 1959).

12 See Edward Thompson's *Suttee: A Historical and Philosophical Enquiry into the Hindu Rite of Widow-Burning* (George Allen & Unwin, 1928).

13 Another gem from Arthur Penrhyn (Dean) Stanley's *Historical Memorials of Westminster Abbey*, op. cit.

14 Bertram Puckle's *Funeral Customs: Their Origin and Development* (T. Werner Laurie, 1926) is the source of much intriguing information – unfortunately not all the information can be corroborated. For example, Puckle says: 'Clement Spelman of Nottingham is immured in a pillar of Nasburgh Church'; despite an intermittent search over a number of years, I have, as yet, been unable to locate Nasburgh.

15 Edinburgh's School of Anatomy has one of the biggest collections of death masks in Britain, including Newton, Charles James Fox, Jean-Paul Marat, William Pitt the Younger, Samuel Taylor Coleridge, John Keats, Dr Johnson, Sir Walter Scott, Carl Maria von Weber and Felix Mendelssohn.
16 Two invaluable sources of last words are Brian O'Kill's *Exit Lines* (Longman, 1986) and Jonathon Green's compilation *Famous Last Words* (Pan, 1977).
17 Willard Gaylin, 'Harvesting the Dead', *Harper's Magazine* (1974), pp. 23–30.
18 William Gaylin, op. cit.

V THE FEAR OF IGNOMINIOUS DEATH

Invaluable sources on royal death are Olivia Bland's *The Royal Way of Death* (Constable, 1986) and Elizabeth Longford's *The Oxford Book of Royal Anecdotes* (Oxford University Press, 1989).

1 See R.C. Finucane, 'Sacred Corpse, Profane Carrion', in Joachim Whaley's *Mirrors of Mortality: Studies in the Social History of Death* (Europa Publications, 1981).
  Cyrus Sulzberger, in his *My Brother Death* (Harper & Brothers, New York, 1961), refers to bizarre African customs regarding the death of kings: the Congolese Chitome, believing the world would perish if their kings died naturally, strangled and clubbed them when they fell sick; the Fazoql hanged their rulers in knife-bladed nooses; the Shilluk kings of Sudan were strangled when they could no longer satisfy their wives; the Samorin kings had their throats cut after they had ruled for twelve years; and the kings of Dahomey knew their end was nigh when their subjects presented them with a parrot's egg.
2 The major source of information was Raymond Crawfurd's *The Last Days of Charles II* (Clarendon Press, 1909).
3 From Arthur Penrhyn (Dean) Stanley's *Historical Memorials of Westminster Abbey*, op. cit.
4 Elizabeth Longford, op. cit, further quotes that Henry's '... nose was elevated, the cartilage even remaining, though on the admission of the air it sunk rapidly away, and had entirely disappeared before the examination was completed. The skin of the chin was entire, of the consistency and thickness of the upper leather of a shoe, brown and moist; the beard thick and matted, and of a deep russet colour.' From Dr Spry's 'A Brief Account of the Examination of the Tomb of King Henry IV in the Cathedral of Canterbury', *Archaeologia Cantiana*, viii (1872).
5 *Great Chronicle*, cited in Longford, op. cit.
6 Robert Carey, *Memoirs of the Life of Robert Carey* (1759), cited in Olivia Bland, op. cit.
7 John Chamberlain, *Letters ... During the Reign of Queen Elizabeth* (1861), cited in Olivia Bland, op. cit.
8 *Gentleman's Magazine*, Vol. xxi (1751), cited in Olivia Bland, op. cit.
9 John, Lord Hervey, *Memoirs of the Reign of George II*, edited by J.W. Croker (1884), cited in Olivia Bland, op. cit.
10 W.H. Wilkins, *Caroline the Illustrious* (1901), cited in Olivia Bland, op. cit.
11 Horace Walpole, *Letters* (ed. Mrs P. Toynbee) (1903), cited in Olivia Bland, op. cit.
12 See 'The Captivity and Death of Edward of Carnarvon' in *The Collected Papers of Thomas Frederick Tout* (Manchester University Press, 1934), Vol. 3. For conjecture about Edward II's final resting-place and whether he managed to escape and wander in Italy, see G.P. Cutting and Thomas Lyman's 'Where is Edward II?', *Speculum*, Vol. 53 (1978), pp. 522–44.
13 A.L. Zevaes, *Damiens le régicide* (1937), cited in M. Foucault, *Discipline and Punish: The Birth of the Prison* (Penguin, 1979)
14 C.V. Wedgwood, *The Trial of Charles I* (Collins, 1964)
15 See Lewin's *Life and Death – being An Authentic Account of the Deaths of One Hundred Celebrated Men and Women with Their Portraits* (Constable 1910).
16 For a recent account of the death of John Paul I, see John Cornwell's *A Thief in the Night* (Viking, 1989).

17 Chris Thomas, psychiatrist, suggests that the first suicide note is in the Erman papyrus in the Berlin Museum. See his 'First Suicide Note?', *British Medical Journal*, 26 July 1980.

18 There is a vast and rapidly growing library on suicide. The best guide for facts and figures is probably Erwin Stengel's *Suicide and Attempted Suicide* (Pelican, 1964, with many subsequent reprints). Emil Durkheim's *Suicide* (Routledge & Kegan Paul, 1952) is a classic text, as are the works of E.S. Schneidman. Other books consulted include Louis Dublin and Bessie Bunzel's *To Be Or Not To Be* (Harrison Smith & Robert Haas, New York, 1933), and A. Alvarez's *The Savage God* (Weidenfeld & Nicolson, 1974). Better still are Forbes Winslow's *Anatomy of Suicide* (1840) and the incomparable *Suicide: A Social and Historical Study* by Henry Romilly Fedden (Peter Davies, 1938)

Readers might find of interest: David Lester's 'Seasonal Variation in Suicidal Deaths', *British Journal of Psychiatry* No. 118 (1871), pp. 627–8; J. Bunch and P. Barraclough's 'The Influence of Parental Death Anniversaries upon Suicide Dates' *British Journal of Psychiatry*, No. 118 (1971), pp. 621–6, and David Phillips and Kenneth Feldman's 'A Dip in Deaths Before Ceremonial Occasions', *American Sociological Review*, Vol. 38 (December 1973), pp. 678–96.

19 See Michael McDonald, 'The Inner Side of Wisdom: Suicide in Early Modern England', *Psychological Medicine*, Vol. 7 (1977), pp. 566–7.

20 Many have long debated whether animals are capable of suicide. The most famous example quoted is Aristotle's horse, who refused to mount his dam. He was eventually induced to do so by the expedient of veiling her. On discovering he had been duped, the animal intentionally flung himself over a cliff. An anecdote from the third century tells of a bird called a porphyrion which called the attention of its master to any infidelity on the part of its mistress by hanging itself.

21 M.D. Faber writes about 'Shakespeare's Suicides' in Edwin Shneidman's *Essays in Self-Destruction* (Science House, New York, 1978). Of interest is Graeme Feggetter's 'Suicide in Opera', *British Journal of Psychiatry*, No. 136 (1980), pp. 552–7.

22 Quoted without source in many books – including D.J. Enright's *The Oxford Book of Death* (Oxford University Press, 1987)

23 Cesare Parvese, *This Business of Living: A Diary 1935–50*, edited and translated by A.E. Murch (Peter Owen, n.d.)

24 Quoted in Henry Romilly Fedden and Forbes Winslow, both op. cit.

25 Richard Friedenthal, *Goethe: His Life and Times* (London and New York 1965), cited in A. Alvarez, op. cit.

26 *Daily Telegraph*, 8 April 1984.

AFTERWORD: THE FEAR OF PLANNING ONE'S OWN FUNERAL

1 See Byron Sher's 'Funeral Prearrangement: Mitigating the Undertaker's Bargaining Advantage, *Stanford Law Review*, May 1963, pp. 415–79.

2 Puckle tells a story in his *Funeral Customs* (1926). A British soldier was laying flowers on the grave of a fallen comrade when he noticed a native carrying food to his ancestral tomb. Amused by such superstitious absurdity, the soldier asked when his ancestor would come and enjoy his meal. 'About the same time as your friend comes to smell your flowers.'

3 In times past the working classes were able, if they so wished, to erect virtually any form of memorial they could afford. Visitors to Hauterives in Frances must make a point of visiting the tomb of postman Cheval – massive, ornate and looking like a Christmas cake. It surely represents a lifetime's savings.

Index